PLACE NAMES OF THE ENGLISH-SPEAKING WORLD

C. M. Matthews

PLACE NAMES OF THE ENGLISH-SPEAKING WORLD

CHARLES SCRIBNER'S SONS

NEW YORK

Contents

Preface

This book is a general study – the first that has been yet
attempted – of the way in which the inhabitants of the British
Isles and their descendants have named the places in which
they have settled during the whole of their recorded history. A
large subject, both in time and space, but one that is so linked
together by the interplay of language, history and tradition
that it may reasonably be taken as a single theme. England is
scattered with Celtic names, the Celtic lands with English, the
new countries overseas with innumerable echoes of both, mixed
with elements that are all their own. The picture, though
diffuse, is interlocking, and in this wide view points of interest
emerge that are not apparent in separate studies.

In so far as is possible I have tried to maintain a continuity
of narrative (though occasional retracing of steps has been
necessary) and to stress the social and historical backgrounds
that affected name-giving; and in each country I have concentrated chiefly on its early history, because it is always the
first period of discovery and expansion that produces the most
names, and those that will be famous later.

Since the extent of my subject is so large I have given the
most attention to those regions where English-speaking colonists
have settled in the largest numbers, and where their influence
on names has been the greatest, passing very briefly over some
large parts of the Commonwealth where native names remain
in almost complete possession. My concern is not with political
affiliations, but with British ideology as expressed in place-
names.

However, within each one of the principal English-speaking
lands that I have taken as my province I have aimed at giving
as complete a picture as possible, including names of indigenous
and other linguistic origins that are typical of the country. One
of the strongest characteristics of the English when establishing
names for places has always been their readiness to absorb

foreign material; it is largely this that has given the place-names of England their rich variety and charm; and a study of American place-names that failed to mention Chicago or California would be as unbalanced as one on English names that omitted London and Devon. But because some hundreds of languages have been involved in naming the whole English-speaking world, some of them very little known, an inequality of treatment has been unavoidable. Where reliable information has been available for important names I have given it to the best of my ability, and have tried at least to indicate something of the character of the principal languages concerned.

With such a vast amount of possible material the problems of selection have naturally been very great. My general principles in choosing names for detailed treatment have been to take those of chief historic interest, those most typical of their place and time and those that are best known; but I have also included samples of the minor names of little places in each country, for these always far exceed the great ones in number and are often more characteristic and picturesque. In choosing names from England I constantly had the younger countries in mind, and where scores of examples existed to illustrate a point I often preferred one that was prominent overseas. Thus the first half of this book, which appears to be devoted only to Britain, contains many etymologies of American and Commonwealth names. Indeed, so many American names are British in origin that they require a study of this sort to explain them.

I make no claim to original research into the origins of place-names, except here and there where a life-long interest in the subject has brought special details to my attention. My task has chiefly been one of accumulation and selection and would have been impossible without the scholarship of others, to which I freely acknowledge my indebtedness. As far as England is concerned, the mass of material in Ekwall's *Oxford Dictionary of English Place-Names* forms a basis on which to build, and to this is added, county by county, the authoritative volumes of the English Place-Name Society which continue to appear in a steady stream, the most important of the series being the two volumes on *English Place-Name Elements* by the late Professor A.H.Smith. There are also two recent books on English place-names in general by the late Dr P.H.Reaney and Professor

K.Cameron, both distinguished members of the EPNS, and to those who wish for a fuller treatment these are recommended.

The chief difficulty in writing on this subject is that there must always be obscurity in the origins of many of the older names, and with so much intensive study in progress new interpretations are often brought forward to supersede those formerly accepted. Where I have given an origin differing from that of Ekwall it is because a later EPNS publication, based on a fuller study of the evidence, has produced a convincing new opinion. An important contribution in this field is *The Names of Towns and Cities in Britain* (Nicolaisen, Gelling and Richards, 1970), which contains some new interpretations that I have used. But Ekwall is still held in high esteem by all these more recent scholars, and the great majority of his etymologies still stand.

For the Celtic countries much less work has been done and reliable publications are few at present. The most valuable is still Watson's *Celtic Place-Names of Scotland* (1926) which contains many references to Welsh and Irish names as well. Not all his findings are still accepted, but the main body of his scholarship, like that of Ekwall, is unassailable. For Ireland we have to look back to 1883 (Joyce's *Irish Names of Places*) for any comprehensive work, and for Wales there is none, but work is in progress and a dictionary of Welsh place-names on the way. Meanwhile the meanings of many Celtic names, obscure to the sassenach, are clearly evident to speakers of Gaelic and Welsh. These and many others that are less obvious may be found in learned periodicals, serious histories, encyclopedias, and the more reputable guide books. In doubtful cases I have found the professors in charge of Celtic studies at the appropriate universities most helpful.

The sources of place-name information overseas are likewise very variable. The chief authority for the United States is Professor George R.Stewart, to whose books I am much indebted. There are short place-name dictionaries for Canada and New Zealand, and both of them as well as Australia and Southern Africa have much information on this subject in their excellent encyclopedias. But on the whole the naming of places in the New World by Europeans is sufficiently recent for the circumstances to be part of well recorded history, and they may

A*

best be found in a wide reading of general sources, such as the journals of explorers, who for the most part have taken name-giving very seriously.

My especial thanks are due to Professor K.H.Jackson of the University of Edinburgh, and to Dr W.H.F.Nicolaisen, former head of the Scottish Place-Name Survey undertaken there; to Professor Melville Richards of the University College of North Wales; to Mr Éamonn de hÓir of the Irish Place-Name Society; to Mr J.McN.Dodgson, Honorary Secretary of the English Place-Name Society; to Sir Alan Burns, the distinguished colonial administrator; to Mrs Elisabeth Ingham, formerly of the House of Commons Library, and to many others who have kindly answered my questions with valuable information.

I must also express my gratitude to my brothers, Philip Carrington, former Archbishop of Quebec and Metropolitan of the Province of Canada, and Charles Carrington, former Professor of British Commonwealth Relations at the Royal Institute of International Affairs, each of whom has placed his wide and deep historical knowledge at my service; and to my sister and her husband, Mr and Mrs B.M.Hulley of Hyannis, Massachusetts, whose help in supplying and checking much of the American material has been invaluable. Nor can I fail to mention my daughter, Carola, and my husband, without whose help and encouragement the enterprise could hardly have been completed.

And, while writing this book, I have also often had in mind others of my family – now dead – who contributed to it unknowingly in the past: my scholarly father who encouraged me at an early age to enjoy words and inquire into their nature, my Welsh mother who gave me a love of Welsh names and a feeling for the language (though I cannot claim to speak it); and two more brothers, Hugh, whose knowledge of exploration in the Pacific was unrivalled and a stimulus to us all until his early death cut short his researches, and Gerard, who as a young explorer lost his life in the mountains of New Zealand, and in whose honour our family name has its place on a peak there, Mount Carrington.

Many families, like ours, are deeply rooted in England, have a Celtic strain, and have been scattered in their working lives all round the globe. Without a background of this sort, I doubt if any amount of pure scholarship would equip one fully to write this book.

C. M. Matthews
Dorset, 1971

Part One

THE NAMING OF ENGLAND

Chapter 1

PRE-ENGLISH INHABITANTS

The great majority of inhabited places in England have names that were given them by Anglo-Saxons in the first few centuries after their arrival in this country. But that is not the beginning of our story or anything like it. The land was full of names long before the English saw it, names belonging to the Celtic language that had been spoken here for a thousand years before their coming and is still spoken in Wales. Many of these ancient names were adopted by the English and are with us still. With them our study must begin.

Five centuries before the coming of the English the Romans had made their first incursion, and earlier still Greek navigators had visited these cold, misty islands at the world's end, noting the names of a few promontories and islands, but apparently not venturing inland. The first of these whose name has come down to us is Pytheas who sailed right round these islands in the fourth century BC. Accounts of his voyage as retold and discussed by later Greek and Roman writers give us our first names, Albion, Ierne (Ireland), Thule (Shetland), Orcas (Orkney), Belerion (the south-west promontory of Albion), and Kantion in the south-east. Belerion is one of those ghostly, long dead names that haunt our early history, for that promontory has been Cornwall for at least a thousand years; but Kantion remains as Kent and has the distinction of being the first recorded name on the mainland of Britain that is still in use.

Among the records of four centuries of Roman rule, over two hundred native place-names in Britain (as the Romans preferred to call it) have been preserved, the most important sources being the great work on geography compiled by the Greek scholar Ptolemy in about AD 150, and the Itinerary of Antoninus, which is a sort of road book of Britain in the fourth century, giving distances from one place to another. With the help of such works and of inscriptions unearthed by archaeologists the names of the principal places of Roman Britain are well known to us, but hundreds more must have existed in the speech of the native inhabitants.

But though the earliest evidence of our place-names comes from the classical world of Greece and Rome, that is not the beginning of the story either, only the beginning of the written evidence. At least two centuries before Pytheas made his famous voyage the Celtic peoples had been coming into Albion and giving the names which the Romans and the English were to find there later. And before the Celts there were other inhabitants, whom we can only call by the modern label of 'Bronze Age people' for want of knowing what they called themselves. All we know of them comes from what is buried in the earth or standing upright in stone; their great monument Stonehenge alone is enough to show that they were numerous, intelligent and well organized, but we do not even know what language they spoke.

Just as the Anglo-Saxons inherited place-names from the Celts (or Britons as the Romans called this branch of them) so it is likely that the Celts, when they first migrated here, also took over names from those who were before them, and it is probable that some of these still exist. The trouble is to identify them, and this can hardly be done with certainty, but when a name is an old one and – according to the highest linguistic authorities – appears to have no affinities with either English or Celtic, then the suspicion is strong that it belongs to an earlier language than either of them. No names of this sort are attached to prehistoric monuments such as Stonehenge or Avebury, nearly all of which have obviously English names. Stonehenge, for instance, means 'stone gallows', a grim thought expressed in total ignorance of the purpose of the structure and given at least two thousand years after its erection. It is indeed a striking fact that no ancient names have survived for such places; we do not even know what the Romans called them. A complete break in tradition is indicated here. The features that do regularly have names of the oldest type are rivers; and among our river-names Humber, Tyne, Severn, Test, Colne, and others belong to this totally unexplained category, and may have been first spoken by those Bronze Age men who were driven away or absorbed by the Celts.

It is a common error to think that all those classical-looking names which appear on a map of Roman Britain are of Roman origin. They are native names taken over by the conquering Romans and given a Latinized appearance. When they built a town or fort close to a British settlement they made use of its name, or if, as must often have happened, it was a place with no previous habitation, then the local name of the nearest natural feature was made to serve. In this way it happened that many Roman cities and military stations grew up in Britain with the Celtic or pre-Celtic names of hills, woods and rivers – but especially of rivers. The city we call Chester was known to the Romans as Deva, the name of the River Dee; Exeter was Isca, the river Exe. Lichfield was Letocetum, which represented the Old Celtic *leto caito* or 'grey wood'. By the eighth century this had become 'Liccid' (pronounced 'Lit-ched'), to which the English added their own word 'field'.

As hardly any British names had been written down before the Roman occupation there was no precedent for their spelling, and Roman officials wrote them in their own style adding the Latin suffixes that seemed appropriate. Then came the Anglo-Saxons who also took over many of the old names, mispronouncing them further and adding endings of their own, so that we never see these names in their purely Celtic form, which often makes interpretation difficult.

The Celtic language, of which British (or Brittonic) was a branch, was unwritten anywhere, and none of its descendants such as Welsh and Gaelic were written until perhaps the sixth or seventh centuries. Existing manuscripts are later than that; and scholars find it hard to date them; therefore, in every respect, they are working at long range in their efforts to master the Brittonic language as spoken before and during the Roman occupation. And yet, from names and phrases recorded by Greek and Latin writers and in stone inscriptions, from comparison with Gaulish names, and chiefly from a study of the oldest surviving forms of Welsh, Gaelic and Breton, a vast

5

amount has been achieved. Until recently the leading scholar on the subject of English place-names in general was Professor E. Ekwall, but now in the particular field of Celtic names Professor K. H. Jackson must be looked on as the first authority. Such scholars have elucidated many words that go to the making of our oldest names, but much obscurity remains, and always must. When the curtain is lifted somewhat we see a little farther, but the darkness has only receded and we shall never see all the way.

Consider London. Little is known of what was there before the Romans established it as a convenient base, and it is first recorded in AD 115 by Tacitus as Londinium. The Greeks – who produced great geographers – called it Londinion, and they were probably nearer to the native version. The Celtic language was inflected in much the same way as Latin and Greek and a regular nominative ending was -on, which the Romans represented as -um, but as all these final syllables were to drop away like autumn leaves by about the sixth century we need not trouble very much about them. When the Anglo-Saxons arrived on the scene, such local inhabitants as were still there were probably saying little more than Londin. Later the vowels suffered some modification, but not a great deal considering the lapse of time. But what did it mean? Scholars agree that it comes from a Celtic root-word londo- meaning 'wild' or 'bold', and probably from a personal name such as Londinos, 'the bold one', which may have belonged to a tribal leader, or a minor deity, for the Celtic people believed in many gods, some of whom were extremely local. But we are peering back into darkness.

The name of London has changed less than some others of the same vintage. York, for instance, was Eboracon in the second century. Its root-word may be definitely identified with Celtic eburos, a yew tree, but once again we cannot know for certain just how it arose. Perhaps from a single significant tree, perhaps from a grove of yew trees sacred in ancient magic, for we know from Caesar that the Celtic priests, the Druids, were much addicted to sacred groves. Professor Jackson translates the name as 'the place of Eburos', but again we are left wondering if Eburos was a man, or a mythical spirit of the trees.

These speculations about mythology are based on the knowledge that all the Celtic peoples were much inclined to religion, and that, though many of their place-names consist of natural description, quite a high proportion are derived from their gods and goddesses. For instance, Camulodonum (now Colchester), the capital of the principal tribe in Britain just before the invasion of Julius Caesar, took its name from a Celtic god whom the Romans equated with Mars. To the British it was Camulo-dun, the fortress of Camulos, and no doubt his temple was an important feature of their town. Again, the magical property of the hot spring at Bath was attributed to a Celtic goddess named Sulis, whom the Romans likened to Minerva, and whose cult continued under their administration, giving this popular spa its Roman name of Aquae Sulis. Neither Camulos nor Sulis attained permanence in these two cities which had once so honoured them, but the early names serve to illustrate the strong religious tendency in the Celtic name-giving. Centuries later the descendants of these same Celts in Wales, Brittany, Cornwall and Ireland were to name innumerable places after Christian saints.

An English town that still preserves the name of a Celtic deity is Carlisle. Latin authors wrote it as Luguvallium or Luguballium, for the Celtic 'v' and 'b' were almost indistinguishable, a soft sound that often faded out altogether. Professor Jackson translates this as 'strong in Lugus', a reference to a god who was widely honoured in Gaul as well as Britain, and whose name is the root of the French Lyons and Laon and also the Dutch Leiden, each of which, in the Roman period, was called Lugudunum, the fortress of Lugus. In Irish mythology Lug, as he was known there, played an important part, a beautiful golden-haired figure, a sort of Celtic Apollo, typifying light. At the first glance Luguvallium may seem very different from Carlisle, but the link between them is well documented, thanks to that excellent person the Venerable Bede. Writing early in the eighth century he describes Saint Cuthbert walking in this town – and incidentally admiring its sights just as any tourist might look at Roman ruins today – and in his careful manner he tells us the Latin form of the name and adds that it is 'now' shortened to Luel. There were still large numbers of Britons in that district, speaking their own

7

language of course, and they called it Cair Luel, *cair* being the early form of the Welsh *caer*, a castle. So, in the course of time, with the aid of some fancy spelling by Norman clerks who understood nothing of the matter, Caer Luel became Carlisle.

The Celts were a remarkable race who began to make their presence felt in Central Europe somewhere about 600 BC. They were clever craftsmen, credited with the practical development of iron as a more serviceable metal than bronze, and this superiority over their neighbours enabled them to spread successfully from Asia Minor to the Atlantic. While the Greeks and Romans were developing their brilliant culture and civilization on the Mediterranean, the Celts were fanning out behind them to the east and west. The Greeks called them the *Keltoi*, but their more general name, used by the Romans, was the *Galli*. Some of them were the Galatians to whom St Paul wrote an epistle; others left their name in Gallipoli on the Bosphorus, in Gallina in Italy, in the districts called Galicia in Poland and in Spain, in Galloway in Scotland, and in Gaul which became France. They consisted of many tribes ruled by many kings, and united only by language, religion and culture. Those who spread into Britain from about 500 BC onwards have – for the most part – been called the Britanni. Some modern historians tell us that this should really be Pretani, a mistake due to early miscopying of manuscripts, but this matter is controversial. Julius Caesar, the first person to give a clear account in writing from first-hand knowledge of these people, called them Britanni and their island Britannia. On his authority the name has stood ever since.

It was not through lack of intellect that the Celts neglected the art of writing. Caesar tells us that they delighted in poetry, and that the education of those of higher rank consisted largely in committing vast quantities of it to memory. He stresses too that their powerful priests, the Druids, discouraged writing, preferring their ancient lore and mythology to be passed on only by word of mouth, and thus kept in secrecy from strangers. This is why the early Celtic people, though one of the great races of Europe, have remained mysterious. Under the influence of Roman rule and later of Christianity they gave up their more barbarous habits and produced Latin scholars and books famous for their visual beauty, but the oral tradition still remained a strong feature of their culture, and right into historic times the bard reciting legendary poems was one of the most honoured persons in the courts of Welsh, Irish and Scottish chiefs.

There is a striking difference to be observed in the fate of the Celtic language on either side of the Channel. The Gallic peoples of the continent were more thoroughly Romanized than the Britons, and when the central power failed and they broke apart into separate states they had lost their own old tongue and were speaking provincial dialects of Latin. Only in the western peninsula then called Armorica, but now Brittany, did the Celtic speech continue and it would probably not have done so there if refugees from Britain – fleeing from the Anglo-Saxons – had not reinforced the local population. For in Britain four hundred years of Roman occupation had failed to weaken the native tongue. During that long period the upper classes and the townsfolk must have been bilingual and official business transacted in Latin, but when, in the fifth century, the legions were withdrawn and the Britons left to themselves to withstand the onslaughts of their enemies as best they could – which was not at all well – they retreated westwards still speaking much the same language that the Romans had heard when they invaded the island four centuries before.

Tacitus, who wrote in the second century AD, tells us that the Britons spoke the same language as the Gauls, but it is not likely that he understood its finer points and there must have been some variation. In Gaul, as we have seen, it vanished away, but the branch of it spoken in Britain has a very lively descendant in modern Welsh. The Gaelic spoken in Ireland and the western fringe of Scotland, though closely related, is not descended from exactly the same source, as the Celts who settled in Ireland and spread from there to Scotland had migrated directly from the western seaboard of Europe without passing by way of Britain. Welsh contains many words of Latin origin, adopted during the Roman occupation – such as *pont* for a bridge – but it has remained entirely Celtic in character, the chief living representative of one of the great ancient languages of Europe.

9

We will return to these Celtic languages when we come to consider the names of the western lands of the British Isles (Chapters 12–15), but first we will think of the names they left behind them in England, littered here and there like abandoned arms on a battlefield to be picked up or cast aside by the victors.

The critical and exciting period when the English invaders swept over the land destroying the Romano-British way of life which they found there has few contemporary written records, and historians gathering together every scrap of information to illume this dark interlude have made great use of place-names. These tell plainly that in the eastern counties, which bore the first brunt of the invasion, there was little communication between the attackers and the attacked, for the invaders learned few of their place-names. In Sussex, for instance, hardly a single Celtic name can be found, though most of the eastern counties have a few and Kent has several. A little farther on, in a broad strip running north and south through the Midlands, far more of the old names were taken over, and in western districts such as Dorset, Somerset, the Welsh border and Cumberland so many of them have remained in use that we must imagine a mingling of the two races who had at last managed to live together with some degree of tolerance. In Wales itself, where the Britons were concentrated, their own ancient names have remained with little interference, and name-giving in their own language has gone on ever since. But whereas Celtic names of all periods abound in the west, such an origin in eastern or central England is a sure mark of antiquity.

The Celtic names of England – names such as London and York – having survived the devastation of the English invasion, are now as nearly immortal as any work of man can be. Others, like Camulodunum, though well known to scholars, have been dead these fifteen hundred years. And yet names in this class are not always so devoid of life as they may seem. The city of Verulamium fell into ruins and was replaced by St Albans; but the earlier name (without the Latin suffix) became a title of honour in the sixteenth century, and has a modern descendant in the town of Verulam, South Africa. And at Morecambe Bay in Lancashire a genuine resurrection has taken place. The Celtic name, as recorded by Ptolemy, was Morikambe, which meant literally 'curve of the sea'. This name was unused by the English until the late eighteenth century when a seaside resort began to grow up there and an enlightened gentleman suggested the revival. In fact no name is really dead if it is still known to living minds.

In this connection we think of those names that live on even though they have lost their local identities: place-names without places. The most famous of them are associated with the heroic Arthur, who is now accepted as an historical character of the Dark Ages even though the trappings with which he has been draped belong to a later date. Because he fought for the British people and their Roman inheritance, it was they who cherished his legend and it was natural that their descendants in the Celtic west remembered the places associated with him by their Celtic names rather than by new ones given by their enemies, the English. The Welsh monk, Nennius, whose *Historia Brittonum* (compiled in about 800 from older sources) gives the earliest account of Arthur, tells of twelve battles that he won, but historians can only guess where they were. His greatest victory was at Mount Badon, which the English monk Bede calls Baddesdown Hill. But where was it? To the unknown root *Bad* it was natural for the English to add their word for a fortified place, *burh*, which would in time produce Badbury. But there are several hills in the west of England with prehistoric earthworks and this very name. My own preference is for Badbury Rings in Dorset standing strategically across the ancient highway from Old Sarum to Maiden Castle, but others argue in favour of Badbury in the Vale of the White Horse, and meanwhile Badon remains only a name.

And what of Camelot? A name that everybody knows but no one can place with certainty. Tradition connects Arthur strongly with the region round Glastonbury, especially with South Cadbury Castle, a fortified hill ten miles to the south, where the remains of defensive work and a large timber hall of the right period have recently been excavated. The Tudor antiquary, John Leland, recorded the local belief that this was Camelot, and names in the neighbourhood are suggestive of it, especially the nearby villages of West Camel and Queen Camel. The syllable Cam- which makes part or the whole of several river-names is generally a Celtic survival, identical in origin

11

with the Welsh *cam* meaning curved or winding. Ekwall derives the River Camel in Cornwall from *cam pul*, curved pool, and these Somerset villages may have a similar origin. Or here we may have another reference to the god Camulos. Serious place-name scholars tend to disregard 'Camelot' because it exists only in legend, appearing first in a twelfth-century French version of the Arthurian tales which had reached France by way of Brittany. But many names have lived for centuries in oral tradition and this one – though its last syllable may show French influence – is strongly Brittonic in its basic character.

Camelot is a ghost name, dimly remembered; so also is Camlann where traditionally Arthur died. But plenty of names of the same vintage and earlier are fully alive in unbroken continuity. Their survival depended on the chance of the Angles and Saxons (or English as we may say) hearing them and starting to use them in their rightful places. The recording of them by the Romans is invaluable, as far as it goes, but their present character and very existence is due to what the English made of them.

Chapter 2

PRE-ENGLISH NAMES OF
NATURAL FEATURES

Throughout the British Isles, and probably in all the countries of the world, the oldest names are those of rivers. As each new wave of invaders penetrates a land, rivers make barriers to be crossed or practical highways for men skilled with boats, and their names, or any words applied to them, are the first to be learned from the former inhabitants.

We can see this happening in periods of expansion that are well recorded, in Virginia, for instance, where Captain John Smith was writing of the Potomac and the Susquehanna in his first accounts of the new colony, and in Canada where exploration was carried out almost entirely by water. In comparison the rivers of England may seem too small to have had such importance, but more than a thousand years ago when they flowed without control, undepleted by urban water-works, flooding freely and spreading out into swamps and marshes, they were something to be reckoned with in an unknown land.

As already indicated, the Celts on coming into Britain must have learned some river-names from their precursors; the Romans adopted wholesale those used by the Celts; and the Anglo-Saxons, in their turn, using rivers far more than the Romans did, picked up and retained far more old names for them than for any other kind of feature.

One might have thought that, the Roman garrisons being gone, the invading English had only to use the Roman roads to traverse the country with ease, but that was not their way. Roads led from one fortified place to another and these were not where they wanted to go. Their method was to strike across country and take the inhabitants by surprise, to find good land and seize it, to make their own settlements and build their own forts. They were barbarians to whom forests and rivers were more congenial than paved highways. Even after they had settled down, they showed surprisingly little appreciation of the Roman roads. We see this indicated in the many stretches of roadway lost, and the number of bridges allowed to collapse and disappear. To give one example from many, the great highway from London to the west had crossed the Thames at a place that must have had two bridges for the Romans called it Pontes. But the bridges went, and in Domesday Book the same place is simply Stanes (now Staines) presumably referring to the stones that lay about there, ruins perhaps of the bridges, while the tribal capital, Calleva, a few miles to the west had lapsed into total decay.

Such examples show that the early English settlers cared little for good roads but took their own course wherever they wanted to go, looking for fords rather than bridges and navigating the rivers in their narrow boats which could be portaged from one to another; and when they questioned captured Britons, the subject of possible waterways must always have ranked high in importance, judging by the words they learned. In their own good time they would themselves name the little brooks and bourns, as they called them, but the great majority of our river-names are pre-English.

One river at least, the Thames, must have been known to the Saxons before they came to settle in Britain, and to the Romans too before their coming. Caesar called it Tamesis, and this makes it (after Kent) the second recorded name in England that is still in use. But the sea-going peoples of northern Europe must have been well aware of that wide estuary, close to the continent, and used a common name for it long before he sailed. The root of the name goes back to an Indo-European word, meaning 'dark', which Ekwall relates to the Sanscrit *Tamasa*, a tributary of the Ganges. By the time it reached Britain it seems to have implied 'dark water', for it became a regular river-name, recurring in many places as Thame, Tame, Teme, Tamar, Tavy and the Welsh Taff.

This brings us to a point which must be made clear for an

understanding of Celtic names, the close relation of 'm', 'v', and 'b'. This may be seen in several European languages, but nowhere in a more active state than in Welsh, in which *mawr*, meaning 'big' can change into *fawr*; and *bach*, meaning 'little', can become *fach*, in a bewildering way to the English mind. Once this is grasped one can see how Tavy belongs to the same group as Tame, and how Dover, a purely British name, was written Dubris by the Romans. It consists of one of the many Celtic words for water, one that still exists in modern Welsh as *dwfr* (pronounced 'dooverr'). The small river on which the town stands is now called the Dour, another version of the same word. The Latin form was a locative plural, literally 'at the waters', but it was the singular that survived, as it does also in Andover ('ash-tree river'), Wendover ('white river'), Dovercourt ('river farm'), Dover Beck and other places.

This early tendency to use a generic term for water, whether still or flowing, has resulted in much repetition among river-names. Avon is simply the Welsh word for a river, *afon*, and there are at least eight rivers of this name in Britain. Five English rivers are called Stour, and to what ancient language it belongs has been much debated. The Wye is identical in name with the Wey near London, with the Dorset Wey that gave its name to Weymouth, and with the second part of Medway. Celtic scholars link it with the Welsh word *gwy* that means 'winding'. Yet another river-name that recurs regularly is Ouse, and this is probably related to Exe, Axe, Esk and Usk which are all forms of the same Celtic word for 'water'. In Gaelic it is *uisce*, better known to the world as 'whiskey'. The Romans who built military stations on the Exe and the Usk called them both Isca, differentiating them by the names of the local tribes as Isca Dumniorum (now Exeter) and Isca Silurum (Caerleon).

The use of such general expressions for rivers rather than individual names has sometimes been explained as arising from verbal misunderstanding. Captured Britons pointing out the way to their conquerors might use some such words as 'water', and the latter take it to be the river's name and use it ever after. This may sometimes have happened, but we must also bear in mind that people who live near a river seldom use its proper name but usually speak of 'the river'. In this way many rivers have acquired very simple names that have stuck to them permanently. The Indus, the Ganges, the Yukon and the Yarra, to name but a few, have the same basic meaning as Avon.

Another point should also be borne in mind. The Celtic race, like the Greeks and Romans, believed in an unlimited number of minor gods and goddesses, each presiding over some hill, forest or stream. This is known from excavated Latin inscriptions on altars and shrines, for the Romans were tolerant of other people's deities, even willing to make offerings to them in their own locality. Above all, the Celts held rivers to be sacred, a natural belief for imaginative people, whose religion is closely bound up in the world of nature. Many races have believed them sacred, and some – the Ganges for instance – are still held to be so. The Arthurian legends which, in spite of the accretion of later detail which has disguised them, did actually originate in pre-English Britain, are full of magical inhabitants of lakes and rivers. And the fact that some of the finest pieces of early Celtic metalwork, swords, helmets and shields have been found in modern times in lakes and rivers seems to confirm that the story of Arthur's sword being thrown back into the lake from which it had miraculously come was a genuine folk memory of an ancient cult. Thus the individual names of rivers may often have been held in reverence: names not to be lightly spoken, especially to strangers. It was perhaps better in common speech to say 'the river' or 'the dark water', or it may be that the true translation of that phrase is 'the dark one'.

Several specific river-names are known to be those of deities. The Lea was earlier the Lygan, derived from the popular god Lugus;* and the Ribble, one of the very few of any size to be renamed by the English, was recorded by the Romans as Belisama, the name of a warlike Celtic goddess. The Brent, now swallowed up in outer London, occurs first as Braegente, which must be identified with the goddess Brigantia, whose name, recorded in Latin inscriptions in Britain and Gaul, apparently meant 'the high one'. A good example is given by the Dee, which the Romans called Deva, a word signifying 'goddess' which was almost the same in Latin and Brittonic.

* Luton, which is on the Lea, appears first as Lygtun.

In modern Welsh the Dee is Dyfr Dwy, 'water of the holy one', but the actual name of the divinity is avoided.

The name Severn has already been mentioned as probably pre-Celtic. As a highway for early ships, with a great estuary to invite them in, the river must have been widely known from prehistoric times. We hear of it first from Tacitus who calls it Sabrina, following the usual Latin custom of writing a Celtic 'v' as 'b'. The origin of the name is unknown but so magical is its quality that we easily share Milton's vision of the nymph 'Sabrina fair ... under the glassy, cool, translucent wave'. Geoffrey of Monmouth who wrote his fanciful *History of the Kings of Britain* in the twelfth century tells us how the river took its name from a beautiful maiden, a king's daughter, thrown into it at the command of a jealous queen. No one believes Geoffrey's stories, but this one serves to illustrate the point that a noble river was sure to inspire the Celtic imagination.

Some of our Celtic river-names can be given more definite descriptive meanings. The Trent and the Tarrant both come from a British *Trisanton* which Ekwall interprets as 'across the path' or 'flooding', and according to Ptolemy's account several other British rivers were known by this name. Some tell of the forests through which the rivers once flowed and, as we should expect, the British oak makes its presence felt from an early date, for Darwen, Derwent, Darent and Dart are all related to the Welsh *derwen*, an oak tree – all rivers among oaks. Frome, the name of two rivers in England, means 'fair' and 'bright'.

Nearly every river-name has produced its crop of secondary names, and in this way the oldest names in England have been multiplied and perpetuated. Sometimes a settlement that has grown up beside a river has been called by its name and nothing more. Some of these have been mentioned. Others include Yeovil, for instance, which took the name of the river Gifle, much distorted in later times by Norman spelling, and Hull, which at one time became known as Kingston-on-Hull but is more often called by its older and simpler river-name. It often happens that a town-name preserves a river-name that is otherwise lost, as at Dawlish in Devon, where the stream was once known by the Celtic words *dub glais*, 'black stream', later

17

contracted and corrupted to Dawlish, but precisely the same in origin as the northern Douglas and the Welsh Dulas. Very frequently, as at Dover, the town has far outstripped its parent stream in importance.

But in the great majority of cases where settlements have been named from rivers, the Anglo-Saxons added some qualifying word of their own, elucidating the nature of the place. Examples are numerous but a few will serve to show how these ancient river-names were given a new lease of life by the English settlers. Tavistock is on the River Tavy; Taunton on the Tone; Wilton on the Wylie, and Wiltshire takes its name from the dwellers in its valley. The Dart has named not only Dartmouth but Dartmoor; Yarmouth in Norfolk is at the mouth of the Yare, Sheffield on the Sheaf. Kendal is in the valley or 'dale' of the Kent, which has the same name as the Kennet and no connection with the county. In every case the second element is English, the first much older.

In Wales and Scotland this type of name is even more common than in England, the prefix Aber- corresponding to the English 'mouth'. Aberdeen for instance stands at the mouth of the Don, another Celtic river name that is found in many lands; Aberdovey, on the Dovey (Welsh *Dyfi*) – 'black water' again – the Celtic race seems to have been fascinated with the darkness of its streams.

For other natural features many names of Celtic or even earlier origin have been preserved, though not in such high proportion as for rivers, and as is inevitable with such prehistoric survivals many have no certain meaning. The isle of Thanet was called Tanatus by the Romans (Tanet in Domesday Book). Ekwall associated the meaning with the Welsh *tan*, 'fire', and suggests that a beacon may have burnt there. The 'h' was a late addition made by pedantic writers just as happened with the spelling of Thames.

The Isle of Wight was the Roman Vectis and although it looks so different it is just the same word; the Roman 'v' represents the sound of 'w'; the 'c' represents the guttural 'ch' as in *loch*, a sound that was later written 'h' or 'gh' by the English, and then lost in speech though it remains in writing to mystify foreigners. The Latin suffix -*is* dropped off, and the

Celtic 'e' changed to an Anglo Saxon 'i', as it very often did. In fact Wight is a word to which everything has happened and yet it is still the same. Its original meaning was 'raised' or 'heaved up', and the thought behind it must have been that the island had risen from the sea.

No meaning is known for the name of the Isles of Scilly, and the chief point of interest in their earliest mention – by a Roman writer, Sulpicius Severus – is that he speaks of 'the island of Scylina' as if it were one island, and this fits in with the many legends of a lost land off the Cornish coast. Archaeologists are seriously of the opinion that the Scillies may once have been joined together in a single island of larger dimensions (alternatively called Lyonesse, another of those 'ghost names').

We are less well informed about the ancient names of hills than of rivers. Roman records seldom name them, and Old English charters which frequently give rivers as boundaries have little occasion to mention hills. Such a well-known name as Helvelyn, for instance, which sounds old and Celtic, is not found before the Tudor period. One whose antiquity is proved by indirect evidence from the Roman period is the Wrekin, a rugged iron-age hill-fort that watches over the upper valley of the Severn. The first appearance of this name is in a charter of 975, as the Wrokene, but it is far older than that, for the Roman town of Viroconium, now Wroxeter, built on its lower slope, was clearly named from it. The abandonment of bleak hill-tops in favour of more comfortable positions lower down was one of the regular processes of civilization, and in hilly country many villages bear names that belonged earlier to the heights above them.

No meaning is known for Wrekin, and many other hill-names that emerge from the same pre-English obscurity have unknown origins. The Chilterns are mentioned in an eighth-century chronicle as 'the deserts of Chiltern' meaning an uninhabitable region. It seems that the densely wooded slopes of this chalky ridge were by-passed by the Saxons in their search for land on which to settle. Such a place would serve as a refuge for dispossessed Britons, some of whom may well have survived here with their prehistoric name.

Just as the Britons had many words for water in its various manifestations, so they had many for hills and mountains of different sorts. The Welsh word for a mountain is *mynedd*, and an early form of this has given us the Long Mynd in Shropshire and the first syllable of the Mendips. For rather smaller hills a common word was *bryn* which often takes the form of *fryn*. Malvern was *moel fryn*, the bare hill, as it still is. Moel, literally the 'bald one', names many hills in Wales.

Another British word for a small hill was *cruc*, which has given several village names such as Creech, Crich and Crick. As the English invaders did not understand its meaning but took it to be a proper name they were inclined to add their own word 'hill' to it. 'Cruc hill' became Crichel in Dorset, while Cricklewood on the edge of London begins with the same combination and might be literally rendered 'hill hill wood'.

The same thing happened with *pen*, a British word for a headland or hilltop. Again the English added their own word of similar meaning, making the redundant Penhill. This ran more smoothly as Pendle which occurs in several places such as Pendlebury in Lancashire, while in the same county Pendle Hill repeats the statement in triplicate.

As we have seen, the English picked up a number of geographical terms from the conquered Britons but seem seldom to have understood them as common nouns, treating them rather as specific place-names. One of the very few that they adopted with comprehension was *cumb* for a deep valley, now coombe in many English place-names, and *cwm* in Welsh. The familiar word 'pool' was common to both languages, the Anglo-Saxons having had it from a Teutonic source and the Britons from a cognate Celtic root, which became *pwll* in Welsh and *pol* in Cornish. In early times it signified something rather larger and deeper than it does now, essentially a good anchorage for boats. It is in this sense that Pol- begins the names of so many Cornish harbours, and we see the same meaning in 'the Pool of London'. It is found all over England and makes the whole name of the town of Poole in Dorset, whose large harbour, almost completely land-locked, made a sheltered anchorage for Alfred's fleet.

It may easily be seen that one cannot separate the names of natural features from those of towns when looking at their origins, for the one often grew into the other; a high proportion of our older cities have names that refer basically to hills or rivers, often in the Brittonic language. Some of these will be considered in the next chapter.

Altogether our heritage of pre-English place-names is large, much of it well understood, much of it obscure, and among the unexplained elements are some that may be pre-Brittonic. This uncertainty gives a background of depth and mystery to the main body of our place-names, which might be a less fascinating study if all their origins were clearly known.

Chapter 3

THE ROMAN LEGACY

It was only natural that the Anglo-Saxons exploring their way across Britain should adopt many names of rivers and hills that they heard from the local inhabitants; and there was another series of large physical objects, which could not be ignored. These were the Roman cities, forts and other military installations which made prominent features of the landscape. The English settlers had no word in their own language for these Roman towns, so unlike anything they would build themselves. They needed a general term for them, something quite different from their own habitation names, and they found it in the Latin word *castra*, which they must have heard the Britons use. To the Romans it meant a military camp, but the English applied it freely to any collection of buildings that was clearly Roman in origin. They must have adopted it very early in the invasion for its use spread quickly among them in every part that they penetrated. In the earliest English records it is written *ceaster*, but its pronunciation soon began to vary in different regions, following the regular sound-changes that gradually took place in the language. It was a normal development that 'c' followed by 'i' or 'e' would turn into a 'ch' sound in the South or Midlands, though it generally remained hard in the North. So the Old English form *ceaster* became either 'chester' or 'caster', and might be further softened or contracted by later influence.

To the Romans this had been an ordinary common noun, hardly ever used as a proper name. The name of their military station on the Dee was Deva, though they might have described it as *castra legionum*, 'camp of the legions'. It was the English who called it Chester. At first they said 'Leganchester', but soon the first element, their version of 'legion', was dropped. They might easily have called it Deechester, which would have been more in line with their usual practice, but in this case the borrowed word was left to stand alone.

For several centuries this useful word must have been hard-worked by the English in their daily speech, for over a hundred of their place-names contain it in some form, often combined with common English nouns, as at Chesterford, Chesterfield, Casterton, and so forth. But even more often an older name was retained and *ceaster* tacked on to the end of it, to indicate the presence of Roman work. Occasionally London appears as Lundenceaster, but it shook off the encumbrance. Just how English this word became in those formative years of settlement is shown by the learned monk, Bede, who – writing in about the year 730 – mentions the Roman city of 'Verulam, or, as the English call it, Verlamcaster'. This particular name did not last but many of the same sort did.

Gloucester was Gloiu to the Welsh (Latin, Glevum), and this meant 'bright'; Nennius calls it Caer Gloiu, which might be translated 'the shining fortress'. Manchester was Mamucion, which must be related to the Welsh *mam* which means 'mother' or 'breast'. This word was often used in the Celtic west to name a rounded or breast-shaped hill, and the first habitations at Manchester must have nestled in such a place. Worcester took its name from the Wigoran, an ancient British tribe that inhabited those parts and gave their name also to the forest of Wyre which once covered much of Worcestershire. To each of these *ceaster* was added.

Dorchester, the chief town of Dorset, has a confusing history. The Romans wrote it Durnovaria and the first element has been identified with the Welsh *dwrn* meaning 'a clenched fist', which occurs in the names of several ancient Celtic strongholds such as Dundurn in Scotland. It was probably first applied to the great Iron Age hill fort now known as Maiden Castle, and later to the important town that the Romans established nearby to take its place; eventually it gave a name to the whole county. But exactly why a fist? Perhaps the great earth ramparts silhouetted against the sky looked 'fist-shaped'; the clenched fist is also an apt symbol of defence.*

Winchester presents us with another puzzle. Its basic element, which appears first (in Ptolemy) as Ouenta, was a regular British place-name occurring in several parts of Britain. The Romans wrote it with an initial V and distinguished the three places of this name where they built important towns by adding their local tribal names, thus making Venta Belgarum (Winchester), Venta Icenorum (Caistor-near-Norwich) and Venta Silurum in South Wales. The last of these three has retained the name, prefixed with Caer, and is now Caerwent, and the surrounding district was formerly called Gwent, the same again. The Venta in East Anglia was left deserted and its name forgotten, while a new settlement which the English called Norwich grew up a few miles away; but the name Caistor for the tiny hamlet where once the Roman city stood shows that at least they spoke of the place though they left it to decay. In the south the Saxons who landed from Southampton Water captured the Venta of those parts, and hearing it called something like Went adopted the name as *Wintan ceaster*, the vowel changing a little as it passed from British to Saxon mouths. The ending -an shows the genitive case, 'the fortress of Went', identical with Caerwent. But what did this *went* mean? It must have been something of a general nature to occur so often – perhaps a market.

We have seen that the Romans, when needing a name for a city, frequently used the local name of the river on which it was built, and the English settlers often carried on these river-names with the addition of *ceaster*. Doncaster is on the Don, Lancaster on the Lune, Exeter on the Exe, Towcester on the Tove, and Cirencester on the Churn. In this last case it was Norman influence that caused the two 'c's to become as soft as they would be in French, instead of remaining like the 'ch' in the river-name. Colchester is on the Colne, and we must pause a moment here to wonder that its older name, Camulodun, famous before the Romans came to Britain, should have been allowed to lapse. Being on the eastern side of the country the city must have been overrun at an early date, perhaps leaving

---

* Dorchester in Oxfordshire had a different first element, recorded first as Dorcic, and thought to be a Celtic river-name, the same as that in Dorking.

no survivors, but the invaders had learnt the Celtic name of its river and called it 'the chester on the Colne'. Leicester seems to be another of the same type. Its Roman name, Ratae, was completely lost, but a twelfth-century chronicler – William of Malmesbury – gives the old name of its river as the Legra (it is now called the Soar), and says that the town was named from it.

Whenever a name contains *ceaster* in any form we can be sure that there were Roman buildings on the spot when the English first saw it. But the converse does not hold true, for not all Roman towns, by any means, received this as part of their names. Some were given a purely English name; others an English addition to what was there before. In the first category we think of Bath, one of the finest cities of Roman Britain. It was called Aquae Sulis, 'the waters of Sulis', from a Celtic goddess who had some affinities with Minerva, and whose shield bearing a ferocious Gorgon's head vigorously carved in stone is the principal relic of her temple. But when the English reached this city, more than a century after their first landings in Kent, what chiefly impressed them, and very naturally, was the sight of the great stone baths flowing with hot water, and that was how they spoke of the place – simply as 'the baths'. The earliest form is plural, but the inflection was soon dropped. Occasionally in early records it is Bathancaster, but the bath was impressive enough to stand alone. A plain name for a gracious city.

Many examples may be found of Romano-British names to which the English added an explanatory word of their own, such as 'field', as at Lichfield (page 32), or 'bridge' as at Corbridge. The latter was one of the few places where the Roman bridge continued in use and was clearly the chief importance of the place to the English. The old name Corstopitum was much too long for them, especially when they had added 'bridge' to it, and nothing of it survives but its first syllable. It may generally be observed that when an addition to a name made its length unwieldy, it was the middle that was squeezed out of existence. The finished product, Corbridge, may be compared with the South African Jo'burg, contracted in just the same way.

The Anglo-Saxons' own word for a fortified place such as they might make for themselves was *burh*. This has come down to us in several different forms of which the commonest are 'borough' and 'bury', and although they never used the borrowed *ceaster* for strongholds of their own making, they did occasionally use 'bury' for a Roman one that they occupied. This is the case at Canterbury where the Romano-British name Duroverneum ('the fort in the marsh') was totally lost, and the invaders called it simply 'the fort of the men of Kent' (*Cantwaraburgh*). In doing so they were coining a new name for the town, but the first element had been recorded by Pytheas as Kantion at least eight hundred years earlier.

Salisbury is another example of a Romano-British town-name with -bury added instead of -chester. This may be explained by the fact that the original site – now known as Old Sarum – was an Iron Age hill-fort whose massive ramparts of chalk were more striking to the Saxon beholders than the Roman buildings they enclosed. The common words that the Celtic builders of such strongholds had generally used for them were *dun* or *duro*, and these the English seem to have understood, for they frequently translated them by their own 'bury'. In this case *Sorvio dunum*, as it was written in the Roman period, had become *Searo byrig* by 552, when it first appears in the *Anglo-Saxon Chronicle*. By the time of Domesday Book it was Sarisberie, which still signified 'the fortress of Sari', or some such word, the original Celtic name having been considerably whittled away by the passage of time. After the Norman Conquest it suffered a further distortion when the 'r' which had been on record for at least a thousand years changed into an 'l', simply because that arrangement of sounds ran more smoothly on the tongues that spoke the name most often at that time. ('R' to 'l' has always been a frequent sound change. One has only to think of Harry becoming Hal, and Mary Moll.) It is always the case that a word of unknown meaning is much more knocked about in use than one that is understood, and nobody knows what Sorvio meant. It was probably already ancient when the Romans heard it and it is unlikely that they thought of it as anything but a name. There is nothing left of the prehistoric name now except the initial 'S', and yet it has a continuous history from pre-Roman times.

The next great change to Salisbury was one of physical location. Soon after 1200 the crowded Norman city which had grown up on the fortified hill-top moved dramatically down to the meadows by the river on the plain below. Innumerable towns all over Europe have started as hill-top forts and gradually spread to lower slopes, leaving the original settlements as citadels above the modern towns. But Salisbury was deliberately moved two miles away. The old site, cold, windy and cramped as it must have been, was abandoned; the massive Norman cathedral built within its ramparts little more than a century earlier was laboriously demolished, and a new cathedral in the very latest style was raised to be one of the glories of England in the meadows by the Avon. And with all the cartloads of good stone and useful rubble, including a mixture of Roman brick that was carried to the new position in this great upheaval, the name came too, so that today after another seven hundred centuries it seems to epitomize, not the bleak fortress that it once was, but the very essence of green pastures and ecclesiastical mildness.

Meanwhile, the authorities of the episcopal city in their Latin records still used the root of the older form of the name, Sar-, with an abbreviated Latin inflection, and this brief form, Sarum, has become the official term for the bishopric, as well as a distinguishing name for the old uninhabited site of the town. Thus the part of the name that signifies a fortress is now attached to the unfortified cathedral town among gentle meadows, and not to the hill-top whose ramparts were built and rebuilt over a period of at least fifteen hundred years.

But the gradual reshaping of the name of Salisbury to its present form was by no means the end of its adventures. The city had enough strategic importance to warrant an earldom, and at the time of the move King John's half-brother, William Longsword, a great crusader and a powerful baron, was Earl of Salisbury. He was the first man to be buried in the new cathedral and may be seen there lying in effigy, while the copy of Magna Carta which he brought back from Runnymede is still in the cathedral library. The point of interest for us is that when a place-name becomes a personal title it acquires a new dimension and even mobility. It was not directly from the English town but from a Marquis of Salisbury, six centuries nearer to us than the crusader earl, that the capital of Rhodesia was named, a city nearly ten times the size of the English Salisbury.

Such names as Salisbury, Canterbury and Lichfield have no particle of Latin in their composition, consisting in each case of a Celtic beginning and an English end. But in spite of this the Romans did influence these names by recording their older elements and turning their sites into forts and cities. By doing so they increased the chances that the names would survive the English invasion, and those that did survive have for the most part attained distinction in England and new honours overseas.

It is a remarkable fact that the Romans who ruled Britain for four centuries left almost no names of their own creation. We may compare this with the rule of the British in India, who respected the names they found there and withdrew having added little to them. The chief contribution of Imperial Rome to our place-names was a small number of common nouns which passed from Latin into English and were used in the naming that took place after the Romans had gone. We have already seen how *ceaster* was used in this way and afterwards allowed to drop out of the language. Other words borrowed from Latin at that time and kept in use ever since include *strata* for a paved road, which makes part of the names of many towns on Roman roads such as Stratford and Streatham, and exists as the modern 'street'; *vallum* for a well-built wall such as the one that reached to Wallsend; and *portus*, a harbour or market town, which is often hard to distinguish from *porta*, a gate, and forms the second element of innumerable English place-names. Some of these Latin words may have been picked up by the ancestors of the English before they left their continental homes, though these were never part of the Roman empire, but *ceaster* was learnt in Britain for it was not used in this way anywhere else in Europe.

The Ordnance Survey Map of Roman Britain gives 236 names of natural features and inhabited spots recorded in classical times, and of these over sixty are still in use in some form, though some are barely recognizable. But a study of these surviving names shows them to be practically all Celtic in origin or at least pre-Roman. The few exceptions may be quickly enumerated. The one with the strongest claim to have descended entirely from a Latin name given in the Roman period is Catterick. This seems to come from the Latin *cataracta*, a waterfall, and may have referred to the rapids in the nearby River Swale; Ptolemy gives it as Katouraktonion. It was then a military station, as it is today.

Portchester consists of two Latin words, but it was the English who put them together; the Roman name was Portus Adurni, the second word probably the Celtic name of the river now called the Adur. Lincoln is half Latin. Its Brittonic name was Lindon, meaning a lake (cf. Welsh *llyn*). The Romans used the place as a *colonia*, that is, a settlement for retired soldiers, and the English hearing the expression *Lindum colonia* telescoped it, in the course of time, into Lincoln. The Roman *legion* survives in the second half of Carleon. Its earlier name was Isca, taken from its river which we now call the Usk, but the local inhabitants must have spoken of it as 'the fort of the legions', for that is what has remained, *caer* being the Welsh word for a fort.

But it should not be thought that Romans in Britain never originated names. It is just that such names as they did give lacked staying power. They called a promontory in the west the Cape of Hercules – all very splendid – but the English when they penetrated so far saw many stags in the neighbourhood and called it Hartland Point. They called a new fort that they built, where they had bridged the river Tyne, Pons Aelius, thereby honouring the family name of the Emperor Trajan who had instigated the work, but we hear nothing more of this place after the Romans' departure until the twelfth century when the Normans built a castle there which was called, very naturally, Newcastle. They called the island of Jersey Caesarea (the equivalent of Kingston as used in British colonies), but the Norsemen gave it a less pretentious name, which probably means 'grass island'. They even renamed London Augusta. The Roman writer, Aminianus, using this name in about AD 380, remarked that elderly people still sometimes called it Londinium.

This regal style of naming has been much practised by later colonizing powers, and in places where there was no strongly established previous name and the new one was in keeping with

B*

the loyalties of its future inhabitants it has generally flourished, as the many Victorias in distant lands bear witness. But London was no new growth in the fourth century. Its British inhabitants had inherited the name from their ancestors, and no imperial edict was likely to change their speech habits. Besides this, the old name must have been widely known among seamen of northern Europe including the Saxon pirates, and it was they who would have the last word on the matter.

In the general failure of the Romans to contribute permanent names to Britain, we must notice two cases which are especially remarkable. Although they left a wonderful system of roads, much of which is still in use, we do not know what they themselves called a single mile of it. The old names that remain for the Roman roads are either pre-Roman – such as the Icnield Way which appears to be connected with the British tribe called the Iceni who inhabited the part of Norfolk to which it leads in one direction – or were given later by the Anglo-Saxons. The Fosse Way includes a Latin word, but it is most unlikely that the Romans would have named a great highway from the ditch that ran beside it, a normal feature of their road-making. *Fossa* was one of the handful of Latin words that the English picked up, though they made little use of it, preferring their own 'ditch' or 'dyke'. In this case they probably used it to indicate that the road had been made in the Roman style, so different from the winding tracks that contented them.

The other gap is even more striking. Roman Britain was an agricultural country and all its central and southern regions, excluding only the mountainous parts, were dotted with 'villas', or large farmhouses. Over two hundred of these have been excavated but not one of their original names is known. They are listed on the Ordnance *Map of Roman Britain* by the names of the nearest village, farm or field, and these names are palpably English – names such as Fishbourne, Lullingstone, Honeyditches, North Leigh and so on. It goes without saying that each villa once had its individual name. In France such names continued and the Latin word *villa* has made the regular place-name element *ville*. In Britain the whole system of Roman villas vanished away, names and all, and remained unknown until the archaeologists began to dig it up. *Ville* never entered our common speech until the Normans brought it in the form of 'village', and has played no part in our local naming except for a very few Norman importations and a few modern hybrids, which still seem alien.

In short, though the English took enough notice of some of the features of Roman civilization to learn the new words 'chester', 'port', 'street' and 'wall', they seem to have shown an extraordinary lack of interest in its farms. This is indeed strange and there must have been a strong reason to account for it since they were farmers by nature, and needed the same things that had dictated the positions of those villas, water, good soil and shelter from the worst of the weather. But rather than use the same buildings or rebuild on the same foundations they preferred to start again at least half a mile away. The fact that their style of living was different seems hardly sufficient to explain it entirely; they could at least have used the barns. In fact those who have thought most about it are led to the opinion that the first English invaders had a superstitious dread of these deserted buildings, strange to them in their luxurious details, and haunted perhaps by the ghosts of their former owners. However that may be, the fact stands out that when the English built their first homes in this island they made a new start, and there is no continuity here from Roman villa to medieval village as there is in France.

With larger towns, as we have seen, there was often continuity, but not always, and the whole subject remains mysterious and intriguing. In some towns, London, York, Bath, Colchester, Chester and others, Roman remains right under their centres have proved that the English occupation began inside the cities. Probably matters of strategic position, prestige or other special advantages could sometimes outweigh the English dislike for the places. There is something incongruous in the picture of the Saxon barbarian camping with his followers in a colonnaded atrium and haranguing them in a theatre or forum. But something of this sort must often have happened, and can be imagined most clearly in those Roman towns whose older names gave place to English ones – towns such as Chichester, which under Roman rule had been known as Regnum, the capital of a native kingdom. The English called it Cissanceaster, the 'chester of Cissa'. According to the *Anglo-Saxon Chronicle* Cissa was a son of Aelle, the leader of the South

Saxons, who landed on the Sussex coast in 477 and after slaughtering a great many Britons became for a time the most powerful king in England. Clearly the conquered Regnum fell to the share of Cissa, and we may picture him keeping his rude court there among the broken columns and the ghosts.

But with some Roman cities the very same thing happened as with the villas; the English town that took the place of the Roman one grew up not within its walls but a mile or two away. Verulam was left to decay and its walls to crumble while St Albans grew on the hill beside it; Lichfield carries on the name of the Roman Letocetum, but the actual site of the Roman town is two miles away, and is now called simply Wall. The name of the cathedral city is given by Bede as 'Lyccid feld' which indicates that its site is not the town of Liccid itself but an open place near it. Viroconium was abandoned, its bridge across the Severn neglected while the English preferred to use a ford a few miles upstream where their important town of Shrewsbury grew up; and only a tiny village near the site of the Roman town carries on the older name as Wroxeter. Calleva, one of the provincial capitals of the south, is un-inhabited and its name gone, while the small village outside its ruined walls has the English name, Silchester, the 'chester in the sallows'.

It may be seen that the continuity of Romano-British towns and their names is very diverse. Some towns continued and some vanished; some names survived and some did not, and these do not coincide neatly with the survival of the towns. Where the Romano-British name has come down to us – however distorted and augmented – we may suppose that some Britons lived on in the neighbourhood, perhaps among the ruins, speaking the name though not necessarily prospering much themselves. Where the city continued and grew, but with an entirely new name as at Chichester, it is more likely that the English who took possession had the place completely to themselves. In between these two situations are many other possibilities, and no very clear pattern emerges, beyond the indisputable facts that far more pre-English names survived in the west than in the east, and far more names of important places than of small ones. We also see that when the English settlers did hear and adopt the earlier name they nearly always telescoped it to something shorter and added a word of their own to it, so that at last it is often barely recognizable except by the expert, who by a study of early records has seen it at every stage of its metamorphosis.

Chapter 4

THE FIRST ENGLISH SETTLEMENTS

We come now to the names that the English made for themselves as they spread across Britain from the fifth century onwards. It took them nearly three centuries to occupy most of the land that would bear their name, and this period was the most prolific of lasting place-names that this land has known.

These completely English names, being part of our own language, are much easier to interpret than the older Celtic ones that the invaders heard and adopted. Indeed, a great many English names, such as Nutfield, Woodbridge and Sevenoaks are still self-explanatory. But we must beware of jumping to easy conclusions. Shipton has nothing to do with ships, nor Gateshead with gates. In fifteen hundred years of use the language has changed greatly; names often preserve old forms; and they too have suffered natural contractions and odd distortions which can easily mislead us.

The great majority of the names of our towns and villages are to be found in Domesday Book, compiled at the order of William the Conqueror in 1086, and we must be grateful for this immensely valuable piece of work. However, it has the disadvantage of having been written by French clerks who spelt the names in their own way, often showing a lack of understanding. Evidence from Old English sources is of far more value, and fortunately a good many such do exist, saved by careful, loving hands, chiefly in monasteries. A series of charters from the seventh century onwards is especially useful because, being chiefly concerned with the ownership of land, they mention so many places. The *Anglo-Saxon Chronicle* is also full of local names, and so too is the history written by the Northumbrian monk Bede who, although he was born in the seventh century when his people were newly converted from heathen savagery, was far more scholarly, conscientious, well-mannered and generally civilized than the Norman king and his scribes four hundred years later. What Bede tells us is good, first-hand evidence. One way and another large numbers of our place-names are recorded in their original forms, and it is from these that language experts can give accurate meanings. Others that occur first in Norman or later medieval records are more open to doubt. But in every case it is the earliest known example that must be studied, rather than the modern form.

The chief characteristic of these English names is their spontaneity. They sprang into life on the lips of practical men of action identifying places, as they came to know them, by straightforward description. Unlike their remote descendants in other lands, these Anglo-Saxons seem never to have coined a place-name deliberately; they simply spoke of what they saw and knew, stressing the points of greatest interest to themselves, and as they spoke the names were born.

That being so, these names can tell us a great deal about the land as those early invaders saw it and about themselves; and if we analyse the component parts of the names as a whole, we can learn the subjects they spoke of most in regard to their new homeland, and the significant points of the places in which they chose to settle. The themes most constantly repeated fall into four main groups: the importance of the tribal unit; dwelling places and with them defence – for these two concepts were at first inseparable; the physical nature of the land; and the personal names of the settlers. Religion occurs as a theme too, but to a much smaller extent than these others.

The tribal theme must be considered first because it belongs chiefly to the earliest phase of the invasion, and it will lead us to some of the regular terms for defensive settlement.

When we speak of tribes we naturally think at once of large divisions, such as the South, the East, and the Middle Saxons, the North Folk and the South Folk, each of which has named a whole county. But we will leave county names for another chapter and turn now to the smaller groups of which the greater ones were composed, groups of all sizes down to the family party. Their names are scattered in hundreds on the map.

The special relationship compounded of interdependence and loyalty that bound such groups together was expressed in Old English by the syllable -ing, and as this plays a large part in the vocabulary of place-names some understanding of its early significance is essential. In the singular form it could mean a son, but could also be used in a less definite sense expressing any close association. In the plural it generally implied a group of dependants, a group who belonged together. Thus the Whittings, or *Hwītingas* as it was written in Old English, were the family and followers of Hwīta (or White), a common early nickname. Their settlements bear such names as Whittingham and Whittington.

But the very earliest of the -ing names have no exact territorial ending, such as -ham or -ton. They consist only of the name of the group, the land they occupied being inferred, and at first their significance must have been fluid, depending on the movements of the people. Once they had settled down the name was localized for ever. In most cases the first element is the name of their leader. Barking in Essex, first recorded as *Berecingas*, means the people of Beric; Worthing in Sussex comes from the followers of Wurth; Godalming in Surrey from Godhelm's men, and there are dozens more of the same sort. The groups varied greatly in size. Reading, for instance, was settled by a large tribe led by Reada (the Red), its early importance being reflected by the size of its manor in Domesday Book. The followers of Hæsta who gave their name to Hastings occupied an area that might almost have become a county; indeed the *Anglo-Saxon Chronicle* as late as 1011 includes it as such in a list of southern shires ravaged by the Danes. This early Hæsta must have been a powerful personality, but no record of him survives except his name firmly planted on the Sussex coast, in a spot that was to be associated with another violent invasion in 1066, about six centuries after his incursion.

Not all the -ing names begin with that of their leader. In some the first element consists of a feature of the land which they had made their own. Nazeing in Essex refers to a group who had settled on a jutting-out spur of land which they called the Naze, or nose. This is the same word which in several forms, Scandinavian as well as English, was to be used for scores of capes and headlands. Epping was earlier *Uppingas*, the people of the upland, and the same expression occurs in quite another district, in Uppingham, the home of the Uppings. Horning in Essex meant the people of the horn, alluding to a sharp bend in the river, and Dorking, the people of the Dorc, the old name of the river there which later became the Mole.

These tribal names had something of the quality of clan names, but the clan system never developed in England, and they survive as place-names only. As they always referred to groups of people, their original form was plural (nominative *-ingas*, genitive *-inga*), but with the passage of time their origins were forgotten and the inflections dropped, leaving the simple ending -ing. A rare example that retained the final 's' is Hastings.

That names ending in -ing are early in date, belonging chiefly to the first century of invasion, is shown by the fact that they are found almost entirely in the eastern and southern counties. As the invaders pressed westwards, breaking up into smaller parties, it became their custom as they established their permanent dwellings to add something more to the group name, a simple word indicating the type of settlement. So we come to the -inghams and the -ingtons, the most typical of all English names, and these too are comparatively early. The -inghams, though more widely spread than the -ings, are rare in the hilly west that was penetrated last, but the -ingtons that developed a little later are widely scattered over all the land.*

Ham, -ton, and the other familiar place-name endings that signify settlement are worth careful study, for they can tell us

* There has been much recent discussion of the precise significance of -ing, which may vary slightly. Wherever early sources show that the original form was plural, as in Basingstoke (Basinga stoc, 990) there is no doubt of its being a group word, 'the meeting place of Basa's people'. But many names of this type are not on record before the Conquest, by which time grammatical inflections were often blurred, especially in the middle element of three, and it is argued that in some cases the -ing may have been singular, signifying direct possession by the person named, without reference to his people. Thus Birmingham, which is generally modernized as 'the homestead of Beorma's people', could more exactly be 'the homestead at Beorma's place'. The matter is fully discussed in *Names of Towns and Cities in Britain*, pp. 17–21.

what these early settlers were seeking in their new homeland, and what they made of it.

The meaning of *hām*, which we know as 'home', has hardly changed since the fifth century: it was a dwelling-place. To Angles and Saxons this implied a farm, for farming was their normal way of life, but already it had that sense of permanence and individual possession that has characterized it ever since.

But *tūn* is almost impossible to translate in a general way because it was constantly changing, and its modern form, 'town', gives an entirely wrong impression of its significance in place-names. Basically it meant a fence, and we may picture a rough stockade, hastily erected as a protection against wild beasts and other dangers. In most cases the meaning was quickly transferred to the enclosed area and the encampment within it, then to the homestead that arose there, and so eventually to a village. Some of our town and village names that end with -ton undoubtedly contain the earliest meaning. Most of our numerous Bartons, for instance, began as enclosures for growing or threshing barley (OE *bere*), a word that in its early use may have implied other grains as well. Another common name, Leighton, is derived from *lēac tūn*, an enclosure for leeks, a native plant that seems to have been much cultivated at an early date, and again the word was used more widely then than now, to include other vegetables. In such places farms and villages grew later. Generally speaking the best translation for *tūn* is 'farm', especially when it is combined with 'ing', as that dates it as comparatively early.

England is peppered with -ingtons and scores of them have never developed beyond this second stage. Within a mile of my Dorset home is a hamlet called Didlington, which is mentioned in a charter of 946 as *Didelingtune*. It consists of a farm-house and two cottages with outbuildings. If Didel and his family were to return now they would of course see many differences, but the position of the buildings, the contours of the land and the curve of the stream might all be familiar, and the population about the same. In contrast we may think of Paddington or Kensington where the ghosts of Padda or Kensig would be sadly lost.

It might be thought that there was little difference between *hām* and *tūn* when either could mean a farm, but the former was essentially a place in which one lived, while *tūn* had a much wider application. This is demonstrated in the name Kingston which occurs in almost every county in England, making over fifty in all. The name generally indicates that the place, whether farm or village, belonged to the king, and most of them are royal manors in Domesday Book. But Kingsham is so rare that there is only one, and that of doubtful origin. We can see at once that kings owned many farms but did not often live in one. They moved about among many residence all larger and better fortified than the simple *hām* would be in the days when such names were being coined. If *hām* and *tūn* had meant just the same thing they would not be regularly combined as they are in Hampton. When a party of pioneers extended their territory and made more settlements subsidiary to their first one they would speak of them in words that became Newton, Weston, Norton and so forth, while the original place remained the 'home *tūn*' or Hampton. When we find pairs such as Warmingham and Warmington in the same district, it may generally be assumed that the former is the parent settlement (in this case of Weormund's people) and the latter an offshoot of the same group.

The word *stede* (modern 'stead') which was often combined with *hām* signified 'place', and seemed to make the *hām* even more firmly rooted. We still feel that a homestead is more substantial than a home. There are many Hampsteads and Hempsteads in England in a variety of spellings, some without further qualification, others with some descriptive addition, such as Nuthampstead, among the nut-trees.

The rich choice of words that the early English used for their small settlements shows the strong feelings that they had for them, differentiating the various types with a minuteness that we can hardly follow. The word *worth* (and its variant form, *worthig*) seems to have been almost identical in meaning with *tūn*. *Wīc*, on the other hand, which has come down to us as 'wick' or 'wich', often shortened to 'ick' or 'ich', varied considerably in meaning from place to place. Its basic idea seems to have been a dwelling-place, but it was often used for an outlying farm devoted to some special purpose. Chiswick was a dairy-farm where cheese was made, and Keswick is the northern form of the same words. Woolwich was concerned with wool, Berwick with barley. Many 'wicks' grew at an early date into commercial centres such as Norwich, which lay to the north of some place which it has long eclipsed, and Ipswich which belonged to a man called Gip (*Gipeswic*, 975). All these common name-endings, -ton, -ham, -worth, and -wick may be freely translated as 'farm' or 'village', and when the Danes invaded England they added their own -by, of similar usage, which became extremely common in the north; but gradually they all dropped out of use except *tūn* which became the universal word for a village.

The sound change to 'town' is perfectly regular. In the same way *dūn* became 'down' and *brūn* 'brown'. But in the unstressed endings of so many names the vowel lost its length, and the Normans, who for the best part of two centuries were masters of the pen as well as the sword, persistently wrote *tūn* as 'ton' (or 'tone'). Thus in place-names the word was fossilized in a different form from what it is in common speech.

Students of local history, seeking out old names of the most detailed sort, find plenty of evidence that even small villages were long called 'towns'. For example, the village where I now live has never had more than two hundred inhabitants, but the bridge leading into it was called the Tunbridge,* and the meadows nearby Tunmead. Again, in the even smaller hamlet of Hailey in Hertfordshire which never had more than fifteen houses from Domesday Book to 1800, the common field nearest the manor house was Tonfield, the 'town field', because all the 'town' shared it. Field names are generally later than village names, and such examples which could be found anywhere show the medieval usage. In Scotland it lasted longer than in the south and in the eighteenth century, as Scott tells us in *Waverley*, a single house was often called a town.

But some villages grew great and the word grew with them, until finally it came to be associated only with larger centres of population and the small, rustic ones, numerous though they were, were left without a distinctive term of their own. And so the French word 'village', which the English had heard spoken

---

* Tonbridge in Kent has the same origin. Ekwall in his Dictionary gives a different derivation, but more recent scholars have rejected this, preferring the straightforward 'town bridge'.

by Normans, began to be used in their own conversation, too. It is a strange fact that this word that has become so typical of English life should be of foreign origin. It came far too late to make any real impact on English place-names but it has taken its place so well in our vocabulary that no one thinks of it as alien.

Every new settlement in a hostile land needed some kind of protection such as the fence round the *tūn*, but a real tribal stronghold built solely for defence was a different matter, and the word the English used for it was *burh*, better known to us as -borough or -bury. The strongholds to which they applied this word were often not of their own making; indeed, as they explored their new territory they must have seen the remains of so many forts, both prehistoric and Roman, that they hardly needed to build anything on a large scale themselves. As we have already seen, they generally called a Roman fort a *caester*, but occasionally used their own word for it, as at Canterbury, which was so near their first landing place that they probably overran it before they had added *caester* to their vocabulary. But the Iron Age earthworks that crowned so many hill-tops were more nearly akin to their own stage of development, and they spoke of them as *burhs* accordingly. In many places that contain this word the primitive ramparts are still visible today, as at Cadbury, Badbury, Bamburgh, Shaftesbury, and many more. In others on lower ground, protected perhaps in the curve of a river, the original walls have been long obliterated by the growth of towns and we are hardly aware of the defensive position, but wherever the word *burh* occurs in any of its modern forms we may assume that the place was well fortified in the past.

The reason for the great variety of forms that this word has taken is twofold. First, there is the final sound represented by 'h' in Old English, and 'gh' at a later date, once similar to the ending of the Scottish *loch* and the bugbear of English spelling. This sound is generally now silent, but it has had a disturbing effect on most of the words in which it occurs. In 'borough' it survives as a whole syllable consisting of an indeterminate vowel sound. In 'burgh' as in Edinburgh we have exactly the same pronunciation though the second syllable is written as 'gh' only. Sometimes the 'gh' has changed to an 'f' sound as in Burgh by Sands in Cumberland which is pronounced Bruff, and this same effect is represented a little more nearly in a number of places spelt Brough, all in the north of England and all sites of Roman forts. When *burh* occurs at the beginning of a name (which unlike *tūn* it often does) the awkward final sound has generally disappeared leaving only Bur-; and almost every one of our many Burtons signifies the 'farm near the fort' or perhaps belonging to it.

There is a second cause that has given *burh* yet another form. Old English was a highly inflected language with many different case endings. Nearly all of these vanished long ago but some have been fossilized in place-names, particularly in the dative or locative case. In the early records many places are mentioned in this way, as 'at the fort' for instance, and this form must have occurred so frequently in speech that it was often the one to become permanent. The dative singular of *burh* was *byrig*, and this became 'bury'. There are on the whole more 'burys' in the South and 'boroughs' or 'burghs' in the North, but both types are found everywhere and in many cases chance must have been the deciding factor.

By the late Anglo-Saxon period this word was in use for widely differing types of place from ancient, uninhabited ruins to new constructions made by the English themselves, including towns and even monasteries, provided they had good defensive walls. We can see the contrast in Aldbury and Newbury, Aldborough and Newborough. It was chiefly in the sense of a fortified town that the word kept alive in the language, and as the chief centres of defence grew more important after the Danish invasion so 'burgh' or 'borough' came to signify a town with special duties in the defence of the realm and special privileges too. So we come to the modern word 'borough' in which the idea of fortification is completely lost, though civic responsibilities remain. Once again, as with 'town', the change of meaning left a gap in the language and a Norman word filled it. In this way 'castle' took the place of the Old English 'burgh'.

But long after 'castle' was in general use there were regions where the older word continued colloquially for a fortified manor house. In parts of Hertfordshire and Essex the principal house in almost every village is called by some local name with the addition of -bury, as Langleybury, Stansteadbury, Haileybury and so forth. Some of these are late formations but the tradition that produced them was unbroken from before the Conquest. In the eighteenth-century manorial rolls of the manor of Great Amwell the heading often describes the court as being held 'at the Bury' or even 'at the Berry', meaning Amwellbury, the manor house, which had presumably been fortified some centuries before.

The chief cause of trouble in the study of place-names is that any of their ingredients, however well understood in general, may sometimes be confused with something else. So it is even with that basic trio, 'ham', 'ton', and 'bury'. 'Ham' may sometimes come from an Old English *homm* or *hamm* which meant a water-meadow, and lingered long in southern dialects. This origin is indicated for Southampton of which the earliest recorded form is Homtun in 825. But it must soon have been pronounced exactly like the more usual *hāmtūn* and thought of in the same way too, for even before the Conquest it was found necessary to add 'South' to distinguish it from Northampton which was a 'home town' in origin.

The regular ending -ton can be indistinguishable from 'stone' when it follows a name with a genitive 's'. Among the many Kingstons a few refer to the 'king's stone', and only the early records can tell us whether it was *stān* or *tūn*. One might expect to find the former at Kingston-on-Thames where there still stands an ancient stone on which Saxon kings were once crowned, but in 838 it was plainly written in a charter *Cyninges tūn*, and that seems to settle it even if there was a famous stone there too.

With *burh* a cause of confusion is the Old English *beorg* which meant a burial mound and survives as the modern English word, 'barrow'. In place-names this has sometimes become -bury, as at Silbury Hill, which the Saxons could hardly have mistaken for a fort as it is so conical that there would be nowhere for the defenders to stand and there are no walls around its steeply sloping sides. It is probable that they thought it a burial mound in spite of its unusual size. Avebury nearby, which must have been even more remarkable when first the Saxons looked on it, did have an encircling rampart and they seem to have classed it as a fort, though it must have seemed a strange one, perhaps 'the fort on the Avon', for any river might have been so called at that early time. Neither of these names is recorded before the twelfth century. Yet another Old English word *bearu*, a small wood, may be confused with either *burh* or *beorg*, and is the commonest source of Barrow as a place-name.

In spite of these and other complications the general truth remains that 'ham', 'ton' and 'bury' in their thousands represent farms and forts, while the element 'ing' suggests a group of early settlers, though this too is, in some cases, open to question.

Of all the elements of English place-names by far the most numerous is *tūn*. It is also the most typically English, for it is all our own. *Hām* has its counterparts in other Germanic languages; *burh* is found all over Europe (*burg* in Germany, *borg* in Scandinavia, *bourg* in France, *burgo* in Spain and so on); but the nearest continental relation of *tūn* is the German *zaun*, which still means a fence. Our word has grown all the way from that stage to the modern urban development, and is still used to coin new names wherever English is spoken.

Among the many adjectives that have qualified this word in place-names the one that has been most often used is the obvious 'new'. The commonest English place-name is Newton; and in every land where names have grown spontaneously this same concept is prominent: Neuville, Villeneuve, Villanueva, Neustadt, Novgorod, Neapolis, Naples, and even Carthage (in the Phoenician language) all mean 'new town'.

Chapter 5

EARLY ENGLISH PERSONALITIES

The number and variety of Anglo-Saxon personal names is almost bewildering, but this multiplicity was natural in a society where men had only one name each. When the regular use of surnames began to be established after the Conquest an enormous change took place in the giving of Christian names. Newly introduced ones with special significance – royal or religious – such as William, Richard and John could be used over and over again in the same community because there was a second name to distinguish individuals. But in earlier times an endless variety was required. Sons were seldom or never called after their fathers or close relations; the names of great leaders were respectfully avoided by their own people; the chief aim in naming a child was individuality, and to this our place-names bear witness.

From the first coming of the English to that of the Normans a good five centuries elapsed during which the English changed from savage, heathen predators to a well organized, peace-loving people, better able to farm their land than to defend it, and capable of producing churchmen and scholars renowned through Europe. The change was effected with remarkable speed during the seventh century by the acceptance of Christianity which, striking almost simultaneously in the south from Rome and in the north from Ireland, influenced the whole country in three or four generations.

Between those heathen English who had ravaged the Roman villas and their Christian descendants who were in turn ravaged by the Danes an enormous development took place, and their style of personal names changed with it. From the first period hundreds of men's names survive in our place-names, consisting each of a single brief element, many totally obscure, names like Woca (of Woking and Wokingham) and Basa (of Basing and Basingstoke); but as time passed the English became steadily more inclined to coin names by putting together two significant words, each expressing something desirable. So we come to the typical dithematic Old English names. Some of them, like Edward (rich guard), Alfred (elf counsel), and Oswald (divine power), are still current; others like Godwin (good companion) and Leofric (beloved ruler) are well known; but literally hundreds more existed, for the double theme gave endless possibilities of rearrangement. All sprang from the English language for the Anglo-Saxons seem never to have thought of giving Biblical or other alien names to their children.

The two styles, single and compound, overlapped considerably. Even in the first stage of the invasion some leaders had double names, and after the Norman conquest many of the old single-theme names were still common among the peasantry, some surviving long enough to be perpetuated as surnames. Wada, for instance, was a sea giant in German mythology and men bearing this name were the founders of Waddington, Waddingham, Wadhurst and other places; and in the post-Conquest period when patronymics were becoming hereditary it was still there to make the surname Wade. On the whole the upper classes had dithematic names by the eighth century, a notable exception being the great King Offa of Mercia, whose name was typical of the older, simpler style.

The oldest names, especially those that soon dropped out of use, are often hard to identify; but a vast amount of work has been done on this subject by distinguished scholars, using all the earliest material, such as charters in which the names of many witnesses occur and early coins, which generally carried the names of the men who minted them as well as local rulers. Then there is evidence from the continent, for many of the invaders had Germanic names that are found in Europe and in the earliest English place-names, although they never took root here in any other way. Such a one is Ægel, which was related to the Gothic Agil, and is clearly seen in the early forms of Aylesford (*Ægelesford*) and Aylesbury (*Ægelesburg*) and several other places. The *Chronicle* tells us that Aylesford was captured from the Britons in the year 455, and Aylesbury in 571: this was written long after the events and the writer is giving the names as he knew them, but it seems probable that in each case a man named Ægel was among the victors and remained in possession of the place which from that time was known by his name. Another such name is Gylla which occurs in three widely scattered Gillinghams, but is not recorded separately as a personal name.

In Old English, unlike Latin, the ending -a was essentially masculine, and never used with women's names, for which the equivalent suffix was -e. The situation has been much confused by historians, writing in Latin, who have often added a spurious -a to a feminine name, producing such forms as Hilda, a man's name, for the saintly abbess who was really Hilde or Hild. The noun *hild* meant 'battle', a popular theme for either sex, which could stand alone or make part of a compound personal name such as the feminine Cynehild. Kenilworth, which was *Kinildewurtha* in the twelfth century, was the farm of a woman of this name.

Some of the short names, especially the later ones, are not really monothematic at all but abbreviations of compound ones. If a man's name was Godric or Leofwine, his friends might call him Goda or Leofa, and such names are frequent, corresponding to the modern Ron and Cliff. Some men, though important locally in their own time, were known by the kind of pet names that are given in infancy and can cling for life, Babba, Lulla, Didda, Dudda. They exist in great profusion; Babbacombe, Lulworth, Didcot and Dudley are examples of these four and many more could be found for each. They serve as a reminder that English place-names are a colloquial growth. It was not the formal name, but what people said, that made the permanent result.

Among the more obscure names for men we may think for a moment of Wassa, which is found both in Durham and Sussex, where men of this name built homesteads, each place becoming Washington, the farm of Wassa's people. The northern one grew into the bigger village of the two, but it might never have been heard of in the world at large had not its principal family come to be known by the village name.

This did not happen until the original Wassa had been dead for about six centuries, and even then this family was to continue using the surname for at least as long again before one of them made it famous. Then suddenly it was raised to the highest importance in a distant land and became a place-name again, and not only one but many. This kind of pattern which weaves from a man to a place, from a place to a family, and so to a man, and then to a place again, has been often repeated, but never more dramatically.

Every name had a meaning once, and many of the old ones that seem at the first sight incomprehensible are revealed as familiar words if the spelling is modernized. Hwita and Reada have already been mentioned, men's names formed from the adjectives that are now 'white' and 'red'; they have been used as nicknames as long as human beings have had variegated colouring.

An equivalent name for a dark man was Dunn or Dunna. As the final inflection would disappear in time it may seem pedantic to insist on this difference which is hardly more than that between Bob and Bobby, but it did have an effect on the resulting place-names, for nouns that ended in -a took -n in the genitive, while most of those ending in a consonant took -es. Thus, in Old English, Dunna's farm was *Dunnan tūn*, which became Dunton, but Dunn's farm was *Dunnes tūn* and then Dunston. The possessive 's' is now so universal in English that it seems entirely natural, but it was not always so, and only a very limited number of our place-names, formed from that of an owner, have this central 's'. The genitive suffix -an has sometimes survived; it is present for instance in Coventry (Cofa's tree), Dagenham (Daga's homestead), and in Bickenhill which belonged to Bica; but more often it disappeared as at Bickford or Bickleigh.

Living, as those early forbears of ours did, in an untamed world where the wild life of nature was an integral part of their existence, they often called each other by names taken from birds and animals, particularly those with fierce, bold, dominant characteristics. Thus we find that Bucca of Buckingham, Bulla of Bullington, Cocca of Cockington and Hafoc of Hawkesbury are really Buck, Bull, Cock and Hawk, names that have clung to Englishmen as nicknames or surnames for fifteen hundred years.

A few animals were held in such high esteem that their names were used not only as nicknames but also as ingredients for making the formal two-part names which continued in favour right down to the Conquest and beyond. Foremost among these was the wolf, who was in some mysterious way associated with the pagan gods, being the special companion of Woden, and, though an enemy to man in the practical sense, appears in their names as a favourite element, as in Wulfric or Ethelwulf. Another animal almost in the same class was the wild-boar, of which the older, more honourable name, used in Anglo-Saxon poetry, was *eofor*. It was the tusks of the *eofor* that decorated Beowulf's helmet, and the same word made part of personal names such as Eorforward and Eorforwine, which we know better as Everard and Irwin. Yet another of the wild creatures which was held in special honour was the raven. Like Wulfa and Eofor this word was a favourite man's name. We see it in many places such as Ravenshall and Ravensburgh and, much contracted, in Ramsgate, which was originally Raven's gate, the 'gate' in this case signifying a gap in the cliffs.

The difficulty is to know when a man is referred to and when a bird or beast, and this cannot always be resolved. Our only guidance comes from the grammatical form which is often evident in early examples of the names. In such a case as Buckingham or Everingham the 'ing' is enough to show that we are dealing with a man. Or again, when the noun in question is in the genitive singular form denoting possession, a man is indicated. Eversley is literally 'Eofor's *lēah*' ('a woodland glade'); in Everley on the other hand the noun appears to be used in an adjectival way to describe the glade as one where wild-boars had been seen. Everton is just 'boar-enclosure' if we take *tūn* in its early sense. This would refer to the animals, in a captive state.

The Wolf- names are particularly difficult to sort out as this element was so very popular for men's names – and women's too – and the animals were also numerous and made their presence felt. Some places that definitely contain men's names are Wolferton and Wolverton, both 'Wulfhere's farm', and Wolstanton which belonged to Wulfstan. One that sounds very wolfish but really contains the name of a highly respectable lady is Wolverhampton. In 985 the lady Wulfrun left a legacy in her will, which still exists, to enrich a church on her property which is described as being *aet Heantune*, that is, 'at the high farm'.* Thereafter it was spoken of as *Wulfrunehantune*, 'Wulfrun's high farm', the last two words becoming in time assimilated to the more common 'hampton'.

Since the more formal, compound names are a later development than the short ones, they are more frequent in the West than the East, but are found everywhere. In some cases, such as Saxmundham in Suffolk and Edmondsham in Dorset, they are barely changed from their originals, but more often they have been contracted to an unrecognizable state. In Huddersfield (Hudred's land) and Godmanchester (Godmund's chester) they are only slightly squeezed, but in Brighton, for instance (Beorhthelm's *tūn*), the compound name has been reduced to a single syllable. The precise origin of such a name could not possibly be deduced from the modern form, but early records can make it clear. In the case of Wimbledon the records are conflicting and we cannot be sure of the man's name, perhaps Winebeald. Sometimes the spelling has preserved evidence of a full name long after its contraction in speech. We still write Cholmondeley (Ceolmund's lea) though we say Chumley, and only in the nineteenth century did the inhabitants of Brighton and their fashionable visitors break away from the spelling Brighthelmstone.

In the North and far West, where time has seemed to move more slowly than in the South, these compound names have more often retained their longer forms. Several northern villages have preserved the name Oswald in full, as at Oswaldtwistle where the second element *twisla* refers to a fork in a river and the tongue of land so formed. In Devon some of the longest one-word names in England may be found, such as Woolfardisworthy (Wulfheard's farm), of which there are two examples, one pronounced as written, and the other, locally, as Woolsery.

It may be reasonably assumed that the women's names

---

* OE *hēa tūn* (nominative) became in the dative *hēan tūne*. *Hèa*, literally 'high' may be used in the sense of 'chief', as in 'high street'.

found in place-names must also belong to a later time than that of the actual invasion. They can only signify ownership, and the frequency with which they occur is a reflection of the remarkable degree of equality between men and women in Anglo-Saxon society, a position hardly reached again until this century. When the Abbess Hild presided at the Synod of Whitby in 663 she was wielding an official authority such as no woman other than a sovereign has held until we reach the lady cabinet ministers of the present day.

But although women's names belong chiefly to the later and more peaceful period, there is evidence for some of them in our earliest records. One notable example is Bamburgh on the Northumbrian coast, the first headquarters of the invading Angles in that region. Anyone who looks now at the towering earthen ramparts and commanding position of the castle on the sea-shore can judge of its strategic importance in the sixth century. Bede who knew that district well calls it a royal city and tells us that it took its name from Bebbe, who was formerly its queen. She was the wife of Aethelfrith, who became king of Northumbria in 593, a vigorous heathen and a great slaughterer of the British in battle. It is likely that Queen Bebbe too was a powerful personality for this fortress to have been called hers. It is recorded first as *Bebban burh*, contracted gradually to Banburgh, and then to its present form.

In 680 Bognor is first mentioned as *Bucgan ora* (Bucge's shore), and although Bucge or Bugge, as it soon became, may seem to us lacking in feminine charm it is well evidenced as a girl's name. The king of Wessex at that very date had a daughter, Bugge, and as Sussex at about the same time fell under the suzerainty of Wessex it is likely that she received an endowment of land on this part of the coast.

These were royal ladies and, as such, more likely than some to hold property, but the number of names of unknown women that survive in this way shows that ownership by women was quite usual at that time.

Although many hundreds of English place-names begin with early personal names there are comparatively few that can, like Bamburgh, be definitely associated with noted historical characters. From the genealogies in the *Anglo-Saxon Chronicle* we know the names of most of the rulers of the early kingdoms, but only a very small number of them can be identified locally. Hengistbury Head in Hampshire would seem to be connected with the first of the invaders, Hengist, who, according to tradition, landed in Kent in 449, but as it is neither in the right region nor recorded early it carries no conviction. Although Old English men's names were greatly varied, they were repeated to some extent, and *hengest* which meant a stallion was just the kind of word that might often be used for a man. A much better authenticated case of an early leader's name preserved locally is that of Cissa at Chichester (page 31).

A number of villages in the Midlands, such as Offenham and Offchurch, do refer in all probability to the great king, Offa of Mercia, in which case they would imply that the farm or church was his personal property or endowed by him. In the cases of Oswald of Northumbria and Edmund of East Anglia, each a devout Christian killed by heathen enemies, it was the fact that they were reverenced as saints that caused their names to be attached to places connected with their violent deaths. We will leave saints' names to a later chapter; among Old English place-names they are not a large class, and all have personal links with the topography.

The greatest Englishman of the age, and one of the greatest of all time, King Alfred, is not immortalized specifically in any place-name that we know of. We know many details of his life and the places most intimately connected with him, but their names were old-established in his day; he spoke of Winchester and Chippenham, just as we do. It is true that the name Alfred does exist in some places, such as Ilfracombe (*Alfredescumbe*, 1249), but there is no reason to suppose that these referred to him. He raised the kingship to a higher level than it had reached before and we see very plainly that his people spoke of him and of his successors chiefly by their royal title. That is why we have so many places named Kingston, Kingsford, Kingsbury, Kingswood and so forth, but few with the personal names of kings.

Athelney, now a little hill among green meadows but once an island among marshes and Alfred's secret hiding place from the Danes, means literally 'the island of the princes'. The form in the *Chronicle*, written in his lifetime, *Æthelinga ēg*, shows clearly that the noun is plural. It is possible that it refers to him and his brother Ethelred, who may have been there together before either of them became king, but this is as near as we can come to a place-name that can be connected with this national hero.

In fact the personal names that occur so freely in our place-names are not commemorative of famous persons but factual, representing the actual occupiers or owners of farms and villages, men and women of whom we generally know nothing except their association with those places. There are some that can be identified with Saxon landowners just prior to the Conquest as recorded in Domesday Book. In these cases they may have replaced earlier names, as occasionally happened when the property came into the hands of someone of local interest, though in general the old name remained. Or, more often, they were additions to what had been previously only a generic term, as we can see happen in Wolverhampton, which was only a 'high farm' until 985 when it was further specified as belonging to Wulfrun. In later times a great many surnames of Norman landowners were tacked on to village names as separate words (see Chapter 10), a continuation of the same process in a different style.

It has never been an English habit to name places deliberately, and the idea of speaking of them by any person's name, other than that of the owner or, more rarely, a saint with whom there was a special link, does not seem to have arisen. The Normans, apart from a greater partiality for saints, showed little change of outlook in this respect, and nearly always retained the English names they found. The great new castle that the Conqueror built on the Thames west of London might have been William's Tower, but instead the old name of the village on the river bank, *Windlesore*, now Windsor, served for the royal fortress. The second element of this ordinary name, *ora*, is the same as in Bognor and means a bank or shore; the first is the Old English form of the word 'windlas', an arrangement on the bank for hauling up boats.

It has been the same through all our subsequent history. I believe it is true to say that there is not a town or village in England bearing the name of a sovereign later than 1066, and very few before. In other countries where the English have settled or exercised their influence it is a very different matter. Jamestown, Charlestown, Fort William, Victoria – such names leap to the mind in dozens, but they are not found at home. We name streets and buildings after sovereigns, railway stations, parks, hospitals and schools, but when it comes to a new town or village we are true to our old habits.

So we come back to the names which do remain in thousands: Didda and Dodda, Bica and Basa, Buck and Hawk, and all the rest of them, and then all the Wulfwins, Ethelhards and so on, who should be multiplied by hundreds to give any true picture of those energetic early farmers who gave the face of England its shape and character. Their great number is a true reflection of a way of life in which personal freedom was taken for granted and the individual ownership of land of the highest importance. This may seem to be a matter of course, but it is not so everywhere, not in the Celtic countries, for instance, where ownership was more a matter of tribes than individuals. In England we see group ownership in the first rush of invasion, but very soon the tribe gives way to individuals in enormous numbers and when a man had built his homestead and laid claim to the land around it, the place was his and his name likely to be there for ever.

Chapter 6

ENGLISH NAMES FROM NATURE

The English settlers had an eye for landscape. Land was what they cared most about; it was what they had come for, and they were connoisseurs of its finer points.

The country was largely covered with forest and in this they felt at home, speaking of it in a rich vocabulary that differentiated all the kinds of woodland with subtle variety. Our familiar word 'wood' has never changed in meaning but it was then supported by many other terms that we have allowed to lapse. Weald, holt, hurst, shaw and grove are just a few of them. The first of these was used for great forests, notably the one in the south-east which the Britons had called Andred and which is now the Weald of Kent. As forests were gradually cleared the meaning of this word, which often became 'wold', changed with the changing nature of the land and came to signify open upland country, so we have the Lincolnshire Wolds and the Cotswolds which are mostly bare, but in older village names, such as Southwold, it generally meant a wood.

A holt was a dense thicket, and might be very extensive too. A hurst seems to have been a small wooded hill, and is especially common in Kent, Sussex and Hampshire. A shaw (or shaugh as it often is in the West) was a small wood, and a grove (often -greave in place-names) perhaps smaller still. This word could apply to a particular group of trees within a larger wood, but at this distance it is hard to differentiate all the finer points of usage.

But what the English wanted most was land for farming. Their word for open country was *feld*, the ancestor of 'field', but very different in meaning from our well-kept enclosures;

however, in many districts there was little of this to be found, and therefore they sought for open glades in the forests which they could clear further. They called such a clearing a *lēah*, which later became 'lea', but appears generally in place-names as -leigh or -ley. Its several forms taken together make it one of our commonest elements. It often stands alone as Leigh, but is rarely the first element of a compound. (For Leighton see page 38).

At first *lēah* seems to have been yet another word for woodland, but the sense of a clearing must have developed early, for by the late Old English period it often implied a stretch of grassland. This is the sense in which it lingered on into the nineteenth century. We see it in a golden poetic haze, the lowing herd winding o'er it slowly; but the Saxon farmer viewed it in a practical light. Most of the -leys and -leighs are village names, because where there was a good clearing someone was sure to settle sooner or later. Our place-names portray a whole series of them that began as pastures for farm animals: Oxley, Cowley, Bulley, Bulkeley (for bullocks), Calverley (for calves), Studley (for a stud of horses), Horsley, Shepley and Shipley (both for sheep); while others are merely described with appreciation as Bradley or Langley (broad or long) or Shirley which occurs in several counties and means the 'bright lea, probably implying that it was open to the sun.

Our Saxon settler was a hunter as well as a farmer and he spoke of many leas while yet in their woodland state by the names of the wild creatures he had seen there – the hart and the buck whom he prized so highly at Hartley and Buckley, boars at Borley, wolves at Woolley, crows at Crawley, cranes at Cranleigh, hares at Harley and so forth. Most of these were well worth hunting as food or killing as enemies, but he noticed the smaller creatures too – the little birds at Finchley, a toad (or perhaps a spate of them) at Tadley, a snake at Wormley – or was there some old legend about the place, for *wyrm* meant anything from a grass snake to a dragon. At Midgeley he was troubled by the midges, and they must have been extremely bad for he was a hardy outdoor type, and in such a damp country midges must have been very common.

One more word that had a similar meaning, though its later development was very different, was the Old English *rod* related to the verb 'ride'. It meant a glade in the woods that was clear enough for riders on horseback to go through. It is now the familiar 'road', but in place-names has often become -royd, a form found most frequently in the north, as at Ackroyd (the clearing among oaks). How many people know that a road is where you can ride?

Yet another word for a clearing is 'thwaite', a word of Danish origin that we must mention again later.

Coming as they did from the low-lying plains of Northern Europe, the English took notice of the least rise in the ground. They had no word for high mountains, but a good many for the moderate eminences which were all they knew, and as they explored across England these words were forced to serve for higher and steeper slopes until they were stretched to their limit, after which the only course was to borrow.

The word they used most in the early period was *dūn*, which developed into 'down' in current speech but is usually written -don as a place-name ending. The question asked by almost every intelligent child on seeing the Sussex Downs, 'Why do you call them Downs when they are Ups?' is easily answered. The word meant a hill first, and when you descended from it you came 'adown' off the down, to a lower position.

In many towns and villages where the name ends with -don you may look in vain for the hill, but we have to remember that such things are comparative. In flat country even a little hillock – such as later building could obliterate – was important as a vantage point, and again the farmer toiling with his heavy plough on virgin soil was aware of the slightest upward gradient. So it came about that the same word that made the principal feature of Huntingdon – the 'huntsman's hill'* – lying as flat and level as the marshy fen-country all around it, has also served for the swelling North and South Downs which stand so massively against the sky, and far in the west when Englishmen adventuring into Wales saw her highest mountain (and it must have been in the winter) all they could call it was Snowdon. An elastic word.

In the course of time there has often been confusion between

---

* In this case the '-ing' is misleading. The original form was *Huntan dūn*. *Huntan* was the genitive singular of *hunta*, a 'huntsman'.

dūn and *tūn* as unstressed final syllables. For instance, Hambleton in Rutland and another in Yorkshire are the same in origin as the two Hambledons in Hampshire and Dorset which both have striking hills. The first element is O E *hamel* which meant crooked, scarred or mutilated. The same idea is expressed in modern form in Broken Hill (Australia). The Hamilton in Scotland which has been reproduced in distant parts of the world had probably this same origin. There are of course many names of English origin in Scotland, especially in the Lowlands where English has been the native language as long as in England itself.

Another common word for a high place, often the jutting-out end of a spur, was *hoh*, which survives generally as 'how' or 'hough'. Many words for natural features are metaphors from parts of the body – head, nose, mouth and so on – and this one meant literally a heel, which shows the kind of shape the speaker had in mind. It makes the first part of many Howtons, Houghtons and Huttons, each one a village built on or near a height, and in its briefest form it supplies the rather unexpected ending of Duddo in Northumberland, and of Bengeo and Ivinghoe in Hertfordshire, the latter a dramatic beacon hill. In several places it stands alone as Hoo (a name that lends itself easily to humorous treatment, especially in conjunction with Ware and Wye), and at Plymouth it has won itself immortal glory as the Hoe.

At Sutton Hoo in Suffolk it turned out that the Hoo, or rather the hoos, for there were several, were man-made burial mounds containing the richest Anglo-Saxon treasure that has ever been found. This brings us to two more words for low round hills whether artificially piled over the dead or natural. *Beorg*, which is related to the German *berg* and used for high mountains in Europe, referred to something much smaller in English speech and survives chiefly as 'barrow' (page 43); *hlaw*, which became 'law' or 'low', seems always to have meant a burial mound in the earliest phase of settlement, and no doubt many of the villages whose names end in this way have ancient burials and perhaps treasure beneath them. But there were so many natural hills in England that in later times both 'low' and 'law' were applied to them. Lewes in Sussex is simply this word in a plural form (961, *Laewes*). It stands on the edge of the Downs but the name is more likely to have referred to a group of minor humps or mounds than to the whole sweep of Downs that dominates the scene.

When the English penetrated far into the West their vocabulary, so rich in many respects, was inadequate for the irregularities of height they found there. Being by this time more in touch with the native Britons than they had been in the earlier stage of invasion they took over many of their Celtic names for individual hill-tops (see pages 19–20) and also borrowed their 'tor' and 'craig' for rocky outcrops. These the English used freely with their own words, making such names as Dunster ('Dunn's tor') and Creighton ('the village by the crag').

It was much the same in regard to valleys. The English had plenty of words for small depressions, such as those we know as 'hollow', 'bottom' and 'dell'. Their most usual word for a valley was *denu* which survives in innumerable place-names as 'dean' or 'dene'; but at an early stage they seem to have felt the need for something more for deeper, narrower valleys, and adopted the Celtic *cumb*. This has become one of our most familiar elements, not only in the West where such names as Widdicombe and Babbacombe abound, but as the first part of our many Comptons, and also standing alone as Combe or Coomb(e), which is pronounced 'coom' whatever the spelling.

In the North it was the Scandinavians who provided most of the words for the more rugged features of the scenery, 'fell' and 'dale' for mountain and valley, 'gill' for a deep ravine. Skiddaw and Scafell are both Norse names, while Helvellyn has a Celtic look, but early records are scarce in the wild north-west and were always more concerned with places of agricultural value than with useless crags, so evidence for these lovely names is somewhat late and uncertain. But the Peak district was written *Peac lond* long before the Conquest. Here the English used a word of their own, making a metaphor from their sharp-pointed weapons. Peak, pike or pick are all forms of the same word meaning a point, and Pike Law is simply a pointed hill.

It is always interesting to watch the fluctuation of words. Some stay for ever, some change their nature, some go. The English 'down' gave place to its compatriot 'hill', which was never far behind it in popular use and has remained unshaken ever since. 'Dean' was dispossessed by 'dale' which reigned supreme throughout the country as the contrast to 'hill' until the French 'valley', very late in the day, superseded them both. 'Mountain', of course, was a French import, too, a word that we really needed; but I fail to see why 'valley' need have ousted, so completely, our coombes, deans and dales, which now scarcely exist except in place-names and poetry.

As every settlement needed a good water supply it is very natural that a watery theme runs through village names; and when they are spoken today we hear the actual words used by the Anglo-Saxons. They talked of 'bourns' and 'brooks', and very often of 'wells' which to them were not man-made contrivances but natural springs bubbling out of the ground and flowing away down the dean or dale. Where there was a spring there was also a stream, and the word 'well' signified both.

Scores of villages that grew beside streams became known by their names, and looking them over one gets the impression that the Anglo-Saxons loved their brooks and rejoiced to hear their cheerful sound. The descriptive words that qualify them consist not only of all the usual variety denoting shapes, sizes, human owners, animals, birds, vegetation and so forth, but there are also epithets that seem to show a pleasure in more than the merely practical aspects. Prittlewell in Essex is the prattling spring, Ludwell in Somerset a loud one. Whitwell bubbled out white and foaming, and in contrast we have the Blackburn which was dark perhaps with peaty water from the fells, or maybe ran in the shadow of tall trees. This is a common image among river-names, more often in the form of Blackwater, and the exact equivalent of the Celtic Douglas. Sherborne and Sherburn, a name which occurs in half a dozen places in slightly varying spellings, means the bright or shining stream.

Some of these names belong only to streams; some only to villages; and there is no distinguishing between these two sorts because they both referred initially to the water. Woburn means the winding stream (OE *woh*, 'crooked') and when someone built his homestead in its curve it supplied a village name. It might well happen that the stream retained another name – for rivers were often called by different names at different points along their banks and only one of these would become permanent – the others remaining attached to farms and villages.

The proper Old English word for a river was *ēa*, an ancient word that is found in various forms all over Europe. The Latin *aqua*, the French *eau* and the Celtic word that gives us the river-names Axe, Exe and Usk are all descended from the same prehistoric progenitor. In England this brief but important word makes the first sound in the majority of our Eatons (of which there are nearly thirty) and the last in many village names ending in 'y' or 'ey'. It is hard to distinguish from another equally important monosyllable, *ēg*, which meant an island, and which also dwindled to a single vowel sound at an early date. It is the 'i' of 'island', and the 's', put in by the Normans but never pronounced, has no right to be there. Scores of village names ending in 'y' have one or other of these watery meanings, and though experts in etymology take pains to sort them out the physical difference in their original situation must have often been very slight. To take the famous Eton, Ekwall explained it as the *tūn* by the river (in this case the Thames), but to more recent scholars it is the *tūn* on an island. In wet seasons it was probably both.

In an earlier chapter it was noted that nearly all the principal rivers of England have retained their Celtic or prehistoric names. But the English, who named the majority of the small streams by which they settled, did re-name a few of the larger rivers too. The Swale, rushing down from the Yorkshire moors, has an English name derived from the same root word as occurs in 'swallow', both in the case of the bird and the action. It is onomatopoeic and refers to that swishing, swooping, swirling, swilling effect that is so delightful in the movement of a bird or a river, and so much less attractive in the act of taking nourishment. The Ribble too is probably English, related perhaps to 'ripple'. The Blythe and Blyth, mean 'merry' river; the Wensum and the Wantsum, hardly more than brooks, are both literally 'wind-some' or winding, and the Waveney, one of the loveliest of names, means 'wavy water'.

Those with more humorous tastes may prefer the Piddle of Dorset with its spate of Piddle or Puddle villages along its banks. The two forms are but variations of the same word which means a flow of water or marshy pool. Affpuddle and Tolpuddle belonged respectively to Affa and Tola, both mentioned as local landowners in pre-Conquest charters. Piddletrenthide consisted of thirty hides of land; and there are several more, Puddletown with its noble church being the chief of them.

There are far more fords than bridges in our place-names for the simple reason that fording was the first way of getting across, and as soon as a place was spoken of as a ford its name had come into existence. By the time the English were moving across the country there were few Roman bridges still standing, a strange fact – they must have been wooden structures, unable to withstand floods without maintenance – but the evidence of place-names is explicit. At Corbridge in the north, and at Cambridge, both Roman stations, the English names tell of bridges, but these are exceptional. In contrast a round dozen Stratfords tell of Roman roads (at this time *stræt* was used for nothing else) that crossed by way of fords, and if one takes a single Roman highway, such as that leading from London to Colchester, one finds Oldford, Stratford, Ilford, Romford and Chelmsford along its course and not one 'bridge'. One has only to glance at a modern road map with its network of old roads converging on historic towns to realize the influence of the ford. Oxford, Hereford, Stafford, Stamford, Bedford, and Hertford each owes its early importance to the fact that travellers came there to cross a river. Eventually the concentration of traffic brought the need for a bridge, but that did not affect the established name.

Of the ford-names mentioned above, Ilford preserves a Celtic river-name, the Hyle; Romford was a 'roomy' or wide ford, Chelmsford and Bedford begin with the names of men; Stafford had a *stæth* or landing-stage close by it, which suggests that there was traffic along the river as well as across it; Stamford is a variation of Stanford, the 'stony ford'; Hereford is the 'army ford', an important crossing-place of the Severn that must have been much used in times of warfare; Hertford a place where deer were seen at an early date, perhaps their regular drinking place; Oxford, as it appears, a place for the oxen to cross.

We could dwell on watery subjects indefinitely. There are still meres and pools to tempt us to linger but space is limited and we must pass over them briefly. 'Mere' was the regular

Old English word for a lake or large stretch of water that could even be the sea, as at Margate. We recognize it when it is written in full, and really should know better than to say 'Lake Windermere'; but we see it less clearly in Cromer, for instance, ('the crows' mere'), or as the first part of many Mertons which once were lakeside farms. But, "Where are the lakes?" we may ask in many cases, and the answer must be, "Dried up long ago." Green and pleasant though England still is, it is a much drier country than it was a thousand years ago, and it gets drier every year, as ponds are drained, streams piped underground, water supplied in millions of gallons to cities, and rivers embanked so that they flow tidily into the sea instead of spreading out into the pools, fens, meres and marshes among which our forefathers looked for dry ground.

It has always been customary in English for the adjective to precede the noun, and thus in our compound place-names the principal feature under discussion is always the last element, and whatever goes before gives qualifying detail. Poulton is the *tūn* by the pool, and we are speaking of the farm or village; but Blackpool alludes to the pool itself, with no indication of a human settlement. The words that our forefathers used for the main features of the country – some of which we have been discussing – are very numerous and varied, but those that add descriptive detail are even more so. A study of these words can bring us closer to the lives of those early settlers, and give us glimpses of the country as they saw it.

We see a land teeming with wild life, much of it now extinct: beavers at Beverley, Cranes everywhere (Cranford, Cranborne and so forth), wolves and wild boar common. Wildboarclough near Manchester dates from the time when wild ones were growing rare.

We see the actual trees. The Anglo-Saxons were expert woodsmen and at least thirty distinct species are mentioned. Of these, oak and ash and thorn, as Kipling rightly observed, are supreme, and it is hard to say which is the most numerous. The older form of 'oak' was *āc*, and this is the distinguishing feature of all our Actons. The sound change from ā to ō was normal, and many Oak- names, such as Oakley, began with Ac- in the early records. But Oakham in Rutland was Ocheham before the Conquest and probably belonged to a man called Oca (a name recorded elsewhere), though generations of its inhabitants must have thought of oak trees since. Particular oaks had special importance and often form the main feature of the name as in Matlock (OE *maethel ac*) the 'meeting-place oak'. Ashes crop up everywhere, Ashby, Ashton and Ashley all being extremely common, and other compounds plentiful.

One reason why there are so many Thorntons is that hawthorn hedges were often planted round farmsteads as a protection. As our place-names show, the tree at first was simply a 'thorn'; the 'haw' which eventually adhered to it meant a hedge or enclosed place, and the fruit tooks its name from the place where it grew, a hedgeberry or haw. Thorns were much used in this ancient craft of hedging which has played such a large part in giving the English landscape its special charm; they also grew almost everywhere, often on windswept hillsides where little else would flourish, and without reaching much height did attain great age, standing gnarled and twisted when taller trees had fallen. They are often mentioned as landmarks in early charters and it is typical that Bishop Asser in his life of Alfred tells us of an ancient thorn tree on the hillside of Ethandune where Alfred won his greatest victory, as if to fix the spot in the memory of posterity.

Willows were also mentioned frequently, because their sinuous shoots could be woven into useful articles. Three sorts were distinguished. The one that they called willow makes the first two syllables of Willoughby and the whole name of Welwyn, the latter being the dative plural – at the willows. The sallow (OE *salh*) occurs at Selborne, Selwood, and at Silchester (where they still grow among the Roman ruins). The withy that loves to grow by water is often found combined with valley-words, as at Withycombe in Somerset, and Widdicombe in Devon, which are the same in origin. Other common trees were the birch (OE *beorc*) as at Berkeley, the hazel at Hessle and Hazelmere, the lime (*lind*) at Lyndhurst, the yew (*iw*) at Uley and the elm at Elmstead, to give a few examples. The beech is not common in early names though it existed in Old English as *bece*. Caesar said there were none in Britain, and though he was making this sweeping statement on very slight personal knowledge it seems that in his day they were not the notable feature of the chalk downs that they have since become. The chestnut is not a native. A few may have been grown by the Romans but they are rare in pre-Conquest names.

The plum, the pear and the apple all grew wild, but the fruit must have been small and sour. The first two have given names like Pirton and Plumpton and indirectly Plymouth (page 112). More attention seems to have been paid to the apple, which was probably the most edible of the native fruits, apart from nuts. There are several Applebys and Appletons scattered round the country. Applegarth in Yorkshire means an orchard, while Appledore which occurs in Kent and Devon is simply the Old English *apuldor* which meant an apple tree. This word made a nice pair with *mapuldor*, a maple. This survives in Mapledurham on the Thames, which has no connection with Durham but was a homestead by a single maple tree.

So much for trees; as for the lesser vegetation that clothed the open country, we see at once that there was a great deal of broom. The hillsides must have been golden with it in spring. The word probably included any kind of furze or gorse, and when we start to list the places that include it, such as Bromley, Bramley, Bromfield, West Bromwich, Brompton, Brampton, Brandon (where the 'd' has affected the 'm') and many others we begin to realize how much clearing the pioneer farmers had to do.

Another common form of ground-cover was fern. The Old English *fearn* is generally Farn- in place-names, or sometimes contracted to Far-. We see it in Farnham, Farnborough, Farnworth, Farndon, Farleigh, and Fareham. It is so widespread that it must refer chiefly to the bracken that still carpets our woods and wastelands. ('Bracken', of Old Norse origin, is found only in a few northern place-names.) Equally common was heath (OE *hæth*) which at first implied rough ground covered with low shrubs, and this is its meaning when it stands alone or in the final position, as in Blackheath. But it also came to signify the specific bush that we call heather that grows largely in such places, and this is its probable meaning as the first element in Hatfield, Hadfield, Hadleigh, Hadley, Headley, and Hatton.

Other growth that is mentioned includes the coarse grass

65

called 'bent', which was the distinguishing feature of several Bentleys; and reeds, generally contracted to Red-, as at Redbourne, and Redmarley, the 'clearing by the reedy mere'. The reeds were useful for thatching but there were too many of them, and on the whole the settlers were against most of these things as they strove to turn the heath and fen and marsh into farmland – which might then be 'acre' or 'mead'. 'Acre' at first meant ploughland and later the amount of it that a team of oxen could plough in a day. 'Mead' is a noun formed from the verb to mow, and meant grass that could be cut for hay. Of course they talked about the soil too, as farmers will; Clayton was a farm on clay, Girton on grit, Chislehurst on gravel, and the many places on sand need no comment.

As for the wild flowers that must have grown in such profusion there is sadly little evidence. Such names as Primrose Hill and Bluebell Wood belong to a much later period, and we do not even know what the Anglo-Saxons called our loveliest native flowers as nearly all their names are first recorded in Middle English and many of them are French. We do know that they spoke of some common flower as *gyld* or 'gold' and this was probably the marsh marigold that grew in damp places. This is contained in Guildford, the 'gold ford', and a few other places, but if they made any comment on the sheets of bluebells and daffodils we are unable to recognize it. They mention clover, at Claverton for instance, but this was good for cattle to eat rather than beautiful, and cress, at Cresswell, but this they ate themselves. There is no avoiding the conclusion that the Anglo-Saxons were practical rather than aesthetic, and yet they have left us authentic word pictures of the countryside as they saw and valued it that have pleased the ears of their descendants all round the world ever since.

Chapter 7

THE RELIGIOUS ELEMENT

For the first hundred and fifty years after the coming of the English to the land that bears their name they were faithful to the heathen religion of their Teutonic forbears, and during the next half century their acceptance of Christianity was only gradual. Out of this pagan period we might have expected a large number of place-names that echo the names of Woden and his mysterious companions, but though such names do exist their numbers – or those that we can identify – are very small.

It may be that the English at the time of the invasion were already growing a little tired of their old gods; the alacrity with which most of them took to Christianity would seem to suggest that their minds were ready for a change; but it is also likely that the small number of heathen names may be largely attributed to the influence of the Christian church which, once it was established, must have done its best to obliterate heathen sites and suppress unseemly names, replacing them with something more decorous. Villages with names like Woodnesborough (in Kent) and Wednesbury (now a large town near Birmingham), both clearly recognizable as strongholds of Woden, must have been very firmly established at an early date to be able to withstand such opposition.

But though these heathen names are few, their interest for us is very great. For one thing they belong unquestionably to the earliest Anglo-Saxon period. Their antiquity is apparent not only in their nature but also in their geographical distribution, which tallies exactly with those Anglo-Saxon burials which have been discovered, showing proof of heathen beliefs. These are found only in the territory that was conquered by the

early seventh century. Beyond that, in the South-West peninsula, the countries bordering Wales and the mountainous North-
West there are no signs of English heathenism, either in graves
or names, for in these regions the Christian Celts held out until
the English who conquered them were Christians too.

Our knowledge of English paganism is very meagre because
no literature has survived directly from that period. We have a
few references in early Christian writings; we have the names of
four principle deities, Tiw, Woden, Thur and Frig (Woden's
wife), preserved for ever in our common speech as days of the
week, and we have perhaps a score of place-names commemorating the first three of these. But this is all the first-hand verbal
evidence that we have of our own ancient gods. Fortunately, the
picture is filled out to some extent by other sources. Latin
authors have left descriptions of the behaviour of Teutonic
tribes on the continent, and the mythology of the Scandinavian
countries, which was closely akin to that of the English, was
much better preserved as they continued heathen to a later
date. From them we learn something of the old religion.

The most important of the gods to the English was Woden,
the one-eyed master of magic, god of the dead, rejoicing in
human sacrifice, treacherous, cunning and wonderfully skilled.
Nearly all the ruling dynasties of the early English kingdoms
claimed descent from this unpleasant deity, and even after they
had taken to Christianity this, the very tap-root of their family
tree, could not be rejected. Woden's name is found in only
seven or eight places, but all are interesting. Wednesfield in
Staffordshire is only a few miles from Wednesbury, mentioned
above, and seems to confirm that this Midland area was once a
vigorous centre of Woden-worship. Another feature of special
interest is the Wansdyke (*Wodnes dic*, 903), a great defensive
earthwork, running from Somerset into Hampshire, which the
Saxons attributed to the magical power of Woden.

To the Scandinavians he was known as Odin; both they and
the English had another name for him too, a more familiar one,
Grim, which meant, literally, a masked person and alluded to
Woden's tendency to appear in disguise. This name is associated
with the Old English *grima* which meant a spectre or goblin,
and the two cannot always be kept apart. When the Anglo-
Saxons saw prehistoric remains, the making of which was a

mystery to them, they were inclined to attribute its workman-
ship to gods or spirits, and when they no longer liked to speak
openly of Woden they spoke of him as Grim instead. So we have
such names as Grimsbury and Grimes Grave, and Grimsdyke
which is just another version of Wansdyke.

Another powerful god was Thunor, whose name was
shortened to Thur, but is better known to us in its Norse form,
Thor. The English name is identical with our word 'thunder',
and the god whose hammer made the skies resound was the
personification of physical strength. The Scandinavians made
much of Thor, but the English seem to have thought poorly of
him compared to the skilled and cunning Woden, apparently
preferring brains to brawn. Nonetheless, his name was honoured
at Thundersley in Essex, Thursley in Surrey, and Thundridge
in Hertfordshire, a village on the side of a hill (or ridge) against
which the thunderbolts may have seemed to strike.

Tiw was a god of war, sometimes equated with the Roman
Mars. His name is found at Tuesley in Surrey and at Tewin near
Hertford. This was the place of the Tewings, or Tiw's people.
Frig, whose name lives on in Friday, does not feature recogniz-
ably in our place-names, except very indirectly in several small
villages called Friday Street, a late name that must spring from
some medieval Christian custom, connected with Good Friday,
possibly a procession to a wayside cross.

There are two Old English words that tell specifically of
heathen worship, *hearg* and *wēoh*, both long obsolete, but with
meanings that are well established. They are used in early
Christian writings to translate the Latin words that mean a
heathen temple or the shrine of an idol. Neither was ever used
for a Christian church. The best known, *hearg*, is now Harrow-
on-the-Hill. There are also villages called Harrowden in three
different counties, each of which began as *hearg dūn* or 'temple
hill'. *Wēoh*, which was the more common word, generally
became Wee- or Wy-. This kind of temple might also crown a
hill-top as at Weedon, of which there are two examples, but is
more often compounded with -ley, as at Weeley, Weoley and
Willey, each of which implied a heathen temple in a woodland
glade.

The best known name that has *wēoh* as its principal item is
Wellington. This ultra-respectable name hardly suggests a

group of idols in a forest, but its three examples in England show in their early forms the distinctive Weo- which points to this meaning. Ekwall considers that they all have the same origin; first there was the temple in a wood, the *wēoh lēah*; then, the people whose special shrine it was were called the Weolings; and, finally, it followed that the village where they lived nearby became Weolingtun. This is the early spelling of the Somerset village from which the Iron Duke took his title, and in his honour were named most of the Wellingtons overseas.

Unfortunately, we have little knowledge of what those heathen temples were like. The Anglo-Saxons built in wood and none of their sacred places has ever been identified except by name. The nearest we have to a description is in Bede's account of how the high priest of Edwin of Northumbria, on being converted to Christianity, himself 'profaned the altars and the temples of the idols and the enclosures that were about them'. His method was to hurl a spear into them and then destroy them utterly with fire. Very clearly they were made of wood; beyond that we can only guess at their appearance. Several Latin authors tell us that when the Teutonic peoples sacrificed an animal or a human to their idols, they often nailed up the head of the victim on a tree or post; and there the skull might remain indefinitely, marking the place of sacrifice. It seems probable that this custom is the origin of such names as Gateshead and Swineshead. The former certainly signified 'goat's head' in the seventh century, for Bede, writing in Latin, called it *ad caput caprae*. This custom may give some idea of the early *décor* at Harrow and Wellington.

As the power of Christianity grew, the names of Woden, Thur and their associates faded out of English speech, but the word 'god' was used with renewed strength in its new context of the Christian deity. With a name like Godshill, or Gadshill, which is just the same thing, we cannot tell what god it first referred to. But as all the places with this name – and there are a round half dozen of them – are in the south-eastern counties that were among the first to be conquered it is highly probable that they were originally pagan. At Godshill on the Isle of Wight the hill is crowned by a medieval church whose fine tower, visible for miles around, proclaims Christianity to the landscape, but the sanctifying of heathen sites was a regular policy of church authorities, and it is probable that many of our parish churches stand over the ashes of long forgotten idols. At Godstow near Oxford a Norman nunnery made the name appropriate – 'God's place'. We have no record of it before 1135, and we cannot tell how old the name was then.

This brings us to *stōw*, a common Old English word that makes a part of innumerable place-names. Its general meaning was a meeting place, or place of assembly, but there is no doubt that such gatherings were often for religious purposes and so it also signified a holy place. Like the word 'god' it made the grade successfully from a heathen to a Christian society, and is sometimes compounded with saints' names as at Felixstowe, which was the holy place of Felix, a seventh-century missionary to the East Anglians, or Bridestowe where the church is dedicated to St Briget.

'Stow' often stood alone and still does in a few places, though more often a later addition has been supplied to distinguish one from another, as at Stow-on-the-Wold and Stowmarket. We cannot be sure that its character was always religious. Plaistow (of which there are four examples) means 'play place', which may be taken as the ancient equivalent of a sports ground, but athletic gatherings are not incompatible with religion. Chepstow was a meeting place for trade (OE *cēap* meant a market), but of course it could have been a holy place first and later one with a market attached. Bristol, when we first meet it in 1063, was Bricgstow, the meeting place by the bridge; soon after the Conquest it was an important religious centre as well as a port, and this importance must have been already old.

With *stōw* we must mention *stoc* which generally survives in place-names as Stoke. These two words are twins. They spring from the same root, and though there are slight differences in use they are hard to pin down and, in fact, nearly everything that has been said of *stōw* will apply to *stoc*.

With Christianity came new words for sacred buildings, one of the earliest being 'minster', used chiefly for monasteries and nunneries. Later, the Norman-French word 'abbey' was preferred, but it does not follow that a church called an abbey is post-Conquest for this word was often added in later times to an early foundation. We have only to think of Westminster, literally 'the monastic church to the west', a description clearly given by Londoners. It was first built as a Christian church in the early seventh century, on the marshy river bank west of the city. Later on, when a king built his palace close by, the name expanded to include the whole royal city that grew up. After that a new designation was needed for the minster that was the nucleus of the whole, and so we call it Westminster Abbey, using a redundancy to make the distinction.

It may be safely assumed that a town or village whose name ends in -minster had a religious house in Saxon times, and in many cases this was the first building in that place. If there had been anything in the way of human habitation there before it would have had a name, and this would probably have endured. This explains how it is that dozens of places famous for their old monasteries, such as Glastonbury (of which the first element is Celtic and obscure) have names that contain no reference to the Christian faith. But Charminster, Axminster, Exminster and so on began as Saxon minsters, their sites chosen by pious men who looked for seclusion from the world and a good water supply with plenty of fish. The three just mentioned take their names from the rivers on which they stand. The seclusion did not last; monasteries soon attracted other habitations and even the most solitary minster was sure to produce at least a village in time.

'Minster' came to us direct from the Latin *monasterium*, but the etymology of 'church' is obscure, and the *New Oxford Dictionary* devotes over a column of close print to its different possibilities without reaching a conclusion. The Latin word for a church, *ecclesia*, had been borrowed centuries earlier by the Britons and still exists in several English place-names such as Eccles, but it made no headway with the English, who preferred their own word 'church' (OE *cyrice*). But although this occurs in a number of place-names it is not among the most common elements. The sites of villages were chosen, often in pagan times, for their natural advantages, and the church came later. The descriptive word most often combined with it is 'white', and in any of the places called Whitchurch we may think of the first little building of wattle and daub washed over with a coat of chalky whitewash making it stand out brightly among the surrounding huts of natural timber and thatch.

Although in a number of towns and villages an ecclesiastical building was the focal point of interest that provided the name, it was rare among the English to name a place from a saint. In the Celtic countries the names of saints form almost the largest category of place-name elements, second only to natural features; in England proper they are comparatively rare; but this statement must be qualified in two ways. Firstly, it does not include Cornwall which is *par excellence* the land of saints. Although officially English, in respect of place-names it is emphatically Celtic, and will be treated as such in Part Two. And to a lesser extent all the western counties that border on the Celtic lands show a sprinkling of saints' names given under Celtic influence and often Celtic in character. It is in the names that the English made for themselves that saints have little place.

Secondly many village-names in England have had the names of saints to whom their churches were dedicated added as distinguishing marks during the Middle Ages under Norman influence, as at Chalfont St Giles or Lytham St Annes. I myself live in Gussage All Saints, which is thus differentiated from Gussage St Michael and Gussage St Andrews, all of them being situated on the same little 'gushing' river from which they take their real name. But the original place-names made by the English contain few saints' names.

For this reason the few that do so are of special interest, and most of them refer to men or women who actually lived or died in the places that keep their names. The most important English town to be called by a saint's name is St Albans, and here the reason for the name is clear and typical. The site on the hill just outside the ruined Roman Verulamium was known as the place of execution of the first Christian martyr in this island, the Roman soldier Alban. He had met his death here long before the coming of the English but they heard his story soon after their conversion and revering, the hill-top for his sake, called it Albanstowe. They built a church on it, which the Normans rebuilt as a great abbey, and round it a city grew. It was Alban's place, in fact as well as in name, and the only question was a matter of language, English or French. Norman influence prevailed; the French word 'saint' was added and the English 'stow' dropped.

The man who brought Christianity to the English, St Augustine, is not commemorated in the name of any city or town, but his name can be found in a little village by the Severn where he sat under an oak tree in the year 603, waiting for the leaders of the Welsh Christians to come across by boat to confer with him. The meeting did not go well, for Augustine failed to rise to greet the Welsh bishops and they were quick to take offence, but the occasion was historic and the spot remembered. Bede, writing about a hundred years later, said that it was then known as 'Augustine's Oak'. Now it is only Aust, but still a point of communication with Wales for it is just at the eastern end of the Severn Bridge.*

The English saint whose name recurs most often in his own land is Oswald, Christian King of Northumbria. Among several localities connected with him (page 50), that of chief interest is Oswestry on the Welsh border, where he was killed in battle in 641 by the heathen Penda. It had an earlier name, Maserfield, but since Oswald was greatly venerated, and several miracles were reported near the spot where his body was hacked to pieces, the place assumed a new significance. Bede tells us that so many people carried away 'the very dust of the place where his body fell, and putting it into water, did much good with it to their friends who were sick . . . that there remained a hole as deep as the height of a man'. In such a spot it was natural that a cross should be erected. The English called it poetically Oswald's tree (a metaphor for a cross which they often used) and this became Oswestry. The early evidence for the name is confused but the Welsh name for the same place, Croesoswald, 'the cross of Oswald', confirms at least that here stood an early memorial to the king.

Much the same thing happened at Bury St Edmunds after the Christian king of East Anglia was murdered by the Danes in 870. Miracles were soon observed in the place where his body had been first buried, and it was transferred to the monastery in the chief town or 'bury' of his kingdom which was greatly

---

* This identification has been disputed but the evidence for it is very strong. As the English side of the best crossing from South Wales, where ferries have plied for centuries, Aust is exactly where the Welsh bishops would have landed. We know that Augustine's name was preserved at the meeting-place for over a century, and no alternative derivation has been suggested except the Latin Augusta, for which there is no evidence.

enriched by the association. As at St Albans the Normans, who were always ready to take up the cults of local saints, rebuilt the minster with a fine church to honour the martyr. The town had once been known as Badricsworth, but this now lapsed, the laity apparently calling it Edmundstow or simply Bury (*Berie* in Domesday Book) while the monks preferred Saint Edmunds Bury. Even today the word order is not fully stabilized, and the local people still say only Bury.

In the same region two other holy men were identified with places that received Norman patronage, at St Neots and St Ives, both in Huntingdon. But almost nothing is known of either. Neot was said to be a monk buried nearby; the other was called Ivo and has nothing to do with the Cornish St Ives. In such cases a final 's' is nearly always possessive and should not be taken as part of the name.

It is much harder to pick out the saints from the purely English place-names in which they are spoken of familiarly without title, as at Felixstowe and Oswestry. One who is seldom recognized is St Botolph of Boston in Lincolnshire. This was originally Botolph's stone (in 1130 it was *Botulvestan*). Botolf is mentioned in the *Anglo-Saxon Chronicle* in the year 654 as beginning to build a minster in an unidentified place. Another early source tells that 'he was a man of remarkable life and learning', and he must have been vividly remembered as several medieval churches are dedicated to him, including one in London. But all the details are forgotten. Nor do we know why his stone was so important. It may have been some ancient monolith which he used as an altar, or as a platform from which to exhort his audience. We can only say that for a time the chief interest of the place lay in holy Botolf and his stone.

On the whole English place-names that are obviously derived from saints have been little used overseas. The Pilgrim Fathers who called their home in New England Boston had probably no notion of its etymology. To them it meant the prosperous little town, set among rich meadows, where ships sailed up the Witham to tie up in the shadow of the tall church tower, a landmark from far out at sea. Masters of understatement, they spoke of it as Boston stump, and in a strange new land their descendants remembered it with love, but not St Botolf.

75

The point has been made that the majority of our old religious foundations are known by pre-Christian names, and if we look at a list of our cathedral cities we see it clearly illustrated. Of the forty-two English bishoprics and two archbishoprics, the names of only three contain any verbal link with Christianity. St Albans is one, St Edmundsbury, recently raised to episcopal status in this form, another. The third is Peterborough, and in this case the great apostle is a late addition, an informal, colloquial one, prefixed in the English manner and not recorded before the thirteenth century. In Domesday Book this town is simply *Burg*, or as we should say, Borough. Long before that there had been a monastery there called Medeshamstede, but it had been destroyed by the Danes, and when a town had been rebuilt there it had good defences so that the local people spoke of it as a stronghold or 'Borough', much as others had done at Bury. When this proved inadequate, the name of the saint to whom the Norman church was dedicated was pressed into service to make it Peterborough, an individual and dignified name. It is identical with St Petersburg, or Petrograd, and actually closer to the latter, being in the vernacular form.

Of the remaining forty-one cathedral cities at least twelve have names of pagan prehistoric origin or partly so, for many like Salisbury and Lichfield have an English tag added to something older. The rest are early English describing in the simplest terms the natural amenities of the places as seen by their first settlers, the excellent water supply at Wells, the profusion of eels at Ely, features that would attract monastic builders at a later date. But there is no hint of piety in them.

Chapter 8

VIKINGS ROUND THE BRITISH ISLES

The Anglo-Saxons had been Christian for over two centuries when a new wave of barbarians, the Danes, burst upon them. And when King Alfred made his famous treaty with them in 886 by which they were expelled from Wessex and permitted to settle only in the north-eastern half of England – henceforward to be known as the Danelaw – the agreement was so binding that its effects may still be seen today. Place-names with a Scandinavian character are almost entirely confined behind the boundary then laid down, which ran diagonally across the country, roughly from London to Chester. These names, created in England by men of Danish speech, are better documented than those made by the early Anglo-Saxon settlers, for the simple reason that the Danish invasion came nearly four hundred years later, at a time when written records were more plentiful. Therefore we see their beginnings with greater clarity.

Just how many Danes made their permanent homes in England at that period can only be guessed at, but enough to name hundreds of small new settlements in their own language, many of which are now large towns. Such names are not equally distributed through the Danelaw. By far the greatest concentration is in Yorkshire and Lincolnshire, while further south in the counties nearer the boundary a mere sprinkling of Danish names shows a much slighter degree of settlement.

Although the contribution of the Danes to our place-names is large, their language was so nearly related to English and their

77

style of name-giving so very similar that we are not conscious of anything alien in the names with which they sprinkled the North Country. Old Norse, as the Scandinavian languages of that time are collectively called, sprang from the same Teutonic origin as Old English, and a large amount of vocabulary was common to both. Such words as land, sea, moor and ness (meaning a cape) were for practical purposes identical, and others differed only slightly. The English and Norse words for an island, *eg* and *ey*, merged together indistinguishably, as also did *burh* and *borg*. Bamburgh (alternatively spelt Bamborough) and Flamborough on the same north-eastern coast appear to be twins, but one was built and named, as we noticed earlier, by English invaders of the sixth century; the other is Norse in origin, and named after a Danish hero, Flinn, three centuries later.

But in spite of similarities there were also marked differences between the languages. Certain words used very commonly by the Danish settlers did not exist in English, or only in some very different form. Of these by far the most prominent is *by*, which meant a dwelling-place or farm, the Danish equivalent of the English *tūn*. The North Country is as full of -bys as the South is of -tons and one has only to glance at their numbers on the map of any area to judge how thickly it was settled by the Danes.

Next in importance is 'thorp' which meant a small or subsidiary settlement, generally an offshoot from a bigger village. This word so often stood alone marking a Danish farm which had grown to a village that in later times many Thorpes had to have additions to distinguish them; we have Thorpe in the Fallows, Thorpe on the Hill, Thorpe Constantine, and so forth, but still a number of plain Thorpes remain. This word has many continental cousins; it is the common ending *trup* in Denmark, *dorf* in Germany, *dorp* in Holland and South Africa. It had an Old English version too in the form of 'throp' which has given the village name of Thrupp, but it was never common among the English.

Another Norse word that lingered long in North Country dialects is 'thwaite'. It means a clearing or meadow and corresponds in its usage to the English *lēah*. Thwaite may also be found alone but is far more often combined with another word, frequently a picturesque one describing the natural surroundings, with a fine disregard of length. Hawthornethwaite and

Brackenthwaite may be compared with the briefer English Thornley and Farley (fern lea); Braithwaite is the northern version of Bradley, a broad clearing.

Yet another characteristic word of Danish origin is 'garth', which meant an enclosure, and is closely related to the English 'yard', and also to 'garden' (which came later from France). The word 'orchard' contains the same element again, but how tame an orchard sounds in comparison with the northern Applegarth. It is this quality of ruggedness that southerners are apt to notice in regard to northern names and it is generally the Scandinavian element that has supplied it. It is fully in accord with the nature of the land, where fells and dales are larger and wilder than the hills and valleys further south (or the downs and denes to use the older words), and it is fitting that they should have their own vocabulary. A list of the principal Scandinavian place-name elements is given on page 337.

Apart from actual words there are very definite differences of pronunciation and spelling between the South and North of England, largely the result of Scandinavian influence. A few of them may easily be grasped. The English sound 'sh' (which was written 'sc' in Old English) is generally 'sk' in the North. We can see the contrast in such pairs as Shipton and Skipton: both mean 'sheep farm' and are English in origin, but Danish influence has been at work in the latter case. Similarly the southern Shelton corresponds with the northern Skelton. Their meaning is a farm on a flat ledge on the side of a hill, literally 'shelf'. A typically Danish name is Scutterskelfe in Yorkshire, a 'shelf' by a chattering brook. An ash tree, in Old Norse, had the sound of 'ask' as we still hear in Askwith (ash wood), and this must have been the commonest tree in the north of England judging by the number of Ashbys. Some of these seem to have begun as English Ashtons which the Danes translated into their own vernacular by changing *tūn* to *by*. But in this case the English 'sh' has remained, making a typical compromise.

Similarly, the English 'ch' has its hard counterpart in the North, giving 'kirk' instead of 'church'. There are a full score of Kirkbys in the Danelaw counties and nearly the same number contracted to Kirby, each one 'a village with a church'. Their large number shows how quickly the Danes took to Christianity. In some cases they may have burnt down the

79

churches they speak of, and looted their treasures, but their frequent reference to them as the outstanding feature of the *by* seems to belong more to a time when they had rebuilt them for themselves. The numerous Kirkbys, like the Thorpes, had to be differentiated in later times, and so we have Kirby Underdale, Kirkby Overblow and other variations.

In the same way the English Charlton, which meant 'the churl's village' and is found in many places, is paralleled by the northern Carlton. A churl (OE *ceorl*) was a free man but of low estate, and such a village would be one where free peasants worked the land on their own account. It was the Normans who gave the good Old English 'churl' a derogatory sense, and put it out of fashion. The Scandinavian *karl* which had the same basic meaning of freedom was held in high esteem and became a favourite personal name. Most of the northern villages called Carlton or Carleton belonged to a group of 'carls', but here and there a man named Karli may have been the owner.

Yet again, the sound of 'g' in many words has contrasting southern and northern forms. We have only to think of 'bridge' and 'ridge' which are 'brigg' and 'rigg' in many northern names, and compare Ashridge in Berkshire with Askrigg in Yorkshire to appreciate the difference.

These are just a few of the variations between the names of the North and South due to Norse influence. Many people would affirm that they reflect the whole character and way of life of the inhabitants of these regions. Certain it is that there is a difference and that the Danish settlement contributed largely to it, but climate has played its part too, and the physical nature of the land. We can find the contrast in many things – for instance in the novels of the Brontës as compared to those of Jane Austen – and it is natural that we see it in place-names.

When we look for differences between Scandinavian and English naming we find plenty but they are mostly matters of detail, and the similarity is greater than the contrast. The whole basic style of naming has the same approach. Every village name is either a natural description showing close observation of the country, or else it is a statement of ownership. Personal names play a very large part, and they are at the same time character-istic of the Norsemen and their speech and also closely parallel with the English. There are the short names like Flinn of Flamborough, already mentioned, and the two-theme ones like Asmund in Osmondthorpe or Asgot in Osgodby. (The change from 'A' to 'O' here shows English influence, for it worked both ways, and Danish names were often anglicized.)

Among the Danes there was a special fondness for nicknames, which were often far from complimentary. Scunthorpe was the village of Skuma, which signifies the squinter. Slingsby belonged to Slengr, the Idler, Brocklesby to Broclos who was without breeches (literally 'breechless'), and Londesborough to Lothen 'the hairy'. Sometimes these characters may be identified with actual heroes in Norse sagas. Scarborough, for instance, was Scathi's *borg*, a fortress built by Thorgils Scathi in about 965, and his nickname meant harelipped. As with the Anglo-Saxons a great many personal names were derived from birds and animals, with the raven and the wolf as special favourites. The Norse form of the Old English *wulf* was *ulfr* and place-names of the type of Wolverton (in English) are found in the North in such forms as Ulverston. The beautiful lake, Ullswater, must have lain within the territory of a chieftain called Ulf, who would have been Wulfa or Wolf among the Saxons.

One way in which the personal names of the Danes differed markedly from those of the English was the familiarity with which the former treated their gods. The English had never at any recorded time called their children by such names as Thunor or Woden, but the Danes seemed to have none of this respect when they were pagans, or aversion when they became Christian. Thor in particular was a favourite name with them. Admittedly it was generally combined with another element to make a name such as Thorsteinn or Thorbiorn or even Thorkettill (the stone, the warrior and the cauldron of Thor). The last, though it seems unlikely, was particularly popular and survives in the surname Thirkell. But these names were almost always shortened colloquially to Thori bringing us back to the starting point of the god's own name. In the case of Odin, whom the English called Woden, the Danes preferred his nickname, Grim, and this too they used freely to name their sons. In the South of England we may be confident that any place-name that includes Thur, Woden or Grim had a pagan religious significance (see Chapter 7), but in the Danelaw counties such places as Thursby and Grimsby were the farms of very human Danish men.

It should not be thought that all the names in the North of England have a Scandinavian character. Those that show it most strongly were very largely new settlements made at the time of the Danish invasion. But every kind of combination of the two languages is found: purely English or purely Danish, English influenced by Danish pronunciation, and vice versa, as well as hybrids. Eventually the English language remained in possession of the field; the Danes influenced it and contributed some useful words, but they have always been good linguists and they learnt to speak it in a northern version.

Nearly all the most important towns in the north had kept their old names established long before the coming of the Danes. Even the Five Boroughs, as the chief strongholds of the Danish armies of the Midlands were called – armies that yielded only gradually to the power of the House of Wessex – include only one new name, Derby, which had formerly been Northworthy, the north farm. The Danes renamed it from the herds of deer that must have been concentrated there, perhaps in some sort of enclosure; the name means 'deer village', and – as is so often the case – the first element could belong to either language. The other four Danish boroughs, Lincoln, Leicester, Stamford and Nottingham, have either English or pre-English names that have been explained already.

In this time of disaster we see the ability of names to survive when all else is destroyed. Famous religious centres that were sacked and burnt by the heathen Danes lived on in name if in no other way. We think of Jarrow where Bede had written his famous history so peacefully. It was obliterated by the Danes but its name was not lost, a very early name of an English tribe called the Gyrwe, who had settled in that place when they were heathen.

The most important Scandinavian centre in all England was York. There Norse kings reigned intermittently in the tenth century, sometimes driven out by English kings but fighting back. The ancient Celtic name had already been remodelled by the Angles who had inherited it from the Britons. It was Eborac(on) (page 6) when they first heard it, but the soft

82

Celtic 'b' sounded much like a 'v' and the English confused it with their own word *eofor* meaning a wild boar. They called it Eorforwic, which would mean 'boar village' and no doubt seemed to them near enough to what they had heard the Britons say. But the Danes evidently could make nothing of it and telescoped it into a single short, sharp syllable more like the bark of a dog than a gracious name. And yet this brief sound, rooted in pre-history and reshaped by two successive waves of barbarians, has attained a dignity that has travelled round the world.

We must now widen our view to consider briefly the great Scandinavian explosion of the ninth and tenth centuries as it affected not only England but other regions of the British Isles. And to begin with we should try to clarify the various names that have been used for those seafaring Scandinavians who so rudely shattered the peace that Celts and Englishmen were learning to enjoy. In England we speak of them chiefly as the Danes because those who attacked our shores and stayed to settle came chiefly from Denmark. But at the same time and in equal or greater strength shiploads of adventurers of similar race and character were setting out from the fiords of Norway. They were known as the Northmen (or Norsemen rather later), and it is to them that the term 'Viking' properly belongs, for a *vik* in their language was an inlet of the sea where boats might be safely anchored and it was from such places that they set out on their voyages. However, this word 'Viking' when applied to the whole violent Scandinavian movement of that period may be taken to include the Danes as well.

A further complication arises concerning that group of Northmen who settled on the coast of France. For them the general term 'Northman' was contracted to 'Norman' and, coming later into England by way of France, had lost its natural plural, so that we speak of 'Normans' rather than 'Normen'; a new word for a highly distinctive racial group.

While the Danes were attacking England, other Viking fleets both of Danes and Northmen were sweeping round to the north of the British Isles, fearless of wild seas and rocky shores, and bearing down on the coasts of Scotland, Wales and Ireland, and all the islands that lie around them. At first it was a matter of

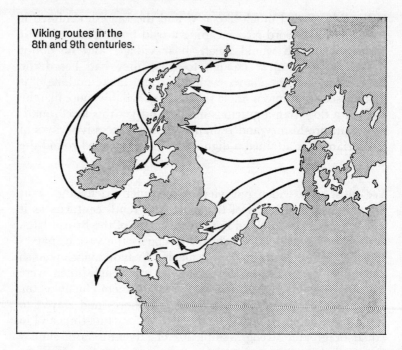

Viking routes in the 8th and 9th centuries.

raids only, the richest monasteries falling the first preys, but soon after came settlement. The Orkneys, the Isle of Man and Dublin became, each one of them, the centre of a Viking kingdom. On the whole Wales got off rather lightly and Ireland suffered worst, and when at last the Irish kings – of whom there were several at any one time – managed to combine for a brief space and drive some of the Vikings out they merely decamped across the narrow seas to the north-west coast of England, and made themselves at home in what is now Cheshire, Lancashire, Westmorland and Cumberland.

Thus this romantic region of England, which still has some of its wildest scenery as well as industrial towns, has a linguistic history more complicated than any other part. First we know it as one of the last strongholds of the Britons, then the Angles overran it and established their rule. Next came Danes invading from the east, and then from the other side Vikings from Ireland with a sprinkling of Irish among them, who had attached themselves to the Northmen in the hope of plunder.

If the people of the north-west counties of England have a character all their own, it is because nowhere else has quite the same mixture of Celt, English and Viking.

The racial distinctions of the north of England are clearly stated in certain town and village names that are often repeated. Normanby, Danby, Ireby and Ingleby were settlements made respectively by Northmen (not Normans in the later sense), Danes, Irish and English; and we are told so in a Scandinavian language. In the case of Normanton, of which there are no less than twelve, and Ireton (two) the statements are English; and lest anyone should think that the Britons (or Welsh as the English called them) have been forgotten in this racial mix up, it should be pointed out that the common name Walton which occurs in many parts of England means in most cases the village of the Welsh, though it has other possible origins as well. Names of this kind generally indicate that the racial group named is in the minority. Where a large district was settled by Danes it would not be natural to specify one village as belonging to them. The three examples of Ingleby, all in the North Riding of Yorkshire, must have been isolated pockets of Englishmen in the midst of Northmen, surviving precariously in their own land.

Whether the Vikings who made themselves so much at home in Britain were Danes coming from the east or Norwegians from the west had some effect on place-names, for, although they spoke almost the same language, there were differences of vocabulary. There is, to begin with, the word *vik* that gave the more northerly race its name. We see it in their own land at Narvik, and farther off in Reykavik, for they left it wherever they went like a visiting card. In Britain it took the form of 'wick', but should not be confused with the Old English *wīc*, meaning a village, a very common element of totally different origin. The Norse 'wick' (an inlet) occurs only rarely in England, for the Danes did not use it, but is found round the Scottish and Irish coasts that the Northmen frequented, for instance in Lerwick (muddy bay) in the Shetlands, Wicklow in Ireland, and Wick in Caithness, where it makes the whole name of a narrow, sheltered inlet on a dangerous, rockbound coast.

Another typical Norwegian word is 'fiord', a larger inlet

D

than a 'wick'. Again, the Danes did not use it, for their coasts are smooth and gentle, and they have no mountains to cause such deep clefts opening into the sea. But the Norwegians had lived in fiords and wherever they found the same configuration they used the word freely. In Scotland it became 'firth' and every firth sheltered Viking ships during the ninth century. On the coasts of Ireland, Wales and Cornwall the same word appears in disguise. One has only to look at the deep and spacious sea inlets at Waterford, Carlingford, Strangford and Helford to realize the inappropriateness of the English 'ford' and the aptness of 'fiord'.

Milford Haven which sounds so English is pure Norse. The first element is not the English 'mill', but the Norse *melr*, a 'sandbank'. Haven is the Norse *hafn*, a word we know well; and we have no excuse for mispronouncing the capital of Denmark as grossly as we do, seeing that we have 'havens' of our own. Copenhaven would be much more reasonable as an anglicized form. Thus Milford Haven is the 'harbour in a fiord with a sandbank'.

This haven must have been well used by the Vikings for they left a number of their names in that region, almost the only part of Wales to have them. A little farther along the coast Swansea is 'Sweyn's Island', while on the other side of the promontory Fishguard is the 'fisher's garth', some sort of enclosure to do with fishing. And all the islands that cluster round that rocky 'land's end' of South Wales, Ramsey, Skokholm, Grassholm and so on have Norse names.* A little further south Lundy takes its name from the Norse *lundi*, a 'puffin', and the comical puffins are still sitting on its cliffs. Caldy Island has been explained as 'cold island', but how could the Vikings who felt at home in the Shetlands and sailed in open boats to Greenland and Iceland have felt cold on the southern side of Wales? It is much more likely that its first element is the Norse *kelde*, a 'spring'.

On the whole they were repulsed from Wales and their chief settlements were around the coasts of Ireland and Scotland and their adjacent islands. Almost everywhere they adopted existing names as they heard them, creating new ones chiefly for their

---

* Ramsey was probably 'Raven's island'. ON *Hrafn* was often used as a man's name. *Skokr* meant a wooden chest or ship's hulk; *holmr* a flat-topped island.

own settlements and for the rocks, headlands and heights that made their landmarks from the sea. In the Isle of Man, for instance, where they established a kingdom that was long un-challenged, their name, Snaefell, 'snow mountain', the exact synonym of Snowdon, stands on the highest peak, and it was they who called the lesser island Calf of Man; but Gaelic names abound as well. The greatest concentration of Norse names in the British Isles is found in the Orkneys and Shetlands where the many 'island' names such as Westray and Ronaldsay are typical and where 'nesses' (capes) and 'skerries' (rocks) are plentiful.

How many people have stopped to wonder why the northern-most county of Britain is called the 'south land', Sutherland. Only the Vikings could have called it so; to them, sailing from Orkney to Iceland, or threading through the tide race of the Pentland Firth and under the towering cliffs of Hoy (the 'high' land) and so on towards the Hebrides and Ireland, it lay always to the south, making the southern part of their watery kingdom of Orkney. It was just a matter of point of view.

The extreme north-east corner of Britain, which was all part of this Viking kingdom, has a curious collection of characteristic Norse names of which Scrabster, Lybster, Thrumster, Ulbster and Vobster are just a few. This ending -ster is the remains of the Norse word *stathr*, meaning a place, and related to the English 'stead'. The Vikings also added it to some old Irish tribal names, making them into Ulster, Munster and Leinster.

Let us end this chapter with a further question of point of view, in regard to the word 'land'. The English and the Scandinavians had it in common but employed it differently. The English, once they had settled down, did not use it very much except in regard to agricultural property; Buckland was land held 'by the book', that is by charter (literally a piece of parchment), Sunderland was an area separated from the rest of some owner's estate. But the Vikings, on their frequent voyages, saw land objectively from the sea as whole territories where they might settle or not as they chose. They named Iceland, Greenland, Finland, even Vinland on the coast of America (but the rest of the world took little notice of that). It was they who added the 'land' to Ireland, which had hitherto had only a tribal name, varying from Ierne to Eire; it was they who called the northern part of Britain first Pictland (of which a corruption survives in the Pentland Firth) and later Scotland. They too made the territories of the Northumbrians, the Westmoorings and a remnant of the Cumbri into Northumberland, Westmorland and Cumberland, and it may be that their influence helped to build the name of England, which is not on record before the tenth century.

One quality that all the Scandinavians possessed in a high degree was adaptability. When they first descended on any district they were extremely destructive, but once they had settled down they learnt the customs, language and religion of their new country with surprising rapidity, so that in a few generations they had ceased to be foreigners. At their worst they were a terrible scourge but they also contributed much to the English, Scottish and Irish way of life.

Chapter 9

THE ENGLISH COUNTIES

By the middle of the tenth century the Danelaw had been reconquered and all England was united under one king, of the House of Wessex, never to be divided again. And already the arrangement of the land in shires – or counties as we call them now – was almost complete.

The word 'shire' comes from the Old English *sciran*, to cut, which also gives us the verbs 'shear' and 'share', and means literally 'a cut off piece' or 'a slice'. It was used for centuries in England before the French 'county' came into fashion.

The establishment of the shires happened at very different dates between the coming of the English and the Norman Conquest. In the south their names arose chiefly from those of the main tribes of Angles and Saxons as they invaded and seized the land or, in a few cases, from older kingdoms that were there before them. Many of these shire names were in use even while the invaders were still on the move. But the northern half of the country was so totally overrun by the Danes in the ninth century that when it was gradually reconquered it was newly organized in defensive and administrative regions, and some of these Midland and northern counties are comparatively late creations. That is to say, they are barely nine hundred years old.

When writing of the early English kingdoms which occupied the land between the fifth and ninth centuries, ebbing and flowing against each other in constant motion, the word Heptarchy, invented by Tudor historians, comes at once to mind. It is out of favour now; there were not exactly seven kingdoms during that time, more at first and fewer later, but it is a convenient expression and gives a rough idea of the state of affairs.

Pride of place must be given to Kent, not only as the oldest county name but the oldest recorded name of any sort that is still in use in England (page 3). As is usual with such ancient words there is doubt about its significance, but the Celtic root word *canto* meaning an edge or rim seems to offer the likeliest explanation, especially when one remembers that this word was first recorded (as *Kantion*) by seamen referring to the south-east corner, bordered by the sea. The Romans called its people the Cantii and though few of them can have survived the English invasion their name did, Kent becoming the first of the dominant kingdoms of Anglo-Saxon England.

To the north of Kent the Kingdom of the East Saxons contained what became the counties of Essex and Middlesex (east and middle Saxons), and it seems that Surrey ('the south region') belonged at first to them too. Meanwhile, the South Saxons founded a small separate kingdom – now Sussex. The East Angles, whose land was spoken of later in a scholarly way as East Anglia, were divided into the north and south folk who occupied, obviously, Norfolk and Suffolk.

The West Saxons deployed themselves gradually over a large region, known from their name as Wessex, and organized at an early date into several shires which were named from their principal settlements. The first of these was at Southampton, a district which appears in the early records as *Homtun* or *Hamtun*. It was here that they made their first incursion in the fifth century, and from this primitive encampment came *Hamtunscir* (755), now Hampshire, its abbreviation Hants showing its descent from the earlier form. This name for a wide region must have been established before the ruined Roman city of Winchester was re-occupied and given importance as a Christian bishopric. The foundations of the cathedral have been dated back to the seventh century, and by the ninth Winchester was the chief city not only of Wessex but of all Saxon England. But the earlier shire-name was never superseded.

Westwards from Hampshire three more shires took names from early West Saxon settlements made by groups who were spoken of as *saetan*, or 'settlers'. Those who made their homes around the Roman city of Dorchester (page 23) became known as the *Dornsaete*, the nucleus of Dorset. A little to the north along the valley of the Wylye lived the *Wilsaetan*, which might be modernized as 'the Wylye set'. Their principal village, Wilton, became the first centre of Wiltshire (*Wiltunscir*, 870). Further west another focal point was Somerton, literally 'the summer farm'. It owed its origin to good pastures where the cattle were driven for the summer, some other place being preferred for the winter months, but it must quickly have developed into a more permanent abode of 'the Somerton set', important enough to name the shire of Somerset by Alfred's reign (as mentioned by his bishop Asser). In later times Somerton has grown little. The county administration was long ago centred on Taunton, and Somerton remains only a village, though a dignified one with its weathered stone houses and market cross.

Another shire that was included in Wessex was Berkshire. Bishop Asser tells us that it was named from the great forest of birch trees called Bearroc. He certainly knew the forest well and the county abounds in silver birches to this day, but the etymology of the name is probably older than he thought for *bearroc* is a Celtic word meaning 'hilly', the ending -oc being typical of the Brittonic language. It seems that as with the river Wylye and the first element of Dorset the Saxons had picked up an old local name.

We have still not finished with the various territories of the West Saxons. In the eighth century they overran and conquered most of the Celtic kingdom of the West which the Romans had called Dumnonia from its inhabitants the Dumnoni, and which we know as Devon. It should be borne in mind that in the Celtic language the sound of 'm' regularly interchanged with that of 'v' or 'f', and thus it is not surprising that in the *Anglo-Saxon Chronicle* these people are first mentioned (in 823) as the *Defnas*, and in 894 we find the first reference to *Defnascir*. What the original root *dumnon* meant is uncertain. Some scholars have connected it with a word meaning 'deep', and the idea may have been that these people lived in deep valleys, or even that they mined, but on this point there is no certainty. They may have had this name in prehistoric times before migrating to Britain.

As the Saxons pressed onwards these native inhabitants fled

further west or across the sea into Brittany, and the advancing and victorious Saxons who settled in the sheltered valleys took over their old name and used it for themselves. That they called the valleys 'coombes' and the hill-tops 'tors' shows that they had absorbed some of the older population, but nonetheless the great majority of Devon village-names are English, though many Celtic elements are mingled with them.

The Cornish long remained a separate race from the English. The first part of the name Cornwall is a Celtic word meaning 'horn' obviously related to the Latin *cornu*. The western promontory of Dumnonia was *Corneu* to the Britons – the land of the horn – and this native form of the word survives in the surname Curno. The second syllable of the county name was added by the English. It is their word *walh* which meant 'foreign', and was what they generally called the Britons. It occurs in many place-names all over England, even as far east as London where Walbrook is 'the brook of the Britons' (or the 'enemy'), and must have been so called at a very early date. This word has provided the English name for the whole country of Wales, and Cornwall means literally 'the Welsh of the horn', yet another name for people rather than a place.

Two great early English kingdoms remain to be considered, Northumbria and Mercia. The former, first recorded as *Northymbre*, meant literally 'the people north of the Humber'. In those days there were Southumbrians too, but they split into various divisions and the name disappeared. At the height of its greatness in the seventh century Northumbria stretched from the Humber to the Firth of Forth, but much of its northern territory was lost to the Scots, and then all was devastated by the Danes. Out of this large kingdom several shires were eventually formed, including Northumberland, which preserves the old name, though only a small part of its former extent and that not near the Humber. The much greater county of Yorkshire takes its name from the old city that was once the capital of the Northumbrian kings, and later the principal stronghold of the Danish armies. The three parts of Yorkshire, known as Ridings, were literally thirds or 'thridings'; but combined with East, West and North, the 'th' merged into the ends of these words and disappeared.

The two north-western counties of Cumberland and Westmoreland, first mentioned in the tenth century, are both named from their inhabitants; Cumberland from the *Cymry*, or 'brotherhood', which is what the Britons called themselves in their time of disaster when driven into the mountains of the West. The Angles, who knew the word, pronounced it Cumbri, but more often called the same people the Welsh. Westmoreland appears first as *Westmoringaland*, that is, the land of the people of the west moors, a typically English name.

Durham, which was one of the last of the old counties to become a separate entity, having been carved out of Northumberland soon after the Conquest, differs from all the others in having an ecclesiastical origin. When the Danish raids threatened the Holy Island where St Cuthbert had died, the monks fled carrying his coffin with them and after many adventures at last found a safe resting place for it on the rocky outcrop where the great cathedral of Durham now stands. Here his cult grew steadily, so that not only the English but also Danes, when they were converted, joined in enriching the shrine. It was the Norman kings who built the cathedral and the castle and established the see, granting the bishops special privileges so that they reigned over their episcopal lands like princes, and it was not until 1836 that their extraordinary local powers were finally vested in the crown. In these circumstances Durham has never had the homely word 'shire' tagged on to it as most of the other counties named from towns have done.

The name Durham is late in origin, being first mentioned in the account of how Bishop Aldhun and his monks were guided by a dream to this hitherto unoccupied site in the year 995, and built on it the first little church as a shrine for St Cuthbert's remains. This was written about the year 1000. The name was then Dunholm, consisting apparently of the English *dūn*, a hill, to which the Danish word *holmr*, used generally for a flat-topped island, was added; the rocky eminence is almost surrounded by the river Wear.* The normal development of this would have been to a sound like Dunnam, possibly spelt

* The Danish element can hardly have been present in the name when the monks, fleeing from the Danes, made it their sanctuary. We do not know what they called it.

D*

93

Dunham, but the place became pre-eminently a stronghold of the Normans and under their influence the 'n' changed to 'r'. The final result is a strong, simple sound that has the advantage of being unique in England.

Another special case was that of little Rutland. The name, which means 'Rota's land', appears first among the personal possessions of Queen Edith, wife of Edward the Confessor, and it continued as an endowment for the Norman queens with its own administration until it took its place among the counties. But of Rota nothing whatever is known except that he lived before Queen Edith and was a man of sufficient importance to own or rule this territory which, though small as a county, is large as the possession of one man.

All the other old counties, including those that make a solid block across the Midlands, once the territory of the great central kingdom of Mercia, were named from their principal towns. This is not a matter of chance but of a deliberate policy, begun by King Alfred and continued by his son, Edward, of defending the land against further Danish attacks and re-conquering what they held. As each district was recaptured a town was chosen and a castle (or *burh*) built and its inhabitants, 'the burghers', made responsible for the defence of the surrounding country. Thus it followed naturally that each strongpoint so appointed became the centre of administration for the district it defended.

Alfred's policy was eventually so successful that less than forty years after his death his grandson Athelstan was King of all England (937), and already the system of shires destined to last over a thousand years was almost complete.

There is an interesting point to be observed in regard to these county-towns built as centres of defence. Although they were all spoken of as *burhs* this word makes part of the name of only one of them, Shrewsbury. They had all been in existence as named places before they were raised to this new importance, and their names tell of much earlier inhabitants than the burghers of Alfred's day. Four of them end in -cester or -caster, indicating Roman origin and in those cases the remains of stone walls must have helped to dictate the choice. No less than five end in -ford, showing the importance of controlling river crossings, and in these cases the same practical considerations had caused the early invaders to settle at these points. Beda, for instance, had probably established himself on the bank at Bedford centuries before King Edward built a castle there; and Hertford, where harts were seen, is on record from the seventh century.

Several of the town-names end in -ham, -ton or -wick, showing them to have begun as encampments of small parties, those that contain -ing being typical of the earliest part of the English invasion. It is not likely that Bucca's people settled at Buckingham much later than the sixth century, and the same applies to Snot, who has lost his 'S' in the passage of time and whose followers built their homestead at Nottingham (*Snotingaham*, 868). Warwick was originally only an offshoot from a bigger farm, a *wīc* by a 'weir' or 'dam', a common arrangement for catching fish. In short, though it was the choosing of these places to be royal strongholds about a thousand years ago that gave them their importance, their names are much older than that.

As they began to dominate their districts, so to each of these town-names 'shire' could be added when speaking of the region. This has resulted in some very bulky words; 'Northamptonshire' is much too long and generally contracted to Northants, and in some cases the contraction took place long enough ago to be established as the correct form, as for instance Cheshire for Chestershire. In the case of Shropshire the distortion that the original name has suffered is so great as to need special comment. Shrewsbury, Shropshire and the abbreviation Salop all go back apparently to a bushy region known as 'the scrub'. This was before 901 when this town was described in Latin as *civitas Scrobbensis*, 'the city of the scrub folk'.* In a rather later English record these people are referred to as the *Scrobsaete*, and the county might easily have become 'Shropset' to match Dorset and Somerset. However, the castle, or *burh*, that was built there had in this case its influence and we next see the town-name as *Scrobbesbyrig*; this contracted to 'Shro'sbury', which is still the correct way of speaking it, though the spelling has gone astray. So much for the town. The county, taking its name

---

* There has been a rival theory that Scrob was a man's name, but I fully agree with Dr Margaret Gelling (*Names of Towns and Cities in Britain*) that the evidence for the scrubby locality is far more convincing.

in the normal way from the town, was written first as *Scrobbesbyrigscir* (it should be remembered that the OE 'sc' was pronounced 'sh'). This being too much for anyone, English speakers soon dropped the 'bury' leaving 'Shrobshire' from which it was a short step to Shropshire; but French clerks, responsible for official documents, found the whole thing impossible. They dropped the 'h', a letter that always confused them, turned the 'r' into 'l', which they were often inclined to do, gave up halfway through and wrote 'Salop', a weak attempt at the native name that they could not master, but one that still survives, if only in writing.

Before we leave the subject of counties, let us look back once more to the even older kingdoms that existed before them. One whose name has seemed most completely lost – though it may yet be revived – is Mercia, the central region out of which so many counties were formed and which for a short time under King Offa held sway over all the others. Mercia is the latinized form of *Merce*, derived from the Old English *mearc*, a 'boundary', and meaning the 'boundary people' or 'borderers'. This makes us realize something of the long struggle to push the Britons westwards and hold them back, along a frontier that was delineated in the eighth century by the building of Offa's Dyke. Another word with the same significance is preserved in Mersey, which is literally the 'frontier river'.

The greater name of Wessex has no present official existence, but is very much alive nonetheless, thanks partly to the novels of Thomas Hardy. But even without them it could not be forgotten. Indeed, the remarkable thing about the 'Heptarchy' which came to an end more than a thousand years ago is the influence it still exerts subconsciously on our view of England. We still speak of the different parts of the land in phrases that roughly tally with those long vanished kingdoms. 'The North Country' almost exactly comprehends the old kingdom of Northumbria, which still has a homogeneous character; while 'The West Country' corresponds more or less to Wessex. Mercia has become 'the Midlands', and the land of the East Saxons is not just Essex, which was only a part of it, but 'the Home Counties'. We still call the bulge of Norfolk and Suffolk East Anglia, while Kent and Sussex have remained as they were.

And each of these expressions, mostly unofficial, represents a region of distinctive character.

If we ignore the changes of our own time and include Monmouthshire (named from the town at the mouth of the River Monnow), which is officially English though practically Welsh, the old counties of England number forty. Of these, twenty-two took their names from their principal towns, and fourteen, including all the older ones, from tribal groups. Among these latter I have included Northumberland and Westmoreland as their earliest forms refer to their people (see above), but they might equally be classed as geographical. Kent and Devon are the nominal survivors of prehistoric tribal territories. Berkshire, of which the first element may be just as old, stands alone in having a name that is purely natural and descriptive – 'the hilly forest'. Only Rutland is derived directly from a man's name without the intervening step of the growth of a town.

This division of England for administrative purposes which was almost complete before the Conquest has its roots in prehistory, but to a large extent stemmed from the brilliant abilities of King Alfred and his family. Now, the first major re-arrangement in a thousand years is being undertaken and new names are needed for ten more counties. The suggestions put forward show how strongly the English cling to their old habit of naming from physical truth expressed as simply as possible, and of adapting old names to the changing scene. So it seems that a number of ancient river-names, some of them prehistoric, will assume a new significance in modern England, giving county names like Teesside and Humberside to regions dominated by growth along these river-banks.

Some of the names discussed in this chapter will lose their county status but that will not cause them to disappear from our speech. Unofficially they will still apply to the districts they have described so long, just as the old regional names of France live on after much more drastic changes than we will suffer. And in distant parts of the world where they have been reproduced so often the old shire-names will still be held in honour.

Chapter 10

NORMAN INFLUENCE

When William of Normandy made his audacious venture in 1066 he conquered a land that was full of old names. Twenty years later thousands of them were recorded at his command in Domesday Book, and thousands more must have been in existence, although not included in that famous report, because the places concerned had no taxable value. Some sites that are now cities were then not thought worthy of mention. Liverpool, for instance, was not included, but its name, meaning a thick and muddy pool – literally clotted – was probably well established in its neighbourhood.

The Norman Conquest was not a large migration of people but a highly successful military coup, and the new rulers who formed only a small minority of the population were well content to find themselves masters of the country, and to accept it as it was, names and all. They changed very few existing names and created only a moderate number of new ones, but those that they did contribute are of very special interest because they show an entirely new approach to the naming of places.

The Normans were really amazing people. In origin they were Vikings, and we have already noted that these Northmen were very adaptable, inclined to adopt the language and customs of whatever people they settled among, and ready to learn what it suited them best to know. The Vikings who settled in what became Normandy were heathen barbarians when they came there, but their contact with the French gave them new qualities and skills, which, combined with their own violent energy, turned them into one of the ablest and most progressive peoples in Europe. Their restless ambition carried them into England full of the zest that is bred by success, and something of this is reflected in the new names they created in England, names that are surprisingly modern in style.

The kind of name that the Normans liked for a new abbey or castle where nothing had been built before and no previous name existed was one that showed a sophisticated pleasure in the chosen site. Beaulieu, meaning 'beautiful place', was a favourite and has survived in a number of places and in several forms. In Hampshire it has kept the French spelling intact but is pronounced like Bewley, the way it is spelt in Kent. In Worcestershire an intrusive 'd' has crept in, making it Bewdley. In Scotland, where the Normans founded an abbey on the Firth of Forth, the pronunciation is like Bewley and the spelling a compromise, Beauly. In Ireland it is Beaulieu again.

A number of names of this type were given in the two centuries after the Conquest when the ruling class were still speaking French. Belper in Derbyshire was earlier Beaurepaire, meaning 'beautiful retreat'. Belvoir (pronounced Beaver) in Leicestershire meant 'beautiful view'. There are several Beaumonts, the one in Essex having replaced the earlier English name which was *Fulepet*. Even Professor Ekwall, whose dictionary of place-names is severely factual, has permitted himself a smile over this change from 'foul pit' to 'fair hill'. Of all the 'beau' names the one that is most completely anglicized is Beachey Head. This was *Beau chef* in which the French *chef* meaning 'head' was used for a headland just as the equivalent word would be in English. But the English reduced it to one word, and not understanding it added their own 'Head' in the same sense, making one of our many redundancies, 'beautiful head head'.

French names in England were doomed to mispronunciation from the start, and the Old French *hault* meaning 'high' was particularly vulnerable. On the borders of Wales a Norman built himself a castle on a hill which he called *Mont hault*. This 'high hill' has become Mold. And on the Yorkshire moors in a spot where the Old English word *twisla* referred to the fork of a river, a French-speaking landowner added *hault* to signify 'the high fork'. This is now Haltwhistle which sounds

99

thoroughly English and like a direction to passing trains. In a more idealistic strain a northern abbey was given the name of *Haut emprise* or 'high endeavour', and that exists today as Haltemprice. This last piece of naming, expressing an abstract idea, reminds us of the Pilgrim Fathers in America with their Concord and Providence. It is completely outside the usual run of names in England, totally unknown before the Conquest and rare at any time.

Another Norman name of an imaginative sort is Freemantle, which belongs in England only to a Hampshire village now swallowed up in Southampton, but has been carried – as a surname derived from that place – to greater prominence in Australia. Literally it meant 'cold cloak' (*froid mantel*) and exists as Fromantel in Normandy, where it began as the name of a forest. Only a poetic metaphor can explain this idea of the forest wrapping one round like a cloak, if a chilly one. The derivation is not in doubt.

Nearly all the great Norman castles have the names that were there before they were built, but one exception is of special interest, that of Richmond in Yorkshire. In this district the Conqueror gave large estates to his kinsman and ally, Count Alan of Brittany, who married one of his daughters and was in high favour. Count Alan built himself a castle on a steep hillside above the valley of the Swale and no doubt chose the site and the name himself, a name that existed already in Normandy, Richmond, or 'the rich mount'. But we must find a better translation for *riche* than the same word which has lost much of its early significance. It was in origin a Frankish word, the same as the *ric* that occurs in so many Northern personal names, and is related to the Latin *rex*. The adjective that the French formed from it might once have been translated as royal, noble, or powerful as well as wealthy, and Count Alan may have thought of it as 'royal'. He became the first Earl of Richmond, and more than four centuries later when Henry Tudor, the son of a later earl, came to the throne of England as Henry VII, he built himself a palace on the Thames near London, and called it Richmond after his family title. That was in 1502. A late name for England, but one that was destined to become famous from its royal association. It is better known than its Yorkshire parent and both are better known than the

little town of Richemont in Normandy which no doubt gave
Count Alan his idea.

This is another new aspect of naming as practised by the
Normans. They brought names with them. If they wanted a
new name for a castle they were building in England, they
might think of their homes in Normandy, and import one from
there. Again we think of the Pilgrim Fathers in America and
new settlers in many countries overseas, and we see how modern
the Normans were compared with the English and Danes of
earlier times who seemed never to look back or consciously
select a name.

One more name chosen by the Normans must be mentioned
as being almost unique of its sort in England – Baldock. Of all
unlikely things it is the Norman-French version of Baghdad.
Mispronunciation of foreign place-names has always been a
commonplace, and in medieval travellers' tales of Western
Europe 'Baldac' is the usual form for this Persian city. The
land in Hertfordshire belonged to the Templars, an exclusive
order of crusading knights who held wide estates in England,
but what whim prompted them – or one of them – to plant this
exotic name in the green English countryside we can only
imagine. Yet again we think of Americans at least five centuries
later calling their new towns Troy and Athens. The same
romantic feeling must have been at work.

But if Norman landowners could show imagination in their
naming, they did not always do so, and some of their names are
as plain and factual as anything that had come from an earlier
time. William the Conqueror himself showed no romantic
feeling for names. He was a man of deeds rather than words,
and the places that owe their being most directly to his actions
have the plainest names imaginable. The abbey that he built
on the hill-side a few miles from Hastings, as his own personal
thanksgiving for the great victory he won there, is simply
Battle Abbey – no saint's name, no mention of victory, just the
fact; and the little town that grew around it has the same stark
name, just Battle and no more. The new castle that he built to
dominate London was simply the Tower, the ordinary French
word for a castle keep, and for the other fortress that he built
on the Thames a few miles upstream from London he was
content to use the ordinary English name that was already

there, Windsor (page 53), coupled with the French word 'castle'. As for the special hunting preserve that he created for his pleasure in Hampshire by laying waste many miles of inhabited country, it has no name but the New Forest. Battle, tower, castle and forest – they were all French words, forerunners of many more that were coming into England, and which the English were going to learn by hard experience.

These then are the two sides of Norman naming, on the one hand the straightforward statement in the French language, on the other something more imaginative and more consciously aesthetic than had been heard in England before.

Complete place-names of Norman origin are not common in England, but when we turn to the double names we find that the second part is often a Norman contribution. I am thinking now of names like Stoke Mandeville and Sutton Valence. Basically these places are Stoke and Sutton, the secondary words, added centuries later, being the family names of Norman owners.

This brings us to the rise of surnames, which developed spontaneously in the early Middle Ages; and although in England its only effect on place-names was to add the surname of a feudal owner to many old village names like the two just mentioned, its later influence on place-names overseas was to be enormous. The need for second names to distinguish individuals had been felt in England even before the Conquest, and surnames were beginning to appear under the later Saxon kings, though as yet the hereditary principal was not established. In Normandy the custom had progressed a little further, and most of the knights who followed Duke William to England had second names that were quite likely to be inherited by their sons.

Exactly the same causes that made it expedient for a man to have a second name could operate also for a village, if its original name was a common one. In early times when each locality had managed its own affairs a name like Stoke was quite sufficiently distinctive within its own neighbourhood, but when government became more centralized some further description was often needed. Of course, this process has been going on since the first settlements were made. The unqualified *tūn* had become the south *tūn* (Sutton), or the high *tūn* (Heaton), or the *tūn* in the wood (Wootton, or by a grove (Grafton), and the additional information has been absorbed into a single word. But at a later stage established names were left undisturbed, and further items added separately as local surnames.

Most of the Norman and early Plantagenet kings were extremely able administrators who liked to gather the reins of government as much as possible into their own hands, and employed an army of clerks (or 'clerics'), the only people who could write, to make lists of all the property they could tax. When the same village-name cropped up in different places, an obvious way of clarifying the situation was to add the name of the owner, who was frequently a Norman knight or baron. So we have Melton Mowbray (this Melton was originally the 'middle *tūn*'), Shepton Mallett (a sheep farm before the Mallets acquired it), Wootton Bassett, Leighton Buzzard, Acton Turville, Kingston Lacy, Stoke Poges, and many more in which the second word is the surname of a Norman family who held the manor in the twelfth or thirteenth centuries. Several of these are derived from nicknames: Basset, for instance, signified a short man but became the name of a great family; Buzzard comes from a hawk-like bird of prey. The others are from places in Normandy. So began the long process whereby place-names were to gain mobility, from their association with men.

But when we speak of villages having surnames like people we must not think only of this type in which the additional word is literally a surname in the usual sense of the word. The additions to place-names besides giving ownership might tell where a place was, as on the hill or in the dale, or they might describe its nature, great or small, stony or fenny. Nor should there be any suggestion that they are mostly Norman in origin. Norman administrative methods did play a large part in creating the need for them and a goodly number are in Norman French, but even more are English, added by the native inhabitants to their own village names. They are so many and so various that we will think of them further in the next chapter. For the present we are concerned with additions to our place-names supplied by the Normans.

Although the Norman Conquest brought a vast number of new words into the English language, very few of them were absorbed early enough to be included in place-names. We talk now freely of villages, farms, rivers, valleys, capes and mountains, all words of French origin, and all to play an enormous part in the naming of English-speaking lands overseas. But in England they are hardly to be found as integral elements of place-names, only as separate words added, often redundantly, almost in modern times. When we speak of the River Avon, Sherwood Forest, Lake Windermere, Burgh Castle, Westminster Abbey and so on, the meaning of the additional word in each case was already expressed in the name.

Of all the words brought in by the Normans 'castle' is probably the one that took root earliest. It is sometimes combined with an English element in a single word, as at Newcastle, and several Castletons. But this word, which comes from the Latin *castellum*, was used by the Britons as *castel* and not unknown to the English before the Conquest. And in any case it was quickly impressed on their minds directly after that event when the Normans began to build castles all over the land using enforced English labour. So much so that the new word that was spoken everywhere completely ousted the native word *burh*, or borough, in the sense of a defensive work, leaving it to live on only in the restricted sense of a certain sort of town.

Another word of French origin that scored a victory over its English equivalent is 'market'. The English word for such a place was 'chipping' which means, literally, buying and selling. It has disappeared from the current language, but lives on in Chipping Camden, Chipping Norton, and others which correspond to the rather later Market Harborough.

Among the French words in our place-names there is one that can best be described as an oddity. This is the article *le*, incongruously preserved in some dozens of otherwise English names, such as Houghton-le-Spring, Hutton-le-Hole, Thornton-le-Moor, and Bolton-le-Sands. The descriptive phrases originally had been completely English – by the spring, in the hole, on the moor, and so on. When Norman landowners and their attendants spoke of these places in French they tended to leave the nouns as they were, but, being able to understand the small connecting words up to a point, they often put these into their own language, as we see them in Chapel-en-le-Frith (in the wood). However, the prepositions varied greatly and the next step for French speakers was the short cut of omitting them, leaving only *le* as a token of the whole connecting phrase. The writing of village-names fell mostly into the hands of lawyers who managed manorial affairs, and lawyers have always loved to preserve traditional forms of words. So it went on until at last even the local inhabitants began to think that the proper thing to call their own village was Hutton-le-Hole.

One respect in which Norman influence was far reaching was on spelling. Since for about two hundred years our business was transacted and our records kept largely by men whose first language was French it is no wonder that many English names came to be written in an un-English way. In the making of Domesday Book the Norman clerks seem on the whole to have done their best to write the English names as spoken by local witnesses, but they often did not hear correctly. It is from that time that the gap between the written symbols and the spoken sound began to exist. For a long time spelling remained fluid and often English pronunciation triumphed and clerks adjusted their spelling at later dates to something nearer to reality; in other cases Norman spelling influenced the sound, but frequently sound and spelling remained apart.

And it was not spelling only that developed erratically under Norman rule. There were several place-names that the Normans recorded tolerably well at first but which they found some difficulty in pronouncing as time went on. We have noted elsewhere that under their influence Sarisbury became Salisbury and Dunholm turned into Durham. This is the kind of unreasonable change made often by foreign speakers. In more modern times the British have mispronounced native names in many regions of the world.

But we must not overestimate the effect of Norman speech on English names. It happens that some of the places where the most marked change occurred are very well known, because the presence of Norman castles and cathedrals has made them important, but the vast mass of English names continued to develop normally, especially those of ordinary villages, and apart from the addition of feudal surnames to some of them the Norman ownership made little difference to their final forms.

The influence of the Normans was not confined to England but also affected the other parts of the British Isles to some extent. We have already noticed some of the 'Beau' names that they made wherever they chose to settle. One more may be added from Wales: Beaumaris, 'beautiful marshland'.

In Scotland they penetrated by peaceful means, until the unsuccessful attempt at conquest by Edward I, but before that a number of Norman families settled there and founded clans with French names, such as Sinclair, Grant and Fraser, and these in turn have given rise to place-names such as Grantown, and Fraserburgh, but they are late and few compared with the ancient native names that cover the land.

From the time they came into England the Normans tried to extend their rule into Wales, and, though it took them two hundred years to complete the conquest, they did secure some footholds at an early date. One of the Conqueror's cousins, Roger of Montgomery, so named for his Norman birthplace, waged constant war against the Welsh and built himself a castle to hold his gains which was also called by the same name. A little town grew around it and two centuries later, when Edward I organized Wales into counties, they were mostly named from their chief towns, Montgomery among them. No other Norman place-name has such prominence in Britain, and most of the Welsh castles built by Anglo-Norman dominance preserve their native names.

The Norman barons who led an army into Ireland in the twelfth century intended to conquer but stayed to settle, and Ireland has a thicker sprinkling of Norman names than the other Celtic lands. The most prominent of them is County Clare which takes its name from the leader of the expedition, Gilbert de Clare, nicknamed Strongbow. But the chief sign of Norman settlement all over Ireland is the word 'castle' incorporated into all sorts of names, often as Castletown, the easy partnership of the two words illustrating the bilingual nature of the invading army. The same name also occurs in Scotland and in the Isle of Man, all telling the same story of Anglo-Norman influence.

In the Celtic countries, as in England, the Norman contribution consisted more of the introduction of new words to the vocabulary than of complete new names, and the great mass of place-names stayed as they were or developed on native lines. As for the Normans themselves, who seemed so alien when they first seized the land, they neither withdrew as the Romans did from Britain or the British from India, nor remained in dominance as the white races have in America. They just merged into the rest of the population so gradually that it is hard to know at what point we should cease to call them Normans.

Chapter 11

THE MIDDLE AGES

Although the origins of the great majority of our place-names are to be found before the Conquest, it was during the two or three centuries after that event that most of them received their finishing touches. It is true that many had been created once and for ever by their first settlers and never received any further addition or change, except to their spelling. In this class belong the simplest names consisting of one element only, such as Hythe which meant a landing place, or Slough which meant a bog. The original inhabitants had built their dwellings beside these features, and the need had never arisen to say anything further about them. But it was more usual for at least one more item of information to be added to the first one, and this might happen when the name was still young or after it had stood unchanged for hundreds of years.

Saltash, near Plymouth, was only Ash as late as 1316. There must have been a noble tree standing there once. What exactly caused the addition of 'salt' is not recorded, but there were many saltworks about the country, especially near the coast, as at Budleigh Salterton for instance, 'the salt works near Buda's lea', and we may suppose that Ash was a place where salt was stored or distributed. Bridgenorth was only Bridge until the twelfth century, an important bridge across the Severn, but the building of others made a further description necessary. At Bridgewater, the qualification was nothing to do with water; it is the first name of a Norman owner, Walter de Douai. One more example of a late addition is Nuneaton. Until about 1200 it was only Eton or Eaton – a river *tūn* – but at that time it belonged to a nunnery, and when it was spoken of as Nun Eton the two merged easily.

So far we have been thinking of building names up, but at the same time the opposite process of whittling them down was going on too. The adding was always done with a clear meaning in mind, giving one more fact about the place. The reducing, on the other hand, was an unconscious process of dropping sounds that were troublesome to make, easing and reshaping the name until it ran smoothly on the tongue, without any thought of meaning. So place-names swelled and shrank again spontaneously absorbing more material in the process. Thus one of the many 'hythes' on the Thames became the 'lamb hythe', because it was used for shipping lambs across from Surrey, but the many tongues that spoke of it soon compressed it to Lambeth.

For one more example – out of thousands – of building up and cutting down, consider Sandringham. First came the encampment of an invading party led by one Deorsig, and so Dersingham; then a small offshoot from this village about a mile from it on sandy soil was known as Sand Dersingham, and soon contracted to one word. So now Dersingham and Sandringham have quite different names.

In many cases the shortening was not completed until after the spelling had become fixed. Examples of this are legion; some have been given on page 50. We end scores of town-names with -wick or -wich and say only -ick or -ich but it is useless to try and give a general ruling on this point as consistency is entirely lacking. Everyone knows that Norwich rhymes with 'porridge', but with Ipswich the second syllable is given its full value.

Names were not shortened overnight but by a gradual process and some of the older pronunciations hung in the air for centuries. One that is preserved in America is Lexington. Because the first shots of the War of Independence were fired there it became famous and was repeated in other states as a symbol of freedom. It is obviously English and typical of the earliest type of group settlement, but it will not be found on the map of England. In its native place, in Nottinghamshire, it has become Laxton, which must be a very late contraction seeing that the older form was current long enough to be carried to America. Where such changes occurred the two forms always overlapped for a time, and we must think of the colonists in America who named the first Lexington there preferring the old form that seemed to them more correct than the shorter version favoured by the younger generation of their native village.

This natural process of erosion that did so much to produce the pleasant-sounding names of Britain has been arrested and thwarted by modern education. A name like North Town, which in medieval England would soon have become Norton, must, if initiated in modern times, remain as it is. And even when a popular contraction has been well established the power of education has sometimes managed to reverse the trend. Cirencester, for instance, had become Cissiter in its own locality, but the traditional spelling and the wish of its inhabitants not to appear ignorant has now brought back the full pronunciation. (Even so, the tendency to shorten is still with us and they are now inclined to say Ciren.)

The instinctive moulding and modifying of names that went on in the Middle Ages may well rank as a kind of folk art. They had been formed originally in a practical spirit, but now an innate sense of euphony was at work, smoothing away any awkwardness, while creating something pleasing to ear and tongue. In this way the river-name Windrush took its final form. It is Celtic in origin, appearing before the Conquest as Wenrisc, the white moor or fen; it was popular English usage that gave the suggestion of wind in the rushes that is at once so musical and apt. Windermere was *Winandermer*, the mere of a Northman called Vinand, but again the idea of wind was irresistible, and the exact arrangement of resonant sounds makes a perfect name for this beautiful lake. Ambleside is recorded first as *Amelsate*; its elements are Norse again, *ā* (water) *melr* (sandbank) *saetr* (pasture), 'a pasture by a river sandbank', but it has come to sound like a stroll along the bank.

The business of slightly reshaping a name to suggest a new idea, regardless of the original meaning, is known as folk-etymology. It is responsible for many charming names, with touches of both poetry and humour. It is folk etymology that turned the 'maiden's hythe' on the Thames, a landing-place used by young ladies – perhaps in connection with a local nunnery – into Maidenhead, and the same sort of popular fancy changed Marybourn, the name of a stream that flowed by St Mary's church near London, into Marylebone, as if it were Mary the Good with a disregard of gender. Old English personal names that had been forgotten were particularly liable to be turned into something else that seemed more meaningful. Dearthington (the *tūn* of Dearnoth's people) became Darlington; the well or spring of a man named Badeca (*Badecanwelle*, 949) became Bakewell; Bada's hurst became Bathurst; and Saxpaenna in Dorset, which was probably a man's name, exists now as the first part of Sixpenny Handley.

It is this kind of thing more than anything else that makes it unsafe to assume that an obvious meaning is also the original one. But though folk-etymology may be an obstacle in the way of finding the truth it has resulted in many picturesque names that may have a kind of truth of their own. A good example comes from one of the remotest parts of Britain, the north-west corner, Cape Wrath. This began as an Old Norse *hvarf*, given by the Vikings. It meant quite simply the corner or turning place. In later years English speakers seeing the furious waves around that windswept headland turned it into Wrath, far more expressive of the spirit of the place than the Vikings' laconic 'corner'.

Among the popular errors that affected place-names during the Middle Ages a mention must be made of 'back-formation', a form of misunderstanding that has changed the names of several rivers. Chelmsford, for instance, began as a ford belonging to a man called Ceolmar (pronounced almost as Chelmer). But when this regular Anglo-Saxon name, and the man who bore it, were long forgotten the local inhabitants began to think that it was a ford across the Chelmer, and that is what the river is now called.

In a somewhat similar confusion the river on which Cambridge stands was turned from the Granta to the Cam. Granta was a Celtic name inherited by the English; the meaning is associated with swamps, and those low-lying willowy meadows must always have been marshy. Before the Conquest the place was called *Grantebricge*, but the Normans who built a castle there seemed to find the arrangement of sounds difficult and during the next few centuries we can follow the changes step by step as the first element became Crante-, Cante- (this is how Chaucer wrote it), Can- and finally Cam-. Then the river-name was altered to match the town. The change was freakish and not fully completed until the sixteenth century. Now the principal river is called the Cam and one of its tributaries the Granta. It may be that long ago it was the other way round. If one of the streams that meander through the meadows to join the Granta had always been called the Cam (and it is a regular Celtic river-name coming from a root that means winding) this would have helped to facilitate the change.

An early case of back-formation produced the name of the river Plym, which was in turn a begetter of many names. The story seems to have begun with a wild plum tree beside which some early settler made his *tūn*. This became Plympton (*Plymentun*, 904). The place was important in Saxon times as the site of a monastery, and (according to Ekwall) the river took its name from the village, which, once the original plum tree had gone, sounded like a *tūn* on the Plym, and gradually came to be so. The place where the river flowed into the sea was inevitably called 'Plym mouth' but the first village that grew up there was known as Sutton, the south town, as distinct from the more important Plympton a few miles to the north. As fishers and other shipmen came to use the splendid anchorage more and more, so several settlements grew up on the sheltered shores around it, and it was not until the fifteenth century that the name of the natural feature, the river mouth, came to comprehend them all as they merged together into one seaboard town. Plymouth was a better name than the undistinguished Sutton in being unique, and if it was a late starter it was nonetheless destined to go far. There are over twenty Plymouths in the world now, all of them sprung ultimately from that wild plum tree.

As we draw into the later Middle Ages – the time of Chaucer – when the language was taking a more stabilized form, the names of all our towns and villages were so well established that further additions were apt to remain as separate words and have done so ever since. Like personal surnames they remain distinct from the first name and are frequently dropped in familiar use. People who live in the neighbourhood of Wootton Bassett speak of it as Wootton, and use the second name only for official purposes or in speaking to someone less familiar with the place than themselves.

Local surnames are a natural growth that has never been brought to order. They may consist of one word or several and they may come before or after the original name. But this variation is not altogether fortuitous; it follows the natural word order of French and English which differ in this respect. The Frenchman normally places his adjective or other quali- fication after the noun, and in writing Latin does the same, but the English have always put their qualifying words first, except in the case of a whole phrase, such as 'on the hill' or 'in the marsh', which naturally follows the noun. This is why we have Much Hadham but Fontmell Magna, King's Langley but Bere Regis.

Surnames of feudal owners nearly always follow place- names because they were mostly Norman. English words referring to the owner come first and are usually general terms of status rather than proper names. Thus we have many places specified as belonging to the king, such as Kings Norton and Kings Lynn, and some to the queen, among them the quaint Queen Camel which has puzzled and amused many; Camel is a Celtic name (page 12) and the village was given by Edward I to his wife Eleanor. Then there are Earls Barton, Husbands Bosworth, Maids Moreton, to name but a few in this class. The earls in this case were of Huntingdon; the husbands were husbandmen or farmers who owned their own land; the maid may have been a young heiress to whom the land belonged for a time.

The word 'girl' was hardly known in England in its modern sense before the Tudor period, 'maid' or 'maiden' being the normal expression for a young unmarried female, whether rich or poor. We see it often in place-names from the earliest times, as at Maidstone, but in what way the maid or maidens were connected with a stone there is anyone's guess, and it may even be that the first element is some obscurer word changed by folk-etymology. In expressions like Maiden Castle it was probably meant to imply that the castle had never been captured, but when added to a village name, as at Maids Moreton, Maiden Newton or Maiden Bradley it is likely to have been a case of ownership.

Among the greatest of landowners was the Church with all its various religious houses, and we still see the titles of abbots, bishops, monks and other dignitaries scattered over every part of England. Because they were the principal users of Latin it was among their possessions that Latin words most often survived, but ecclesiastical titles are often expressed in English too, and examples may be freely gathered in both languages: Abbots Langley, Milton Abbas; Bishops Stortford, Kingsbury Episcopi; Monks Risborough, Zeal Monachorum; Canons Ashby and Whitchurch Canonicorum. It should be noted that Kingsbury had been a king's castle before it came into the hands of a bishop, and that Zeal, which preserves the West Country pronunciation of the *sealh* or sallow (a kind of willow) was known by the tree name only, before the monks came on the scene. A pleasing name in this class is Ashby Puerorum ('of the boys') of which the rents were devoted to the upkeep of the boy choristers of Lincoln Cathedral.

Driving through England and seeing these absurd remnants of monkish learning on the signposts one wonders how they could ever have become so firmly rooted in the countryside. But it may be observed that the most ponderous and unlikely of them belong to the smallest villages. In populous places a large majority of ordinary English inhabitants rejected pedantries and unreasonable excrescences, but in a tiny village a religious community could form a high proportion of the population and speak with an authority that commanded respect.

Again it should be understood that the Latinisms in question were generally translations of English words which were there first and continued in use even while the monks were writing them in Latin. When one looks through medieval manorial documents – and the originals still exist for hundreds of English villages – one sees that most of the names were written in a partially latinized form in all of them, but only in a small minority did this have a lasting effect on the name. For example, that delightful Dorset pair, Toller Fratrum and Toller

Porcorum, literally 'Toller of the brothers' and, 'Toller of the pigs', appear in medieval records sometimes written in Latin as above, and sometimes as Monks Toller and Swine Toller, which is what the natives were actually saying. (Toller incidentally is a Celtic river name.) But the natives were few and in the end the official version prevailed.

One might have thought that the dissolution of the monasteries would have put an end to this monkish Latin, but the tradition was carried on by the lawyers. In the manorial courts of small villages, which copyhold farmers attended right down to the nineteenth century, the steward presiding on behalf of the lord of the manor was a person of influence and if he chose to use the pedantic form of the village-name the humbler tenants would follow suit.

Surnames of villages belong roughly to three classes: ownership, locality and description. Of ownership enough has been said. Of locality little comment is needed; names like Stratford-on-Avon and Harrow-on-the-Hill explain themselves. Yet we are tempted to linger, because now we are in the realm of poetry, even though it was an unconscious art that made them what they are. Bourton-on-the-Water, Moreton-in-the-Marsh, Shipton-under-Wychwood and Stow-on-the-Wold – they fall on the ear like music. These four were all on the old Cheltenham and Banbury Line and the porters calling them out in rich West Country accents made them sound like a ballad. The well-educated young ladies who make announcements now over microphones do not have the same effect. The Cotswolds are particularly rich in these phrase-names. There are some splendid ones too in the North Country, and it is there that the Norman *le* (page 104) has most often lingered in place of the English prepositions.

Locality may also be expressed in a single word, often the name of a natural feature, a river or hill perhaps, by which the village is situated. Dorset is a great county for double village-names, mostly connected with rivers. When a string of villages grew up along the same stream they all were known by its name differentiated by further detail. There are nine Tarrants within as many miles along the valley of the gentle little Tarrant, whose name is identical with that of the great Trent (page 17). From a distance one speaks of the group as 'the Tarrants', but their own inhabitants speak of going over to Monkton, or Crawford or one of the other secondary names. Tarrant Monkton belonged to Tewkesbury Abbey, and at Tarrant Crawford the crows wheeled above the ford. Winterbournes are even more plentiful. A winterbourne is a stream that dries up in the summer, a common feature of the chalk downland. There are fourteen villages of this name in Dorset, and seven more nearby in Wiltshire. Their additional names make them very varied ranging from Winterbourne Gunner, which belonged to a Norman lady called Gunnora de la Mare, to Winterbourne Steepleton, which had a church steeple.

Secondary names of a descriptive sort may be simple adjectives such as Great, Little, Upper, Nether, or rather more expressive ones as we find in those two bad patches on a great Roman road, Fenny and Stony Stratford. Others mention some special feature of the place, as at Hatfield Broadoak, or Newton Poppleford which had a 'pebbly' ford. At Midsomer Norton a traditional fair was held at midsummer that gave the place local fame. At Saffron Walden wild saffron was gathered in the fields, a herb much valued for its colour and subtle flavour.

Many writers of fiction have invented English village-names but they cannot surpass the real ones either in comedy or charm. Everyone has his own favourites. For myself some of the funniest are Great and Little Snoring, Nether and Over Wallop, Steeple Bumpstead and its twin Helion Bumpstead, Sheepy Magna and Parva, Cricket St Thomas and Little Ann. None of these was quaint in origin. Snoring is a very early tribal name, 'Snorri's people'; Wallop means an enclosed valley (OE *hop*) with a stream or 'well' in it; in Bumpstead the first element may be a personal name or a word for reeds which is also found in Bunny; Cricket comes from the Celtic *cruc* meaning a hill; Ann is a Celtic river name.

For pure rustic charm I would put forward Church Honeyborne and Cow Honeyborne. They stand close together on a West Country stream where wild honey must have been found on the bank. One had a church and the other a cow. What could be better? But for an evocative sound my choice must lie among the many Willow names, especially those that make use of alliteration, Walsham-le-Willows, Willoughby-on-the-Wolds, and Willoughby Waterless. But the last has a melancholy note, for how could the willows live without water?

Poets in their lighter vein have made play with village names and none more successfully than John Betjeman.

> Rime Intrinseca, Fontmel Magna, Sturminster Newton, and
> Melbury Bubb,
> Whist upon whist upon whist upon whist drive, in Institute,
> Legion and Social Club

begins a Dorset poem in which all the place-names are genuine. The 'mel' in Fontmel and Melbury (the latter having belonged to a Saxon called Bubba) is the Celtic 'bare hill' that we have met as Moel in Wales. Rime, which sounds so odd, is only a form of the familiar 'rim', meaning an edge or bank, while the absurd Latin Intrinseca indicates that it was inside some boundary. There was once a Rime Extrinseca outside to contrast with it, but it was very small and it died young. It reminds one of Newton Without in Wiltshire, which must have provoked an incalculable number of people to ask, "Without what?"

These double names and phrase-names have never been popular as exports. Colonists wanting to give their new homes names from Britain have always preferred single names, avoiding anything comical, or too much bound up with the aristocracy or the church. And so it is that the long complex names remain one of the special charms of Britain, where the narrowest lanes, leading to the smallest villages, need the longest signposts to accommodate these echoes of medieval life.

By Shakespeare's day English place-names were very much as we know them now. To him they were already rich in historic association and he could make magic out of ordinary town-names, adding more glamour to them as he did so:

> Then shall our names
> Familiar on their lips like household words,
> Harry the king, Bedford and Exeter,
> Warwick and Talbot, Salisbury and Gloster,
> Be in their flowing cups richly remembered.

He had no nonsense about the spelling of Gloucester. It was later pedants who revived the archaic form.

E

By the end of his life some adventurous Englishmen were beginning to invent names for the new lands overseas, but there was no need to do so at home, for there were names everywhere. Of course, others have been added since, and we will return to them, but they are few and insignificant compared with those that were already old in Shakespeare's time.

Part Two

THE CELTIC WEST

Chapter 12

LANGUAGE AND LANDSCAPE

The recent investiture of the Prince of Wales, televised to many countries, brought to the attention of the world as never before the existence of a second living language in Britain. Even so it is little understood abroad that Welsh, the older native language, and unrelated to English, is still so much alive. In the middle of the fifth century the Brittonic language from which it is descended was spoken over the whole island except the extreme north, while English, newly arrived in the south-east, was just beginning its encroachment. Today the position is reversed; the Cornish branch of Brittonic is dead, and Welsh is fighting for its life. The census of 1961 gave the number of Welsh speakers in Wales as just under 700,000; there are others scattered about Britain, their numbers unrecorded, but the total throughout the country is probably under a million, at most two per cent of the population. Yet those who do speak it do so eloquently and mean to continue. The great tide of English that has flowed right round the world has not yet completely engulfed this island.

The strange thing is that these two languages have existed side by side for fifteen hundred years without the least tendency to amalgamate. Norman French was at last smoothly blended into English, different though they were. But no half-way house between English and Welsh was ever evolved. Welshmen have learned English as a second language; Englishmen have not learned Welsh. Many English words have been adopted into Welsh, and a few Welsh words into English (How many English people realize that 'Dad' is Welsh for 'Father'?) but no merger has taken place. They remain like oil and water.

A little farther afield that other Celtic language, Gaelic, the language of Ireland, the Scottish Highlands and the Isle of Man has survived less well. In 1961 only 70,000 Gaelic speakers were recorded in Scotland and their numbers are declining faster than those of Welsh. At the time of writing only one genuine speaker of Manx remains alive. In Ireland the native tongue was fading away fast at the end of the last century, but vigorous efforts at resuscitation have brought it back to a semblance of life, just how effectively remains to be seen.

Gaelic and Welsh, both purely Celtic, are somewhat distant cousins, having branched apart in separate migrations from the continent at an unknown prehistoric time. Although Gaelic is physically more remote from England than Welsh, its Scottish form is better known to the world at large, thanks largely to Sir Walter Scott whose immense literary success in the nineteenth century made his country romantic to English readers everywhere. Queen Victoria's love of the Highlands continued the process of making them fashionable, with the result that a number of Gaelic words for natural features have become widely known, although the language as a whole is a closed book to almost all. *Glen*, for instance, a narrow valley made by a stream, has had an enormous vogue, much more so than the Welsh equivalent *glyn*. *Strath*, a broad valley, is fairly well understood by people who would look blankly at the Welsh *ystrad*. *Cairn* has passed into English with the meaning of a pile of stones, but the Welsh *carn* is less familiar, except to climbers. Everyone knows what a Scottish *loch* is, while far fewer understand the Welsh *llyn*, an unrelated word, but the general one for a lake in Wales. And yet it was not Gaelic but Welsh in its early form that contributed so largely to English place-names. As far away from Wales as the Norfolk coast Kings Lynn preserves the same British word for the harbour pool that had named it long before an English king laid claim to it.

In Chapters 1–3 an attempt was made to review some of these Brittonic place-names that remain in England like fossils left in rocks by seas that have receded for ever. Now we take a brief look at the western lands where the Celtic peoples – British and Gaelic – have remained in occupation, and where such names have continued as part of living languages to a greater or lesser degree right into modern times. The subject must be approached with diffidence for the language barriers are formidable, but a little study reveals them as less fearsome than they first appear.

The most alarming thing about Welsh is its habit of mutating some of its initial consonants, according to the sounds that precede them. Thus a simple commodity like bread can be *bara*, *fara*, or *mara* in varying circumstances, and the place-name Bangor can, in Welsh conversation, turn into Fangor or Mangor. This is disconcerting, but as a compensation Welsh spelling is completely phonetic, a claim that no one would make for English. A language looks difficult in proportion to ones own ignorance of it; to the English a name like Whitchurch looks simplicity itself because its component parts are easily recognizable; but to a foreigner it may appear as a fearful conglomeration of consonants. To most people Welsh seems baffling on sight, but once you have grasped a few different spelling conventions (given on page 340) together with the commonest local words you can approach Welsh place-names with some confidence. One useful point to remember is that there is no 'v' in the Welsh alphabet. When Welsh places are spelt with this letter it is as a sop to the English. In Welsh the 'v' sound is represented with a single 'f', the double 'ff' being reserved for the normal 'f' sound. Thus the Welsh word for a river which the English know as Avon is written *afon* but the consonants are pronounced as in English.

Irish spelling on the other hand makes things more difficult. We English are open to criticism for the way we go on writing the symbols of sounds that we have not pronounced for centuries, such as 'gh' in innumerable words, but our spelling is child's play compared with that of the Irish. They are a people with a tremendous sense of the past. Their proper names, both personal and local, have come to them from very remote times, and though in the course of many centuries they have been softened and modified in speech to pleasant sounds like Sullivan or Kevin, modern Irish scholars insist on writing these very names as Suileabhain and Caomhghin. This does not make things easy for themselves or anyone else. The trouble arises from the fact that the native tongue, in the last century, was divided into many dialects and spoken only by the illiterate, and when the great revival took place the enthusiasts brought back the classical spelling of the early Middle Ages. In recent years there has been a serious attempt to modify this, but it has not gone far enough, and the visitor may often be baffled by place-names that he sees in writing, although he would know them if he heard them spoken.

In dealing with Celtic names one must always keep in mind the close connection between 'm', and 'b' and 'v', especially the last two. The Celts had a soft sound that was half-way between them. The Romans generally wrote this as 'b' (as in Sabrina) but when it survived it generally did so as 'v' (Severn), but often it grew so soft that it ceased to be sounded at all. In Gaelic it is written 'bh' or 'mh' and has the sound of a soft 'v' or nothing. We can see it in the Gaelic *dubh* which means 'black', a useful word to know, since it occurs in so many names. We have met it before as the first element of Douglas, the black stream, which has named places in Scotland and the Isle of Man, and it also forms the first syllable of Dublin, the black pool; but here the pronunciation has been influenced by the generations of Norsemen and English who made this harbour their headquarters. A Gaelic speaker says it as Du'lin or Duvling.

This same word makes part of many personal names both in Ireland and Scotland, such as Macduff and O'Duffey, that have come from the nickname, 'the Black'. Its Welsh and Cornish equivalent is *du* or *dhu*, and Poldhu on the Cornish coast is identical in meaning with Dublin, and also – to jump languages completely – with the English Blackpool.

One characteristic that is common to all the Celtic languages and makes their place-names so different in style from English ones is their habit of placing the noun that forms the principal feature first and qualifications after, as in French. Bryn Mawr, for instance, is literally 'hill big'. It was not always so, and it is a strange fact that in the earliest recorded Celtic names, such as those given by Roman writers, it is always the other way round, as in English, but from about the sixth century we find that this inversion has taken place and is henceforth universal. This is helpful in dating names and shows that those like Douglas and Dublin that begin with the adjective have the greatest antiquity.

Very often the second element is a noun in the genitive case which an English speaker would place first. We say St David's Head; the Welsh, Pen Dewi. They say Penmaenmawr, literally 'head of the stone great'; we would put it all in reverse. They always start with Aber- or Inver-, both meaning a river mouth or confluence of waters, but we put it last as in Dartmouth, which is identical with Aberdare, 'mouth of the oak-tree river'. This Celtic word-order has persisted strongly and even influenced the English spoken in the regions where the two races have mingled. It explains such forms as Kirkoswald (Oswald's church) and Kirkcudbright (Cuthbert's church) and Bridge of Allan, which would have been Allanbridge further south. And in England wherever one finds such an arrangement as Castle Cary (i.e. belonging to the Cary family) one can be sure that it has arisen under Celtic or Norman influence, for the English left to themselves would say Cary Castle.

In every country the most basic element that is bound to occur in endless village names is the one that stands for a farm or homestead. In Wales and Cornwall this is *tref*, generally shortened to *tre*. Everyone knows the Cornish Tre-s because so many families have taken their surnames from their places of abode in Cornwall that Tremaynes, Tresillians, Trevelyans and so on have gone all round the world. Welsh surnames, on the other hand, are nearly all patronymics and the many Welsh villages beginning with Tre are known only on their local merits. An exception is Trevor, which is now used as a boy's name having been a surname first. There are several places of this name in Wales, and its meaning is simply 'big farm'.

In Gaelic the same meaning of a homestead or, later, village, is expressed by *baile*, which has been distorted in Ireland to the ubiquitous Bally. In Scotland it has become Bal- or Balla-. Ballantrae is a village on the sands; Ballachulish is on the narrows. On the Isle of Man it is said that there are over two hundred farms and hamlets beginning with Balla, but no one could ever count all the Ballys of Ireland; some are towns but many are only farms and the total must run into thousands. The best known Scottish Bal- is probably Balmoral, which is said to mean 'the house of the laird' but its etymology does not go back very far. The Irish *baile* that has the largest namesake overseas is Baltimore in County Cork, in Gaelic *baile an tigh mor*, the village near the big house.

E*

In the north-eastern part of Scotland the first element of many names is Pit-, a Pictish word for a farm or piece of land. It occurs only in the districts where other evidence shows this mysterious race to have been most thickly concentrated, but as almost nothing is known of their language – such Pictish inscriptions as remain have never been deciphered – little more can be said of it. It is often combined with a Gaelic word as at Pitlochry, 'village among stones', and Pittenweem, 'near caves'.

These Celtic words, tre(f) and baile and the Pictish pit are the equivalent of the English ham, worth and tūn, but their position as the first feature of the name makes them seem much more prominent. The commonest Welsh element and one that is often taken to mean a village is llan, but as its significance is largely religious we will reserve it for another chapter.

Less numerous than these settlement words but more dominating in the Celtic scene are the principal words for fortified places. From the earliest recorded times the Old Celtic dunon was in use all across Europe, and its principal places of survival are Ireland and Scotland, in the many Gaelic names beginning with Dun. In Wales it generally became Din- or Tin-, and makes the first elements of Denbigh and Tenby, each of which was din bych, the 'little fort', before English spelling made them seem so different. In Cornwall the same development took place, and the first syllable of Tintagel, that natural stronghold by the sea, shows that it was indeed primarily a place of defence, although the earliest of its ruins, dating from the fifth century, have been identified as religious in purpose.

This Welsh and Cornish word developed a secondary form, dinas, which is still in use in Welsh with the meaning of 'town', but has also been applied from ancient times to hill-forts, such as Dinas Bran above Llangollen. This is sometimes translated as Crow Castle, for bran is Welsh for a crow or raven, but it may well have taken its name from the legendary hero, Bran the Blessed, whose decapitated head was considered potent for warding off Saxon attack.

About the time of the Roman withdrawal another word for a fortress came into use among the British. This was cair, now written Caer- or sometimes Car- under English influence. It is probably related to the Latin *castra*, though not directly descended from it; but whatever its ancestry it has long held a distinguished place in its own right, especially in Wales. We tend now to associate it with the great castles built there by the Normans, but the names had nearly all belonged to earlier strongholds on the same sites.

Caernarvon means the castle in Arfon, that is the land 'opposite Mon', the Welsh name for Anglesey with the 'm' mutated to 'f'. Cardiff is the castle on the River Taff; Caerphilly, the castle of Ffili, of whom nothing is known. Carmarthen has the distinction of containing both *caer* and *dun*, the latter in the final position of early times. The Romans recorded it as Moridun(um), the fortress by the sea (*mor* is still 'sea' in Welsh). The next time we meet it – in the writings of the eighth-century monk, Nennius – it is Cair Mardin, literally Fort Seafort. When we speak now of Carmarthen Castle we express the same concept for the third time. In the Middle Ages the Welsh began to think it was 'Merlin's Castle' for his name in their spelling is Myrddin, but this piece of folk etymology has not obscured the true history of this ancient name.

The majority of Celtic place-names are descriptions of the natural scene in which a few simple words often recur, so that even a slight knowledge of vocabulary can give an understanding of many names. *Pen*, literally a head but often used in the sense of an end, is very common in the Brittonic regions – Wales, Cornwall and the north-west counties – but is not found in Gaelic where the equivalent word has taken the form of Kin-. Thus Kinloch in Scotland means the end of the loch, and Kintyre – like the Cornish Pentire – the end of the land. The south-west promontory of Wales preserves a different word for land, *bro*, which was earlier *brog*. When the Normans planted a colony here in about the year 1100 they heard the inhabitants call it something that sounded like *Pen broc*, which they rendered as Pembroke, and as such it is known to the world, though in Welsh it is Penfro (the 'b' mutating to 'f'). Pembroke, Pentyre and Kintyre are all synonyms of Land's End.*

* The Brittonic Pen- and Gaelic Kin- are actually cognate, and the regular relation between their initial sounds has caused the two languages to be classified as P-Celtic and Q-Celtic.

An element that is common to all the Celtic countries is *ros* or *rhos*, its meaning varying slightly from place to place. In general it signifies a high, upsurging, rocky moorland, where nothing but heather will grow, and as the Celtic countries are full of such places, many of them jutting out into the sea, it is often used for headlands. In Scotland it has named the whole county of Ross and makes part of scores of village-names. In some places where English or Norman influence has been strong it has changed to the milder sounding 'rose', as in that charming Cornish village St Just in Roseland or the setting of the Scottish abbey of Melrose. In the latter case the first syllable is contracted from the word that we see in Wales naming many bare hills as Moel, literally 'the bald one'. Melrose was originally the bald-headed moor, but the Christian buildings in the valley below added a gentler beauty to the landscape in which the concept of a rose does not seem out of place.

As the Celtic lands abound in rocks and hills they have many words for such things. The Welsh *carreg*, a rock, occurs in many places, as at Carreg y Druidion, the Druid's stone, while in Ireland the same word in the form of Carrick or Carrig has made the first or only element of over a hundred towns and villages.*

As for mountains, the Celtic languages offer a rich choice of words. The Gaelic *ben* meant originally a horn, and as the Scottish Highlands have the sharpest peaks, so they are the true home of the Bens; but Ireland has them too, sometimes surviving in the form of Ban-. Bantry means the peaks by the sea shore.† In Wales the same word may go unrecognized because of the mutation, which the English can never get used to. It is present in the name of the beautifully pointed Tryfan, which is recorded in a Welsh poem, written about the year 600, and which means three peaks. But in Wales *mynydd*, *moel* and *carn* are more commonly used, and many peaks have individual names such as Plinlimmon, 'five lights', which must refer to some special occasion when five fires burnt there. The commonest Gaelic word for a round hill is *cnoc* which has helped to make many picturesque names such as that of the

---

* As listed in Bartholomew's *Gazetteer of the British Isles*.

† *Bannoc* in the Gaelic lands means 'rocky' as in Bannockburn, the rocky burn, hence also a kind of 'rock' cake.

Knockmealdown Mountains in Ireland in which the latter part is a personal name, Maelduin, from legendary times.

We might linger indefinitely among Celtic mountains – and what could be pleasanter – but there are other words for natural features to which we must give a rapid glance. There is the Welsh *dol* (generally *dal* in Scotland) which means a water-meadow. Dolgelly, or more properly Dolgellau, means the meadow by the cells, perhaps referring to monastic dwellings; Dalkeith the meadow by the wood. Another useful word to know, since so many Celtic towns are near the sea, is *heli*, meaning salt water. Pwllheli is the pool of salt water, and Hayle in Cornwall consists of just this word. This also was the earlier name of the Helford river, to which the Vikings added their 'fiord', the little town that grew there taking its name from the Celto-Norse hybrid.

In Welsh the definite article 'y' or 'yr' is often preserved in the name although the preposition that might go with it is omitted. Pontypool is the bridge (by) the pool; Betws-y-coed, the 'bead-house', or shrine for prayer (in) the wood. *Pont* is an old borrowing from Latin, and there are many of these in Welsh, which is only natural seeing that the forbears of this race once lived under Roman rule. Their word for a church, *eglwys*, comes from the Latin *ecclesia*, learnt when Christianity came to Roman Britain. We see it in place-names, not only in Wales – Eglwys Fach, little church – but also in Scotland where Ecclefechan has just the same origin. In Cornwall it occurs in Egloshayle, the church by the salt water, and in Lancashire as Eccles.

These simple statements of visible features with which the Celtic world is very largely named, and of which many examples have already been given, range from single words to whole phrases of three or four that make pictures of the landscape. In the first category we may mention Perth which meant a copse or thicket, Bray, a hillside, the same in origin as the Highland 'brae', and Derry,* an oak-wood. The commonest arrangement is of two elements; Glasgow, green hollow; Belfast, crossing-

---

* Of the many Derrys in Ireland the best known became Londonderry as a result of its being granted to the Corporation of London after the confiscation of the O'Neil estates in 1609. It was 'planted' as a colony by twelve City Corporations; but its old, simple name has remained in colloquial use.

place by a sandbank; Drogheda, bridge by a ford; Harlech, fine slab of stone; Barry, hill stream. Longer descriptions include Linlithgow, lake in a damp hollow; Glendalough, valley with two lakes; Pontypridd, bridge by a house made of earth; and Penrhyndeudraeth, the end of the cape with two beaches. Lists of the commonest topographical words in Welsh and Gaelic to be found on pages 338–341 will help to clarify some of these and other meanings, but many names are too old and have been too much corrupted by time and ignorance to be explained on sight.

In this chapter I have tried to take a wide view of the speech habits of the Celtic peoples in regard to the naming of their lands, noting particularly how much they have in common. Among their names natural description predominates to an even greater degree than it does in England, where, although physical features play a large part, they are constantly intermingled with the names of the persons in possession at the time that the names were coined. But in the Celtic countries where conditions of society were more tribal, more nomadic and pastoral, the land was named chiefly by its rivers, rocks, moors, woods and lakes, and compared with these permanent features human ownership counted for little.

The only personal names that occur in large numbers in these regions are of those who were reverenced locally as saints, and to these we will come presently. There are also some names of legendary kings and heroes – for the Celts have always loved to cherish their history. We will look at these in the next two chapters.

Chapter 13

INHERITANCE OF THE BRITONS

In the last chapter we glanced at some of the Celtic place-names that picture the natural scene in very similar style down the whole length of the west of Britain and in Ireland. Others, more closely allied with human activity, demand some understanding of the historic background, and for this we go back to the Dark Ages to see what became of the Britons when the Angles and Saxons had occupied more than half their island. We left them retreating westwards, still speaking their ancient Celtic language, though with a smattering of Latin words, still Christian, but deprived of the civilized amenities which they had enjoyed under Roman rule.

Fortunately these so-called Dark Ages are not so dark as they used to be. In recent years work done by linguistic scholars, archaeologists and others has thrown considerable light on the period and much that was once dismissed as myth and fiction is now taking its place in the area of established fact.

Our first glimpse of the Britons from their own point of view after Rome had abandoned them is given by the Welsh monk Gildas, writing early in the sixth century. He is a very incoherent writer, but at least he knows at first hand what he is writing about even if he fails to make it clear to us. From him and other scraps of evidence we see that the Britons, left to fend for themselves in a time of disaster, have fallen apart into a number of separate kingdoms, ruled by Christian kings, but kings of whom the indignant Gildas has a low opinion. Of native kingdoms in the eastern half of Britain we hear little for they were speedily overcome by the English, but in the west several kingdoms can be clearly identified stretching from

Cornwall to the Clyde, and corresponding closely to the local British tribes mentioned earlier by Latin authors.

In the south-west the kingdom of Dumnonia extended over all that is now Devon and Cornwall. Its king, Constantine, is mentioned by Gildas as 'the tyrannical whelp of an unclean Lioness', but Gildas was an outspoken man and perhaps this British king, whose family was to produce both saints and heroes, was not so very bad. His name lives on in the village of Constantine overlooking the Helford river. Or it may be one of his descendants who is commemorated there, for there were other Constantines among them and identities are hard to establish at this date. But in any case this classical name which seems so unlikely in this remote corner of the once-Roman world is a link with those British tribal rulers who still felt themselves inheritors of Roman culture.

A little later a king named Geraint was ruling in Dumnonia, an heroic if misty figure, referred to in early Welsh poetry and genealogy as the companion and cousin of Arthur. And there seems no reason to doubt that Arthur was a prince, though not a king, of this royal house, who won lasting glory against the English. His battles were not fought in Cornwall for the invaders did not penetrate so far in his life-time, but wherever leadership was most needed, which was throughout the west-centre of Britain as far as the Firth of Forth. He alone seems to have been able to unite the quarrelsome British kings against their common enemy, so that battles were won and the tide turned back for a generation. After his death it flowed again engulfing the scenes of his victories, and those of his people who survived to cherish his memory wrapped it in such a cloak of poetic fancy that the very truth of his existence has been obscured by it; but the tendency of modern scholarship is to re-establish him as an important historical character.

Among the mass of indirect evidence for Arthur's life are the widespread occurrences of his name in sites of natural grandeur, such as Arthur's Seat near Edinburgh, which Giraldus Cambrensis recorded in the twelfth century as 'Cathedra Arturi'. (The Greek word *cathedra* which meant a throne came into English first for a bishop's throne and was later used for the whole 'cathedral' that contained it. In Welsh it was simply a chair, and as *cader* is still so used.) Such names are found all over western Britain, formed at various dates, and though they do not prove that the real Arthur was ever in those places, they do show that a folk memory of him lingered there.

It was not until the eighth century that the Saxons spread over the part of Dumnonia that we now call Devon and as this county is no richer in Celtic place-names than Dorset or Somerset it must be supposed that a large proportion of its native inhabitants crowded westwards into Cornwall or fled over to Brittany, which took its name from these British refugees. Gildas describes their going, 'their lamentations sounding like singing under the bellying sails'. The last recorded king of Cornwall was another Geraint who was defeated in a battle against the Saxons in 710, according to the *Anglo-Saxon Chronicle*, and whose name survives on the headland called the Gerrans. The final inclusion of Cornwall in the English kingdom was a gradual process of which there is little record, but it has never lost its separate character, and even today its people can speak of 'going to England' as to another land.

The vast majority of place-names in Cornwall belong to its own language, which gives them a foreign appearance to the majority of Englishmen, who can make no guess at the meanings of such names as Mevagissy, Perranzabuloe, Gweek, Looe and Truro. The first two of these contain saints' names (page 151); Gweek is the same word as the English 'wick', both being descended from the Latin *vicus*, a village; Looe is the Cornish form of the Gaelic 'loch'; and Truro is thought to have been *tri erow*, meaning three measures of land, but the size of the Cornish *erow* is not known.

In many cases the Cornish name has received an English addition, as at Helston where the final 'ton' gives an English appearance. The original name was Henlis which meant 'old court', and it must be truly old as the adjective *hen*, which still means 'old' in Welsh, precedes the noun as it did only in the earliest recorded Celtic names. The word *lis* is inadequately translated as 'court' and has no real modern equivalent. It implied the dwelling of a king or chieftain, but such a place in primitive times involved only ephemeral buildings of timber and thatch and was more like an encampment than a palace. Another *lis* not far from Helston was the *lis airt* or high court, probably established somewhat later. This has become, by folk-etymology, the Lizard, and as the rugged promontory with rocky headlands jutting out this way and that is somewhat like a lizard in shape the name has a certain aptness. This same word *lis* is found in all the Celtic lands, and frequently, for tribal chieftains moved about and had many such dwellings. For example, Lismore in Ireland is the great court, and Listowel in Wales the court of Howel, one of the native princes.

The largest territory that the Britons managed to hold was what we now call Wales. In the sixth century this consisted of several kingdoms of which Gwynneth in the north was ruled by a dominant dynasty of princes who would eventually unite the whole country under its sway. Its founder, Cunedda, had established himself in Anglesey (or Mon to use its native name) in the last years of the Roman occupation, perhaps under Roman authority, and his many sons, according to Welsh annals, included Ceredig, whose territory, *Ceredigion*, is now Cardigan, and Merion who had Merioneth for his portion. In mid-Wales both Brecon and the county of Brecknock owe their names to Brychan, another dynastic figure, said to be the father of so many sons and daughters all of such saintly character that one cannot but feel some element of doubt about so many virtues. However, Brychan was a real ruler of the fifth century and no doubt did have a notable family. Further south the realm of Gwent (page 24) was ruled by several successive princes of the name of Morgan, and their land became *Glanna Morgan* or Morgan's shore, now Glamorgan.*

But these princely names from the Dark Ages are not the earliest known Welsh place-names, for the Romans had colonized this part of Britain and classical writers have recorded about twenty of its names, at least half of which are still in use in recognizable forms. Most of the Roman stations took their names from the rivers on which they were sited: Conovium from the river we call the Conway (Welsh Conwy, 'glorious river'), Nidum from the Neath (Welsh Nedd, 'shining'), and the modern towns in these places still bear the river-names. Segontium, which became Caernarvon, stood on the river now

---

* Two other famous kingdoms of this period were Powis and Dyfed, whose ancient names are reappearing in current use in the present regrouping of the counties.

known as the Seiont. At the confluence of the little Gafenni with the Usk the Romans built a fort that they called Gobannium; now it is Abergavenny. They also knew the Ystwith, which means 'winding', at whose mouth stands Aberystwyth. Caerleon, Caerwent, and the Usk, which they called Isca, all rich in Roman associations, have been mentioned earlier.

The island of Mon was well known to them as a great stronghold of the Druids, captured after a fierce battle. Its name seems to be closely related to that of the Isle of Man, which is derived from the Celtic sea-god Manannan. Ptolemy wrote them Mona and Monavia. The English name Anglesey means the island of the Angles, an unreasonable claim that can only have been made by the Angles themselves. Soon after the year 600, when they were extending their kingdom of Northumbria westwards, they won a great victory over the Britons at Chester, and a year or two later Edwin of Northumbria, according to Bede, 'ravaged the Menevian Isles', which are taken to be Mon and Man. It is this raid and this only that caused the Angles to speak of Mon as theirs; but they retained no hold on it. The Welsh king, Cadwallon of Gwynneth, fought back vigorously and, with aid from Penda of Mercia, defeated and killed Edwin in 633, after which the Northumbrians turned their energies northwards, and never penetrated Wales again. Anglesey is a pleasant sounding name with happy associations for many of golden sands and gentle hills, but considered as a statement it is an empty boast.

In the ninth century Wales was united as one nation under the rule of Rhodri Mawr (Roderic the Great) of Gwynneth, and for the next three hundred years maintained its independence until in 1283 it fell before the power of Edward I. Since then, in spite of seven centuries of political unity with England, it has kept its language alive to a remarkable degree, and although this is now threatened by modern pressures the thousands of purely Welsh place-names, coined and used by speakers of the same language in unbroken continuity from the earliest recorded times, are in no danger. In comparison with them, the place-names of England have suffered far greater upheavals.

Along the border and on the coasts a moderate number of English and Viking names have encroached, but in some

135

counties one can hardly find a name that is not Welsh. In Caernarvonshire, for example, almost the only one is Snowdon, so called by English travellers from the eleventh century onwards; but, of course, the Welsh have their own name for it, Yr Wyddfa (pronounced Wythva), the view-place or look-out. Wherever one finds an English name in Wales one may be sure that the native one exists beside it. One of the very few English names in Merioneth is Barmouth, in Welsh Abermawdd. This refers to the mouth of the Mawddach river, but the English turned the river-name into 'mouth' and reduced Aber to Bar, perhaps because there is a sandy bar across the estuary, an example of total confusion. Many Welsh names are normally spelt in English style, but the correct local forms exist and are still used by Welsh speakers. On the whole the place-names of this small country are more homogeneous and better preserved than those of any other part of the British Isles.

North of Wales other British kingdoms of the Dark Ages survived less well. West of the Pennines a king named Urien was ruling in the middle of the sixth century. His people were one with the Welsh, though cut off from them by land after the Northumbrians had reached the mouth of the Dee, and it was in this time of increasing disaster that they began to call themselves the Cymri or brotherhood. But the Angles overwhelmed this northern kingdom of the Cumbri (as they pronounced their name); all that remains of it, besides the name of Cumberland, are a number of British place-names, such as Penrith, 'hill ford', and Carlisle (page 7), with those of later comers.

Further north still, in what is now Scotland, another dynasty of British kings ruled on the banks of the Clyde. This great river, whose name is given by Ptolemy as Clota – in Brittonic Cluth – was their frontier against the Picts. They called their chief stronghold, on a rocky headland, Alcluth, 'rock of Clyde', but others spoke of it later as *Dun Breattann*, 'fort of the Britons', and this has come down to us as Dumbarton. This kingdom, which was known as Strathclyde, lasted longer than its Cumbrian neighbour, but it too was overcome at last by attacks from all sides, and absorbed into the rising realm of Scotland.

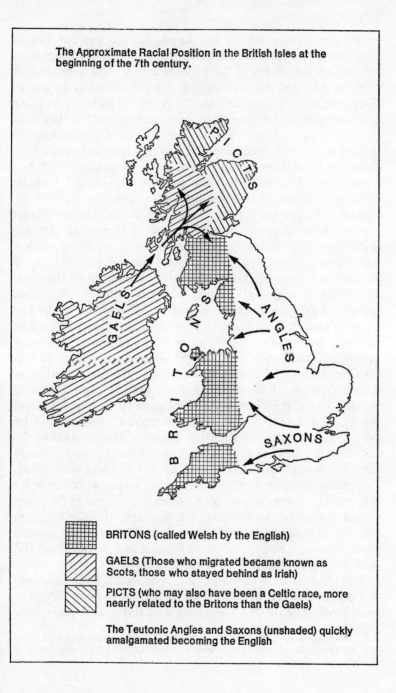

The Approximate Racial Position in the British Isles at the beginning of the 7th century.

PICTS

GAELS

BRITONS

ANGLES

SAXONS

BRITONS (called Welsh by the English)

GAELS (Those who migrated became known as Scots, those who stayed behind as Irish)

PICTS (who may also have been a Celtic race, more nearly related to the Britons than the Gaels)

The Teutonic Angles and Saxons (unshaded) quickly amalgamated becoming the English

On the eastern side of the Lowlands yet another British kingdom stood as firmly as it could in the threatening sixth century on the shores of the Firth of Forth. And here we will linger a moment, for although as a separate entity it was to disappear entirely, yet through the poetry of its bards its spirit was to win an immortality little known in England but cherished in Wales. Its principal fortress was Eidyn, a simple enough name that meant a steep slope, in this case crowned with a fort, known in those days as Din Eidyn, but to us as Edinburgh.*

It has often been said in the past that Edinburgh took its name from Edwin of Northumbria, who expanded his territory northwards after his raid on Mon. But Celtic scholars of this century have disposed of this theory as a case of popular etymology. Before Northumbrian power reached so far north – and there is no evidence that Edwin himself ever did so – a British bard writing in his own language immortalized the royal household of Eidyn. His poem, which is called by the tribal name *Gododdin*, has been dated on internal evidence to the last years of the sixth century. It gives what may be our earliest intimate picture of social life in the island of Britain. We see a group of young warriors picked from the noblest British families from all the western kingdoms, feasting together at Eidyn. We see them drinking from golden cups, adorning themselves and their horses with bronze and gold trappings, and finally after a year of preparation, inspired by mead and by poetry, riding south together in a desperate venture against the English. It was useless. The battle – fought probably at Catterick – continued until all of this heroic band were killed, excepting only their bard, Aneirin, who escaped to compose his lament. The name Eidyn which occurs many times in the poem is now definitely identified with Edinburgh. But the kingdom which had stood as an outpost against the Picts since Roman times was swept away, and its songs, such as survived at all, did so in Wales, the last retreat of the Cymri.

The Angles, who had annihilated this rash force of young aristocrats in about the year 600, pressed on to more successes, conquered most of the Lowlands and did a few years later

---

* This kingdom was called Manau Gododdin. The first word, which is identical with the British name for the Isle of Man, survives in Clackmannan, the 'Stone of Manau'.

reach and occupy Eidyn which they called their *burh*. Before the century had passed they were beaten back again by a combined force of Picts and Scots, but they must have left behind them many Anglian settlers whose cultural and linguistic influence has remained ever since. From that brief period of Northumbrian domination which reached its peak in the seventh century English has been the language of the Lowlands, and many of its place-names such as Haddington and Hamilton (page 58) are of typical English character. But the Brittonic tongue that had been there earlier has left behind it many landmarks in the form of names whose common elements, such as Aber-, Car-, Pen-, and Lan-, show their close relationship to Welsh. In Scotland they remain as fossils in an English-speaking land, but in Wales they are still part of a living language.

The Lowland union of Celt and Angle is typified in the name Edinburgh, Celtic 'hillside' and English 'fort'. To Gaelic speakers of the Highlands it was for centuries 'Dun Edin', and as such has sprung to new life in the Antipodes, where in the south of New Zealand one may hear it spoken in Scottish voices on the shores of the South Pacific.

As we have seen, the Lowlands right up to the Clyde and Forth were once occupied by the same Brittonic race that later survived chiefly in Wales. Beyond that natural barrier the first inhabitants that we know of are the Picts, a mystery race about whose origins and language almost nothing is known. Eventually they were overrun and absorbed by the wave of migrants from Ireland who became generally known as the Scots, and whose language and culture spread over the Highlands just as that of the Angles did further south.

Of all the Celtic lands Scotland has the most complicated history and this is truly reflected in its place-names, which are the hardest to elucidate, for here five separate races, speaking five languages, met and mingled. First the Picts, who lie like an under-carpet beneath all the rest, and whose unknown language must be responsible for a large proportion of the place-names that cannot be explained. Next the Britons pushing up from the south even as far north as Aberdeen, an unmistakably Brittonic name that might easily belong to Wales. Then the Gaels (or Scots) from Ireland, sweeping across through the western isles to invade the mountainous mainland and absorb the northern Picts so that they seemed to disappear; and at the same time the Angles from Northumbria swallowing up the Lowland Britons in much the same way. And, as if this were not enough, there came in the ninth century the fleets of the Vikings, adding their names around the coasts as a sort of crust. A slight sprinkling of Norman names in the Lowlands was to complete the mixture.

Of all these elements it was Gaelic that was to provide the largest number of permanent place-names, and to understand something of the Gaelic race we must turn to Ireland.

Chapter 14

THE GAELIC LANDS

Compared with Scotland the early history of Ireland is simple indeed. If we were to plunge into details of tribal feuds and the rivalries of minor kings we should find complications in plenty, but taking only a broad view from a distance we see a country unique in Europe for its unity of culture, having stayed aloof and undisturbed for the best part of a thousand years. The Romans never attempted to conquer it, though Agricola looking across the sea thought he might do so with a single legion. The Angles and Saxons did not even complete the conquest of Britain. It was not until the ninth century, when the Norsemen fell upon them, that the Irish found their way of life disrupted from without, and then the effect was devastating. Three centuries later came the Normans by way of England, and from then on English domination and influence varied only in degree.

Although the Romans never invaded Ireland, navigators from the classical world must have sailed round it and made some contacts, for Ptolemy records some Irish names, chiefly of rivers, and as we should expect from a Celtic country they are linked with pagan deities. The Boyne, given by Ptolemy as Buinda, is associated with a goddess called Boinn, literally 'cow-white', a name well suited to a pastoral people whose wealth was chiefly in cattle. The Shannon, Sionainn in Gaelic, means 'the old one', a splendidly suggestive name for this lovely river.*

* Another name recorded by Ptolemy was Oboka, now written Avoca, the 'place of waters'. This valley is the meeting-place of the Avonmore and Avonbeg, the great and little rivers.

Many Irish place-names like these two are of an antiquity that is undatable. Early Irish literature, like that of the ancient Greeks, begins with mythology, passes imperceptibly into legend based on truth, and so on to factual history. The stories of Conchobar, of Cuchulain, of Deirdre of the Sorrows, of Con of the Hundred Battles and many more, all dove-tailing with complete genealogies and wedded to the physical features of the land, such tales are based on memories passed down through generations, but enriched by Irish imagination. The trouble is that nothing was written down before the fifth century, and the earliest surviving manuscripts are copies made at least four or five centuries after that. The dating of these transcriptions and their contents is a matter on which the scholars are not in agreement; therefore, with the oldest names we cannot say when they were first recorded, only that they occur in legends that seem to take us back even to the first century.

To this legendary pre-Christian period belong the names of the five old provinces, once rival kingdoms. The root-words of Ulster, Munster, Leinster and Connaught are all the names of tribes who feature in the oldest of the legends as the *Ulaid*, the *Mumu*, the *Laigin* and the *Connachta*. Meath, a little later than the others, meant the middle kingdom. Other tribes whose names survive from the same remote period include the people of Con mac ne Mara (Connemara) and the Eoghain, whose land, *Tir Eoghain*, is now Tyrone.

The datable history of Ireland begins with the coming of Christianity, for that brought writing as its accompaniment. In about the year 433 St Patrick preached before the High King at Tara, and soon afterwards founded a bishopric at Armagh. His activities give the first evidence for these two names, but they were there before he knew them. Tara, in Old Irish *Teamhair*, signified a hill or view-point; Armagh was *ard magh*, the 'high plain', its word-order showing the old style of speech. *Magh*, generally translated 'plain', implied only a flat, open space, not necessarily large; it occurs in many Celtic names, such as Mayo (*magh eo*), a level clearing among yew trees.

Most of the details of Patrick's ministry come from lives of him written one or two centuries after his death. One story tells how he preached at Cashel and inadvertently drove the spike of his pastoral staff – clearly a practical implement – through the foot of King Angus of Munster who stood beside him; and the king, thinking it part of an initiation ceremony, bore it silently until Patrick noticed the mishap at the end of his sermon. Cashel is one of the very few names of Latin origin that had reached Ireland at this early date. It comes from *castellum*, 'little fort', which the Britons had learnt from the Romans and used in Wales in the form of *castel*. In the late Roman period the Welsh coast was fortified against raids from Ireland, but they continued and this word, picked up by the raiders, was carried home with more tangible booty. In Ireland it became *caisal* or Cashel, and as such named the great limestone rock where the kings of Munster ruled in barbaric splendour, many centuries before the Normans brought the same word to England in the form of 'castle'. As is well known the raiders also carried off the boy Patrick, who later made his way to Europe, but returned in manhood to convert his captors.

The rapid spread of Christianity in Ireland brought links with the church in western Britain and Gaul and with them a few more Latin words, but nothing like the number to be found in Welsh. One word, however, picked up from Latin authors at about this time was destined for prominence, the word 'Scot'. Its origin is unknown, but in the fourth century it was what other races, including the Romans, called the inhabitants of Ireland, and when Irish monks began to read and write Latin – as they did with Christian zeal – they learned to write of themselves as Scotti and their country as Scotia; but in their own language they still described themselves as Eireann or Gaedel (Irish or Gaels) as they had from prehistoric times.

Towards the end of the fifth century when the Roman Empire was falling apart and the Angles and Saxons pouring into Britain from the east, the Irish, Gaels or Scots (whichever we choose to call them) were also inclined to expand. From Derry in the north it is a short way across to the western isles of 'Scotland', and it was easy for adventure-loving men to cross from island to island until they reached another mainland, and so on up sea-lochs to found a new kingdom of their own in a region that they called *Airer Gaedel*, that is the 'coast of the Gaels', now Argyll.

This infiltration into the north of Britain was a gradual

affair, but certain events stand out like beacons. In the year 563 St Columba, leaving his native Derry, established a monastery on the tiny island of Iona, and just as Patrick had been the chief missionary to the Irish so Columba became to the heathen Picts. It seems as if the Christian ardour of which his life was typical inspired the Gaelic people of that time with an extraordinary vitality, for their influence stretched out over that wild, mountainous land to its even wilder inhabitants whom even Rome had failed to conquer, so that not only the Christian faith but also the Gaelic language was triumphant among them.

Eventually the Scots united with the Picts to drive the Northumbrian Angles out of Edinburgh and became gradually the dominant partner in such enterprises, until in 848 a Scottish king, Kenneth MacAlpine, became ruler of Pict and Scot alike. His descendants consolidated and increased his kingdom, and by about the year 1000 were reigning over most of what is now Scotland and calling it by that name.

We have been dealing with a time of great ambiguity in regard to names. For at least two centuries 'Scotia' or 'Scotland' could mean either Ireland or the new kingdom in North Britain, but the matter sorted itself out as such things will in time, the old tribal name derived from Eireann being confined to one and that from Scotti to the other, while the wider term Gaelic could be applied to either. The word 'Gael' makes part of many place-names in these two lands but often much disguised as in Argyll. There was another word, *gal*, meaning a foreigner, which may easily be confused with it, and the two occur together in Galloway, originally *Gall Gaidel*, the land of the stranger Gaels.

Until about the tenth century Gaelic as spoken in Ireland and Scotland was the same, but as their later histories diverged so minor differences developed. In regard to place-names we see the same elements repeated right across both countries, as indicated in Chapter 12, and many of the simplest names such as Glen More (great glen) are common to both. In other cases we see the slight variation we should expect; Tipperary is the well by the river Ara, while in Scotland the same first element is found in Tobermory, the well of Mary, and the same river-name in Inverary.

But more than mere words the Gaels brought with them their

myths and legends, and Scotland like Ireland echoes personal names from Irish folk-lore. There were, for instance, several fanciful names that the Irish applied to their country, personifying it as a woman or goddess. One was Banba, a term of endearment, literally 'little pig'. In Scotland it seems to have been used first for a stream, and then for the village that grew there; the modern form is Banff. It is true that this could have arisen in a natural way from an actual animal, but Celtic people had a strong tendency to associate rivers with their mythology. Another poetic name for Ireland was Fodla, and this is contained in Atholl (Gaelic, *ath Fodla*) which is generally translated New Ireland; and yet another is found in Elgin (little Ireland) and in Glenelg. For such ancient names there is no exact proof of origin, but the repeated echoes of Irish mythology are inescapable.

Scottish river-names are nearly all Celtic in origin, whether Gaelic or Brittonic, or of an earlier, unknown origin. Some are identical with Celtic river-names in England, some, such as the Ayr (which has named a town and a county), link up with prehistoric river-names found all across Europe, the Aar, the Aire, and so forth. The river Ness (whose mouth gives its name to the city of Inverness) and the loch from whence it flows have the same name as a legendary Irish queen, mother of Conchubar, who according to the genealogies was reigning in Ulster at the time of the life of Christ, but the river-name may well be older still. It is first recorded in the life of St Columba, written by a seventh-century abbot of Iona, who tells how the saint rebuked a monster in Loch Ness (Nesa) which was about to swallow a monk who was swimming across. The rebuke was effective and the monster withdrew, having entered the pages of history in one of Scotland's oldest documents.

A striking element in Gaelic place-names is the great number of Dun-names. Nowhere has the regular old Celtic word for a well-defended site survived more strongly than in the Gaelic-speaking lands. We see it all over Ireland, as for instance at Dun Laoghaire (pronounced Dunleary, and long known to the English as Kingston). This was the stronghold of Laoghaire, the king of Meath who allowed Patrick to preach to his court at Tara but was not himself convinced. In Irish names the Dun has sometimes been corrupted in sound, as in Donegal, the castle of the strangers, Downpatrick where St Patrick is said to be buried, and the county that takes its name from this once fortified town.

This word is even more common in Scotland. It was the Gaels who called the Britons' stronghold on the Clyde *Dun Breattan* (now Dumbarton); Dunkeld was the 'fort of the Caledonians', who had dominated the central Lowlands in the Roman period; Dundee and Dunfermline seem to preserve personal names as their second elements, perhaps of early chieftains; Dunblane keeps the name of a saint, Blaan, who helped to convert the Picts. Dunmore (several of them) means the big fort, Dunbar the fort on the hill-top, Dundrum on a ridge, Dunoon on a river, Dumfries by a little wood.

Because the duns were the principal centres of defence in each district many of them have grown into large towns, as the English boroughs did, having begun in the same way. In contrast, the places beginning with Rath-, though also numerous have seldom become large centres of population. Rath- had the same meaning as Lis- (page 133), the court or dwelling of a chieftain, but was more distinctively Irish. A typical rath consisted of a circular rampart of earth inside which the prince or chieftain lived in primitive pomp with his household of warriors, his family and dependants and his bard to sing tales of his ancestors. There are more Dun- names in Scotland – perhaps because the different racial elements made for more serious fighting – and more beginning with Rath- in Ireland, where the perpetual rivalry between the kingdoms consisted often in little more than cattle raids and fierce skirmishes between small numbers. Each tribal leader had probably several raths and moved from one to another with little sense of permanent occupation. Tara, for instance, was the principal dwelling of the High Kings for several centuries, but when a holy man cursed the place in a quarrel with King Dermot in the sixth century the king abandoned it and set up his court elsewhere. Today Tara is a stretch of smooth green turf, with only grassy banks to show the dimensions of the Hall of Kings. So it was with many raths. They were remembered as everything is remembered in Ireland, and the word makes the beginning of many village names such as Rathlin, the rath by the pool, but none have grown into big towns. Indeed, it is useless to look for towns in Ireland before the coming of the Vikings.

The isolation of Ireland had been little disturbed by the gentle coming and going of holy men, but in the ninth century it was shattered for ever by the Viking raids. Something has already been told in Chapter 9 of the Norsemen's activities round the coasts of Scotland and Wales, but nowhere suffered more severely than Ireland, and its way of life was never the same again. There was tragic destruction of works of art as well as of human life, but positive results too, for the Vikings in their permanent footholds around the coasts established the first real towns and the beginnings of commerce. Nothing illustrates more clearly the unworldly nature of the Irish than the fact that they had never felt the need of money until the Vikings introduced it.

The principal towns on the Irish coast are all Viking foundations. Waterford, Wexford and Carlingford each ended originally in the Norse 'fiord', the last of them evidently having belonged to an old woman (ON *carline*). Wicklow was the Vikings' meadow (*Vikingu lo*); Cobh, disguised by Gaelic spelling as effectively as these others are by English, was the Norse *kofi*, first cousin to the English 'cove', which is how the Irish name is pronounced.

But although the pirates destroyed so much, they often adopted place-names, if they happened to hear them, for they were quick to learn as well as to plunder. At Cork and Limerick, for instance, both great centres of Norse activity, the Gaelic names (derived from *corcaigh*, a swamp, and *luimnaich*, bare land) remained in use; plain names, one might say, but rich in ancient associations.

The chief headquarters of the Vikings in Ireland was the harbour of Dublin, which retained its old-style Celtic name, *dubh linne*, the black pool. Here throughout the ninth century fleets from Denmark and Norway clashed in rivalry as the anchorage changed hands between them. In later times it became the capital of the invaders from England.

For this reason Irish nationalists have tried to reject the name of Dublin for their capital, even though it belongs to their own language, as having too much association with foreign domination. They preferred a name that features in their own ancient poetry, the tale of a cattle raid across the Liffey in the 'heroic' pre-Christian period. As the story goes, the men of Ulster were stealing cattle from Leinster and threw down hurdles in the shallow water to help drive the animals across. At this point the Leinster men caught up with them and a fierce fight ensued. The spot was remembered as Baile Atha Cliath,* the 'village of the hurdled ford', not far from the 'black pool'. Now it is all swallowed up in one city, and though an attempt has been made in recent years to persuade us all to use the longer, legendary name, it has come to nothing, except for Gaelic speakers. Too many associations had gathered round 'Dublin' for Irishmen or others round the world to think of that city by another name.

Wherever the Vikings settled we see the same mixture, Norse names frequent on the coasts, but far outnumbered by those of native origin. Although Norsemen dominated the Western Isles for centuries, most of them still bear the names that were known to the Greek navigators of ancient times. The Hebrides, Skye and Mull, for instance, appear in Ptolemy's *Geographia* as Hebudes, Sketis, and Malaios, just recognizable, but of unknown meaning. Other Scottish Isles have names that are known Gaelic words, such as Muck, which means 'swine', a common element in Irish place-names: Muckross (swine moor), Ballymucky (swine farm).

As for Ireland, in spite of the Viking settlements and all the later English influence the vast majority of place-names are still Gaelic.

It was the menace of the Vikings that inspired the various kingdoms of the British Isles to find their nationhood. In the century that followed the first Viking raids, the Welsh became united under Rhodri Mawr; the Scots under Kenneth MacAlpine; and the English under Alfred, although the task remained to be completed by his grandson, Athelstan. It was a little later that the Irish under Brian Boru drove out the main body of Danes, but real unity was never attained, and the lack of it caused them to fall an easy prey to the Anglo-Norman invaders of the twelfth century.

Of the three chief Celtic lands, Scotland, though more mixed

* Pronounced Bally a Clea.

148

in race than the others, resisted English domination best and was never conquered; but owing to its confused early history, the number of languages involved, and the lack of early records, its place-names, though fascinating to the scholar, are the hardest to interpret, and many famous ones remain mysterious. No definite origin can be given for Ben Nevis, nor for Stirling, which was first recorded in the twelfth century as Strevelin.

Confusing the issue further is the mass of folk-lore that has gathered round so many names. The Coolins or Cuillins of Skye are said to be the mountains of Cuchulain, and an old rhyme tells of a Pictish king with seven sons, of whom one named Fib inherited Fife. Scholars reject these tales, but have nothing definite to put in their places. Fife may well have been a personal name; Angus certainly was so – probably of the eighth-century Pictish king of this name of whom there is some record. But with early Scottish names one is seldom on firm ground.

Irish names are more easily interpreted than Scottish ones because they are largely in one language, but they have suffered even greater distortion through centuries of use by a ruling class that was non-Gaelic speaking, while those who did speak the language were mostly illiterate. This is in great contrast to the situation in Wales, where the native language has not only been spoken, but also written by men of education continuously from the Dark Ages to the present day. Now, at last, in a national effort, the Irish have restored many of their old names to their earlier forms, but the pendulum has swung too far, and excessive zeal for archaic spelling has made the manœuvre more difficult than it need have been.

Chapter 15

THE CELTIC SAINTS

Caesar, in the earliest detailed description of the Celts, stresses their religious nature and the power of their Druid priests. Their religion was then a cruel one, involving human sacrifice, while in contrast the Christian saints of the early Celtic church were a pattern to the world in the virtues of gentleness and loving-kindness to all living creatures. There was indeed a great change of heart, but the large place of religion in the people's lives remained the same, and no characteristic is more clearly expressed in their place-names than their respect for their spiritual leaders.

It was under Roman rule that the Britons first received Christianity and through all their troubles they clung to it firmly. Indeed, the more they lost their lands and worldly possessions the more they gloried in the faith that could not be taken from them, despising the Anglo-Saxons as heathen barbarians, which they then were. Long before St Augustine landed in Kent to convert the English there were simple little churches forming centres of British worship in the west, from Cornwall to the Clyde, and the gospel news had spread from Britain into Ireland whence it rebounded into the land of the Picts.

Some of the Celtic saints of the Dark Ages are very well known and documented. Patrick, David and Columba, to name the three greatest, are as historical as Julius Caesar or William the Conqueror. But a vast number of other men – and women too – who devoted their lives to the service of God in the Dark Ages are totally unknown except for their names which exist still in the places where they were loved and remembered.

We think of Cornwall at once as a land of saints – not of the great Biblical saints such as the Apostles whose names are found all over Europe, but chiefly of local ones. Immediately examples leap to mind: St Ives, St Austell, St Mawes, St Just, St Keverne, St Columb. But there are also many Cornish villages that are named from 'saints' without the use of that word. In fact, though often inserted in official records and preserved in the final names, it was clearly not used in colloquial speech. The little town of St Austell was only Austol to the Cornish in the Middle Ages, and St Ives was Porth Ia, 'Ia's harbour', Ia being an inspired virgin who came from Ireland to settle and build a church at the little harbour that bears her name. (She had nothing to do with St Yves of Brittany, nor yet the one in Huntingdon.)

Thus saints' names in Cornwall are even more numerous than at first appears. The villages of Ruan (Major and Minor), Sennen, Mullion, Mawgan, Zennor, and Feock all have the names of saints, though hardly anything is known of their lives. Indeed, the last two, Senara and Feoca, are so obscure that even their sex, probably female, is in doubt.

Often these names are compounded with Cornish words, as at Polruan (Ruan's pool) and Porthleven (Levan's harbour). Ruan, whose name comes ultimately from Romanus, seems to have come from Brittany. Levan was a hermit, and the path from his cell to the rock from which he regularly fished was said to be always greener than the rest of the turf on the cliff.

At Perranzabuloe (Piran-in-the-sands) the ruins of a tiny stone church of the sixth or seventh century still stand among the dunes, built perhaps by those who had personal memories of its saint. Perranporth nearby was his harbour and may have been used by pilgrims coming to visit his shrine, for Piran became the patron saint of the Cornish tin-miners and his relics were venerated and displayed on special occasions until the Reformation put a stop to such things. Ten miles away Perranarworthal (Piran-in-the-marsh) was perhaps a daughter church, offshoot of the first foundation. So through the names we see the cult of this holy man, but hardly know anything else about him.

Mevagissey incorporates two names, those of St Mewan and St Issi joined by the Cornish ag, meaning 'and'. The second of the pair is sometimes written Idi or Ida (*Mew ag Ida* is one early version) and is wholly obscure except that there is another village nearby called St Issi which is probably the popular form of the same name. But Mewan was one of those adventurous missionary monks who helped to convert the more pagan parts of Brittany and founded a monastery there. His faithful companion and beloved friend was Austell, whose name stands close beside his on the coast. It is said that when Mewan was dying he told Austell not to weep as they would be together again in seven days. Sure enough Austell died a week later and when the monks re-opened the grave to lay him beside his friend it was found that Mewan had already moved over to make room.

Sometimes the saints' names are compounded with the English 'stow' (page 71). Morwenstow is the place of St Morwenna, who came to settle there from Wales, being, according to legend, one of the many holy daughters of King Brychan. Padstow was Petroc's stow, and among the multitude of obscure Celtic saints Petroc is one who stands out as an important and definite person. He came from Wales in the sixth century and founded several monasteries and churches in Cornwall. Most of his life seems to have been spent at Padstow, where he set an example of austerity by rising always at first cockcrow and standing in the cold water of the estuary reciting psalms until the sun was up. He is said to have died a hermit on a lonely moor, and the monastery at Bodmin (*bod myneach*, 'the house of monks') founded on the site of his hermitage retained his relics, which were still highly enough prized six centuries later to be stolen and carried off to Brittany, and it took the power of the king, Henry II, to get them back.

It is not known what saint was reverenced at Penzance. It was *Pen sans*, the 'holy head', like Holyhead in Anglesey.

Although the Celtic world had broken up into several kingdoms during the Dark Ages, from the point of view of Christianity they were all one, and nothing illustrates better their unity of culture than the legends of their saints. When we try to study the saints of Cornwall we find that most of them have come from Wales, Ireland or Brittany, but this is balanced by finding Cornish saints in all those countries. A typical figure is a

King Constantine of Cornwall (page 132), who gave up his crown to retire into an Irish monastery and was later martyred in Scotland.

There was a constant traffic across the sea, the men of God delighting in dangers as they set forth in flimsy little boats from one stormy rock-bound coast to another. There was great freedom of action in the early Celtic Church that enabled each man to follow his own inspiration. Some priests stayed in one place ministering to their people; some lived in monastic communities; some preferred to isolate themselves; others set out on adventurous travels, trusting in God to guide them to do his will. It might be missionary zeal that drove them but more often – where we have records of their thoughts, as we have for St Columba for instance – they went in a spirit of asceticism. In such a spirit Columba left his native Derry (the land of oak trees) because he loved it so much.

Our knowledge of the Celtic saints comes chiefly from Latin lives of them written between the seventh and twelfth centuries in the monasteries they had founded. In most cases this was more than a century after the saint's death, and long enough for a considerable body of legend to have gathered around the facts. The trouble for us is that the main object of the writers was to show that the holy men were blessed with divine power. Any remarkable event in their lives was stretched into a miracle, and there are more miracles than facts in the stories. As is to be expected a great many of the wonderful events are concerned with the sea. The saints who travelled did so by the most unnatural means: St Piran came from Ireland on a mill-stone; St Ia on a leaf; St Budoc, who has given his name to St Budeux near Plymouth, sailed from Brittany to Cornwall in a stone trough; St Cadoc was wafted from Wales to Italy on a cloud; St Brendan, sailing with his company of monks for seven years, had fantastic adventures with birds, beasts and fishes on magic islands in a Celtic Odyssey.

Absurd though many of these stories are, we must not let them obliterate what is true. These people did exist, as the places that keep their names bear witness. They carried their faith about adventurously, and founded monasteries and churches that continued into historic times. Even the miracles, exaggerated though they are, tell us something of the truth. St Brendan was, undoubtedly, a great explorer; St Cadoc did go to Italy, besides founding a monastery in Wales. They all did something worthy of remembrance.

There were various ways in which a village might come to be known by the name of a holy man. It might be the place where he had lived and worked, so that it was, literally, his church. An obvious example is St Davids, which in Welsh is *Ty Dewi*, 'Dewi's house', or it might be that the church had been founded by one of those active monks or bishops who travelled about organizing religious communities, in which case the founder's name would be held sacred. Or sometimes the name might be that of a founder who was not a cleric at all, but the local landowner who built the church and was buried in it and remembered with honour. Years later, a recovery from illness, or an escape from disaster, might be attributed to his merit. In that age of faith, people were always hopeful of miracles, and local rivalry must have played some part. If a neighbouring church had a founder and patron with some miracles to his credit you would not wish your own church to be behind. Those who are on the look-out for marvels are seldom disappointed. So any church builder could become a saint.

In some cases the parish name comes from the dedication of the church to a more generally known saint – as it does in England where St Mary's or St John's is often added to the original name. But the speciality of the Celtic countries is the great number of place-names arising from personal links with local saints, largely unknown to the rest of the world.

In Wales the word that indicates a religious centre as an origin is *llan*, which for all practical purposes implies a church. Originally it meant an enclosed place, like the English *tūn*; but whereas the English put their fence around their homestead and their *tūn* became a village, the Welsh were more concerned to enclose the sacred place where they had built their little church and where they buried their dead. So *llan* came to imply the churchyard and the church, and as this was the centre of village life it became the commonest place-name element in Wales. It is of interest that the name of Bangor has a similar origin. It was a word for a special kind of plaited wattle fence that must have been used chiefly by monks, for the towns of this name in Wales and Ireland began as monasteries.

Occasionally the word that follows *llan* is a natural description. Llandovery, for instance, is the church on the waters, Llandaff the church on the river Taff. But in the great majority of cases the second part is a saint's name, and they are as numerous and obscure as those of Cornwall.

Even well-known saints may not be recognized because the Welsh habit of mutating certain consonants is so disguising. St Mary's Church, for instance, is Llanfair in Welsh, pronounced Llanvair; St Peter's becomes Llanbedr, and St Michael's Llanfihangel, literally, church (of) Mich Angel. As there are many churches with these popular dedications some further description has often been necessary, such as at Llanfairfechan (Little St Mary's) or Llanfihangel y trethau (St Michael on the Sands).

Welsh place-names are famous for their length. A small village in Anglesey, finding itself renowned for its long name, has taken a pride in preserving every part of it, some of which might more naturally have been dropped. It may be seen at the railway station written along the full length of the platform as Llanfairpwllgwyngyllgogerychchwyrndrobwllllandysiliogogo-goch. It means 'the church of St Mary in a hollow of white hazel near a rapid whirlpool and St Tysilio's church by a red cave', and is composed of two parishes united in one. But of course the full title is not often spoken. The local people refer to the two places as Llanfair and Llantisilio, or if they want to specify the former more precisely they find Llanfairpwllgwyngyll quite sufficient.

Dedications to well-known biblical saints are comparatively late, and the older names arising from local saints are often as hard to identify as in Cornwall. Llantwit is the place where St Iltyd had his monastic school, in which David himself was trained; Llanbadarn is the church of Padarn, a companion of David; Llanbedrog commemorates Petroc, whom we met in Cornwall. Llangattock (of which there are several) is the church of Cadoc who, despite the many strange tales told about him, was an influential abbot of the sixth century. But many of the best-known 'Llans' commemorate the least known saints. Of St Tudno (Llandudno) only the legend remains that he had a whetstone that would sharpen a brave man's sword in an instant, but destroy the sword of a coward. St Elli (Llanelly) is supposed to have been one of the many daughters of King Brychan. St Collen (Llangollen) was a hermit, and of St Peris (Llanberis) nothing at all is known, except that he was alive at the end of the sixth century.

Sometimes several are associated with the same little church. Llanddeusant is 'the church of two saints', Llantrisant 'of three saints' and Llanpumpsant 'of five saints'. They are five of the sons of Brychan, sleeping here side by side, and when they wake, or so we are told, Wales will return to its former glory.

In Ireland and the Gaelic-speaking parts of Scotland the element that regularly signifies a religious origin is Kil-. It began with the Latin *cella*, meaning a small habitation for a monk or hermit, and as the spirit of Christianity in Ireland found its strongest expression in austere monasticism so 'the cell' became the nucleus of religious life in all parts of the country.

St Patrick established bishoprics in Ireland, but in the following century, as we begin to see a Christian country emerging out of obscurity, no central organization appears, but only independent monasteries each ruled by its own abbot. As buildings they were unpretentious, each with its little church of wattle and thatch surrounded by the huts of the monks, where they lived in extreme hardship. But as the fame of such centres grew, so more and more people gathered round them, and in time many of these communities – that had begun perhaps with a single hermit – grew into large centres of culture.

We have noted that the Irish had no tendency towards creating towns, and that even the habitations of their kings were apt to be moveable; but a monastic foundation, however humble, had a permanency that nothing could destroy. Though the buildings were transitory, the spot where they stood acquired a sanctity often marked by a stone cross on which was lavished the skill in carving and sense of design in which the Celts excelled. Within the enclosure the burial of the founder and other monks continually added to the holiness of the place, and it only needed the report of a miracle to draw more people to the neighbourhood. This is why in Ireland and wherever Irish missionaries carried their faith there are so many towns beginning with Kil-, which, like the Welsh Llan-, may be translated 'church'.

There are many Kilpatricks, and even more Kilbrides (at least seventeen in Ireland and six in Scotland), but the important monastery founded by the much-loved St Bride does not bear her name. It is Kildare (*cill dara*), the 'cell' by the oak. Kilmuir and Kilmory may both be rendered St Mary's, but Kilmore, of which there are at least twelve in Ireland and Scotland, is generally 'the big church'. Kilkenny takes its name from Saint Kenneth, a companion of St Columba; Kilkierran from St Kieran; Killeedy from St Ita, an abbess who founded a nunnery there. Kilmartin in Skye is easily interpreted. The great St Martin of Tours was personally known to St Patrick and a strong influence on the Early Celtic church. With Killarney we have a natural origin again, 'the cell among the sloe trees'.

But though a few easy names have been selected there are far more of this type that are extremely difficult to interpret. Not only are many of the saints obscure, but the Irish had a habit of using familiarities that are most confusing. Consider Kilmarnock. The saint in question was probably Ernan, a nephew of St Columba and later himself a bishop, but his admirers turned his name into Ernoc (-oc being a diminutive ending often applied to personal names as in Petroc, Cadoc, etc.), and then spoke of him as Ma Ernoc, *ma* being a term of affection, so that Kilmarnock is really 'the church of my dear little Ernan'. St Ernan's head was long preserved at Kilmarnock. It was washed every Sunday and the water given to the sick, from which they derived great benefit.

Added to this tendency to alter names colloquially is the mispronunciation that many of them have suffered. Another difficulty is that there are one or two other words that have sometimes taken the form of Kil- in place-names. *Coille*, meaning a wood, which has often become killi- as in Killiecrankie (the wood of aspens) and *caol*, meaning a strait or narrow sea passage, which generally takes the form of *Kyle* (the Kyles of Bute for instance) may both occasionally appear as Kil-. But

F*

the majority of Kil- names do denote an origin from a monastery or nunnery – or just one hermit in a hut or cave, or even living up a tree, as some of them did – and that may be followed by a saint's name, recognizable or not.

Not every monastic foundation in the Celtic world has a name with a religious origin. Some famous monasteries were founded in places where older names existed and survived. Such a one is Iona, which had its name before Columba settled there. As usual with extremely old names there is some doubt about its true meaning. The earliest form of the word has excellent authority, for it occurs many times in the life of Columba written by one of his successors as abbot within a century of his death. But it is always given as an adjective, *Iova Insula* the island of (possibly) Io or simply I.* Bede, writing at nearly the same time, calls it Hi. Professor Watson, in his book on Celtic place-names, suggested that the original word should be identified with the Irish *eo*, which meant a yew tree. There were Druids on the island before Columba landed and turned them out and it is well known that they were inclined to function in groves of ancient trees. We think of York (page 6) and also of Mayo, an important monastery in the West of Ireland, whose name, *Magh eo*, again refers to yews. Then we remember Kildare (the church of the oak) where St Bridget founded her monastery, and we seem to see a pattern of pagan religious sites turning Christian.

But to return to Columba's island of Io, or I, or Eo, one thing that is clear is that the adjective Iova, miscopied by later scribes, has given us the form of Iona which has long been so firmly established that nothing can shake it. The Gaelic people were inclined to call it Columcille (Columba of the churches) after their beloved saint, and this form is perpetuated in Shakespeare's *Macbeth*, but in the end it was the older name, misread but attractive in sound, that came through to posterity.

Before we leave Celtic religious place-names one more should be thought of, St Andrews. In this case, exceptionally, an older name has been replaced by that of a non-Celtic saint. The place was one of the strongholds of the Pictish kings of Fife and the

* If we were dealing with English, this could signify 'island', but in this time and place that is out of the question.

oldest known name for it was in Gaelic, *righ ma naigh*, 'royal hill'. A legend tells that Angus, an eighth-century king of the Picts, vowed that he would build a Christian church there if successful in a battle. He won his victory and built his church, and the place became Kilrimont. So far we can believe the story, but we are told also that soon after the building of this church the keeper of St Andrew's bones in Constantinople, whither they had been taken from Patras where the saint was martyred, had a vision of an angel telling him to take these sacred relics to the land of the Picts, and that he did so. Relics at Kilrimont were believed to be the apostle's, and the priory church dedicated to him became a place of pilgrimage that dominated the town to such an extent that its old name was lost. This was during the time of Norman influence, as is reflected in the form the new name took. It is perhaps a pity that the cult of this international saint was introduced and given such prominence in a land so rich in holy men of its own. St Columba, or Columcille, as his own people called him, should have been patron saint of Scotland.

Part Three

THE NEW WORLD

Chapter 16

THE APPROACH TO THE NEW WORLD

The end of the fifteenth century, with its sudden outburst of discovery across the oceans, marks the beginning of a new era of place-naming, not only because of the vast extent of the new areas to be named, but rather the new spirit in which this naming was approached. In the explorers and colonists of the New World we see from the start a tendency to think names important, to choose them with deliberate care, conscious art and serious purpose, often using them to express deeply felt loyalties and ideals. This is in striking contrast with the Anglo-Saxon settlement of England in which names were left to develop in their own way.

At this stage we cannot confine ourselves to names created by the British. All the maritime nations of Western Europe were competing in the same field, and Portuguese, Spanish, French and Dutch pioneers were unwittingly to contribute place-names to the modern English-speaking lands. First we look westwards across the Atlantic where an unknown coastline, extending for thousands of miles, barred the way to the East which everyone hoped to find, and where the settlements of several nations grew and fluctuated, each uncertain of its own extent. In this exotic setting some names grew spontaneously as they always will everywhere, but many were given ceremoniously, the places marked with crosses and inscriptions, set up to the accompaniment of drums, trumpets and solemn Te Deums, nothing being omitted to make the christenings auspicious.

Among the innumerable transatlantic names in use by

English-speaking peoples today, only a small proportion can be chosen for mention. These must include the most famous and also those that best illustrate the different trends of naming among the extremely varied groups of people who made their homes in the new lands. Nor can we ignore the native names, without which no picture of America would be complete. To them we will return later. For the present we turn to the first coming of the white explorers, and try to identify the oldest European names in the new world.

At once we are faced with difficulties, for it is a common-place of history that when one studies a traditional starting-point one finds that it is not the true beginning. One thing is certain. Columbus was not the first European to reach the western shores of the Atlantic. The Vikings had been there, and possibly Irish and Welsh voyagers. There are Celtic legends of great voyages to strange lands, and though they are full of fanciful details, they could be based on truth. It is a fact that when the Vikings reached Iceland in the sixth century they found Irish monks there before them. Those who could sail to Iceland could sail to Greenland, and from there it was only one more step to the North American coast. But if the Irish did get there, any names that they gave are lost in a Celtic mist, and though the Vikings did record some names of a practical sort, Markland, Haluland and Vinland, the actual places have never been identified.

The Vikings lost the urge to make great journeys and their discoveries faded from men's knowledge. But still there were legends of lands across the western sea. There always had been, even before the Vikings sailed. The ancient Greeks had believed in the island of Atlantis, which took its name from the Atlantic sea which lay beyond the Pillars of Hercules, and the sea was named from the god Atlas who stood in the mountains at the end of the earth holding up the sky on his back. When the Portuguese and Spaniards first ventured far out into this ocean they used this name, Atlantic, for the part near the Straits of Gibraltar, calling the farther expanse by such makeshift terms as 'the western ocean' or 'the ocean sea', and it was only very gradually that the old Greek name was stretched across the second greatest ocean.

All the sea-going countries of Europe believed in western

islands. The Greeks and Romans told of Atlantis and the Hesperides. The Welsh and Bretons believed in the mysterious Avalon to which Arthur was magically borne to be healed of his wound. The Irish had wonderful stories of St Brendan's Isle, and some continental map-makers were still placing this in mid-Atlantic in the eighteenth century. Another island that appears on several European maps, made even before Columbus sailed, was called Antilha, the island of Seven Cities. Yet another – and one that was placed in very different regions on early maps – was called Brazilia, the name of a red dye that was much prized in the Middle Ages, but this was the least explained island of them all. Some of these names were to be given real locations in the course of time. The first was Antilha, for when Columbus returned from his first voyage saying that he had found the Indies, the Portuguese, who did not accept his theory, turned Antilha into a plural form and put his islands on their maps as Las Antillias. That is why in several European languages the West Indies are the Antilles, but this name never caught on with the English, and if we are looking for the very first names those given on the spot by Columbus must have precedence.

But were the names given by Columbus really the first? In contrast to the legendary tales, there is genuine evidence, though indirect and lacking in detail, showing that all through the fifteenth century both Portuguese and English sailors, and probably Basques and Bretons too, were catching cod regularly off the Grand Banks that lie so close to Newfoundland that surely they must have known of its rocky, inhospitable shore at least a generation before Cabot officially 'found' it. The Portuguese, under the inspired direction of their great prince, Henry, whom they called 'the Navigator' though he had hardly been to sea, were particularly enterprising, but they told other nations very little of what they found. There are Portuguese names on the Newfoundland coast that could be pre-Cabot and pre-Columbus too. The earliest European name may exist among these northern coasts, but until Cabot's voyages (1497–8) we have no specific evidence. Columbus's first voyage was five years earlier and much better reported, and so we come back to him for the first recorded names, bearing in mind that the northern group are close to him in date.

The first name that Columbus gave was his famous error, 'the Indies'. That he was wrong was suspected at once by some and a certainty before his death, yet the name stuck, and the fact that it was based on a misconception does not make it any less a living name. It was certainly the first for which he was responsible, for he was talking of Indies before he sailed, and as soon as he saw islands he hailed them as such. He even used the phrase 'West Indies', writing 'Las Indias occidentales' in a letter about his voyage. Presumably he meant the islands he had reached by sailing west as distinct from those known of already in the east, but he believed them all to be close together and near to India.

Antilles would really have been a better name, or Caribbees, which is what English seamen tended to call them for a time, taking the name from the dominant race of natives who inhabited the islands, or any name unique to that archipelago. But Indies had taken the fancy of a wide public and there was no stopping it.

> From the East to Western Ind,
> No jewel is like Rosalind

wrote Orlando of his love, and Indies remained in possession of the field, for Englishmen at least, while Caribbees faded away. When prefaced with West, for the sake of clarity, it served just adequately, but led to another and far worse error when the term Indian was applied not only to the natives of these islands, but to the millions of human beings inhabiting two great continents, from the forests of the north to the plains of Patagonia, leaving a legacy of ambiguity to the world that can never be shaken off.*

Columbus took name-giving very seriously. He was a mystic and a fanatic, and the names he chose expressed his intense religious feeling as well as his wish to please his royal patrons. He had to the highest degree that arrogance, common among explorers, which made them feel that anything they found was theirs to name regardless of its own life and history. Sailing

---

* This disaster in the field of international name-giving nearly spread even farther, for in the log-books of eighteenth-century seamen the natives of Australia, New Zealand, and all Pacific islands are called Indians, but the influence of a more enlightened age checked this tendency.

happily among his new-found islands and observing their friendly inhabitants with interest, he often noted the native name but invariably gave another, as if conferring a benefit.

But planting names in exotic surroundings is rather like planting flowers. Some live and some do not, and the causes of failure are very various. One is neglect; if no one is there to speak a name it can hardly continue. Another is a strong native growth that smothers the tender young plant in infancy; and yet another, a rival planting by another person. But place-names, once they have survived the early stage of vulnerability and taken root well, are likely to be more permanent than any vegetation.

The names that Columbus gave so freely on his first voyage were almost a total loss. As is well known, his landfall was in the Bahamas, but he did not touch upon the island that bears that particular name, an unexplained native word by which the whole group was later to be known. He landed on an island which its natives called Guanahani and which he named – with every kind of pomp and ceremony – San Salvador, in gratitude to his saviour. But this was a plant that died quickly. It was so completely forgotten that for centuries no one really knew or cared where Columbus had landed. Only in this present century has the matter been settled by careful research, and in 1926 the name was officially restored. It is, indeed, the first recorded European name given in the New World, but it cannot qualify as a genuine survival.

Having given this name Columbus sailed on looking for Asia and, passing several more of the Bahamas, gave each one a splendid title, either religious or royal. All that the Spaniards who came after him did for these islands was to take away their gentle inhabitants to be slaves in Cuba where they died from overwork and cruelty. And so the Bahamas remained uninhabited for more than a century, except by pirates and castaways, until the English moved in. Even then development was somewhat haphazard and Columbus's stately names were replaced by very casual English ones. San Salvador became Watling Island, named from one John Watling, 'a hardened old pirate' who settled there for a time in the seventeenth century. The next two islands, named Fernandina and Isabela in honour of the sovereigns of Aragon and Castille, became

Long Island and Crooked Island, and – worst fall of all from grace – Santa Maria de la Conception became Rum Cay. 'Cay' comes from the Spanish *cayo* meaning a low, sandy island, a word that the English soon picked up in the Caribbean.

After the Bahamas he came to Cuba, which he christened Juana in compliment to Prince Juan of Castille, but here the native name (first recorded as Colba, of unknown meaning) was too strong to be supplanted.

Then there loomed up before him another large and beautiful island known to its natives as Haiti, which meant 'mountainous', and admiring the island greatly he coined the charming name Hispaniola, or Little Spain. This lasted for almost two centuries but after a stormy and sanguinary history the island was divided politically, one part reviving the native Haiti, while the other became known by its principal city, San Domigo, and is now the Dominican Republic.

On 6 December 1492, when he had sighted but not yet named, Hispaniola, Columbus landed on a small rocky island close to its northern coast and named it Tortuga, or Turtle Island, from the number of the creatures that he saw there. This is a very simple name by his standards, and one that has been repeated elsewhere, but it outlasted many of his more ambitious efforts. It is, perhaps, appropriate that it was not one of his religious names for the place became a nest of pirates – most of them English – and in a part of the world famous for bloodshed and iniquity was one of the most notorious. The modern French-speaking inhabitants of Haiti call it La Tortue, but that is merely a translation. There are a few other names on Haiti that echo Columbus's choice, most of them slightly altered, but Tortuga was the first, and if we disqualify San Salvador as having failed to stay the course we must award the prize for the first European name in the western world to wicked little Tortuga.

After this more Spanish names came quickly to this part of the world, and many to islands that are now British or American. A few months after his triumphant return to Spain Columbus sailed on his second voyage and this time the names he planted were more enduring. He took a more southerly route, and on 3 November 1493 landed on a beautiful, mountainous island which he called Dominica, from the day of the week, Sunday. From there he passed on north-westwards through the chain of islands that English seamen have since called Windward and Leeward, bestowing names on all he saw. These include Marie Galante (from his flagship), Guadeloupe, Antigua, St Christopher, Santa Cruz (known by the French as Sainte Croix) and the Virgin Islands.

His original names were much wordier than these. Guadeloupe and Antigua were given in honour of particular churches in Spain, in full, Santa Maria de Guadeloupe de Estemadura (a famous place of pilgrimage) and Santa Maria la Antigua de Sevilla. These cumbersome phrases were soon reduced in practical use to one item each of their qualifying detail. Antigua means simply 'old', but it was St Mary's church in Seville that was old and not the island. The Virgin Islands commemorate the eleven thousand virgins who were said to have been martyred with St Ursula. Columbus must have sighted many islands on that day. Of special interest is St Christopher, for that island was the first in the Caribbean to be settled by the English (1623), and its name forms a personal link with Columbus being that of his own patron saint. Typically, the English treated it in familiar style, calling it St Kitts.

On the same voyage Columbus discovered Puerto Rico and named it San Juan in honour of the Baptist, but a few years later the Spanish explorer Ponce de Leon established a settlement on a fine harbour there which he called Puerto Rico, literally 'rich port'. This came later to be used for the whole island while San Juan was confined to the port. A curious interchange. Next Columbus found Jamaica and christened it Santiago, but, as in Cuba, there were many natives there speaking their own name for their island, recorded first as Xmayca, the 'land of springs', so that even the Spaniards picked it up. This name achieved a lasting place in the world though the native race it belonged to was exterminated.

On his third voyage Columbus named still more islands, among them Trinidad, the island of the Trinity, so called because as he approached it he saw three peaks. The French translate this as Trinité, but the English have always kept the Spanish word.

Other Spanish explorers who followed Columbus took little interest in the small islands, pressing on to the mainland in search of gold. But they lay sufficiently in the seaways for Columbus's names to be remembered and kept by both English and French settlers when they began to establish themselves there more than a century later. By then a few more islands had received Spanish names which we may notice now. Very Columbian in style, though not given by him as far as we know, is Nuestra Senora de las Nieves, Our Lady of the Snows, which became Nevis, an island where a white cloud on the mountain top often gives an appearance of snow. Anguilla is a simpler name, Eel Island. Tobago is 'tobacco'. Barbados meant the bearded ones (*los barbados* in early records) and alluded to the trees with trails of moss hanging from them.

Bermuda sounds like a native name, but a Spanish sea captain who sighted it in 1519 reported that it had been dis-covered earlier by his compatriot Juan Bermudez and called it by his name. On this island, in 1609, an English gentleman, Sir George Somers, was wrecked with all his ships' company, and there they lived for several months until they had built a boat to carry them to the mainland. This incident caught the public imagination in England and inspired Shakespeare to set his last play in such an island. For a time there was a tendency to call it Somers Island, and the association with summer-time would have had a certain aptness, but there was a magic about 'the still-vexed Bermoothes' as Shakespeare wrote it, and the older name has shown the better staying power. The final 's', part of the original personal name, has been treated as a sign of the plural and dropped when only the principal island is referred to.

Thus the first recorded names in the New World belong to West Indian islands and are either native or Spanish. Many of the islands have since been filled with typical English names – romantic Jamaica divided into Cornwall, Middlesex and Surrey – but that came long after Columbus.

If we ask next what is the earliest English name in the western hemisphere we must look northwards to that other gateway to the new continent, the islands that guard the mouth of the St Lawrence. But here the matter is far less decisive, for John Cabot who sailed from Bristol with a charter from Henry VII to find new lands has left no narrative or charts of his voyage, or none that has survived. We are dependent for information on letters written by geographers in several royal courts on the continent, who exchanged news of the latest voyages; on accounts given by Cabot's son, Sebastian, long after the event; and on information collected in the next generation by that splendid Elizabethan scholar and recorder of voyages, Richard Hakluyt. From these various sources we catch glimpses of what Cabot saw, the sea so full of fish that it 'sometimes stayed the ship', and the great white bears that plunged into the water to catch fish. But hardly any names are mentioned.

We only know that at five in the morning of 24 June 1497 the first land was sighted, and Cabot named it Prima Vista, or 'first seen'. This should be a famous name but it is gone, and its very position lost, more irrevocably than that of San Salvador. However, the evidence is almost conclusive that it was not part of Newfoundland, as many have thought, but of Cape Breton Island off the coast of Nova Scotia. Within a few years of Cabot's voyage, ships from other nations were exploring these coasts and tentative maps were being made. A Spanish map made in 1500 (by Juan la Cosa) marks a point that appears to be Cape Breton as *Cavo Descubierto*, 'the cape that was discovered', and an opening beside it (which was really the mouth of the St Lawrence, though that was not understood) as 'the sea discovered by the English', and old Sebastian Cabot in the map he made for the King of Spain forty years later wrote 'Prima terra vista' at about this same point.* Then, too, the French, who were the first to occupy Cape Breton Island, called its best harbour Havre des Anglois, until they renamed it Louisburg. By the use of these names Spain and France admitted that England was first in this region, but they were soon forgotten and when Jacques Cartier sailed this way a generation later the island had become *la terre des Bretons*.

Wherever John Cabot landed first, he did also find the coast of Newfoundland. On his second voyage he reached a more northerly coast where 'even in the moneth of July he founde monstrous heapes of ise swymming on the sea'. This must have been Labrador and it was probably then that it received its name. We can hardly count it as the first English name, for it is Portuguese, the name or nickname of a man who seems to

* These early maps are not accurate enough for identification to be exact.

have been with Cabot on this voyage and to whom we will return later. From there they coasted down past Newfoundland – missing the mouth of the St Lawrence – and perhaps almost as far as Florida before they turned homewards, but they left no record of any names that have lasted.

But there is a name that emerges from this period that is pure English, and undoubtedly the first permanent one to be given beyond the British Isles. It is Newfoundland, a splendidly spontaneous phrase that grew into a name in the mouths of English sailors at sea and merchants in Bristol. It belongs to the old tradition of English name-making, in sharp contrast to the exotic Prima Vista. (After all, Cabot was an Italian by birth, though he sailed an English ship, and that may account for his choice.) No exact date can be given for 'Newfoundland', but it occurs in separate words as 'the new-found land' in English documents from 1498 onwards. At first the expression was vaguely applied to all the land in that region, for no one knew if or how it was joined together, but when gradually a large island was revealed the English attached their name Newfoundland to that alone.

As soon as the news of Cabot's voyages had spread, the Portuguese sent several expeditions to reconnoitre this coast, and made maps showing their own names for its bays and promontories. Some of these are still there: Conception Bay, for instance, a name that no Englishman would ever have chosen, and Bona Vista (fine view). Some have thought that this last might be Cabot's landfall because of the similarity of the name, but the other evidence is against it, and this name, in the more usual contracted form of Boavista, was a great favourite of the Portuguese, who have used it often in their colonies. The most notable of the Portuguese names in Newfoundland is that of the nautical landmark that we call Cape Race. It was originally Cabo Razo, the bare or shaved cape, and appears so on many charts from 1502 onwards. But the English, inspired no doubt by racing tides, have turned it into something of their own.

We have no such early maps made by English sailors to show the first lasting names that they placed on this coast. But reports collected by Hackluyt tell us that they were there from the beginning of the century. From that time English, French and Portuguese fished those waters together and seem to have done so fairly amicably for there was plenty of fish for all; but whereas the others took their catches back to their homelands in salt, the English preferred to land and dry them in the sun on the beaches. Of course, they had names for every sheltered cove and stretch of sand, where they made themselves at home and built their summer huts, and every harbour that they used. By chance one of these names was recorded far ahead of all the others. On 3 August 1527 an English seamen named John Rut who had been sent by Henry VIII wrote the king a letter from that place which he describes as 'a good harbour called St John'. The name seems to have been there before him, and must have been given by an Englishman, because it does not appear on any of the maps made in that century by the French or Portuguese (not even as St Jean or San Juan), and cartographers always put in the names given by their own explorers.

Fifty-five years after that letter was written Sir Humphrey Gilbert sailed into the same harbour to proclaim the annexation of the island in the name of Queen Elizabeth. The bay was crowded with fishing boats and one of his companions there described it as 'a place very populous and much frequented'. But another generation was to pass before there was any official attempt at permanent settlement on the island. This began early in the next century and from then onwards the English names around the coast are gradually revealed in the scanty records. They are mostly far less formal than St John's, real sailors' names, each one given after a man's own fancy to his summer camping-ground or anchorage. Among those that still survive are Heart's Content and Heart's Ease, Bare Need, Pushthrough, Come-by-Chance and Seldom-come-by (now called Seldom), Witless Bay, Doting Cove and Cuckolds Cove. A river is called Exploits and a hill that makes a landmark from the sea, Main Topsail. Most of these are undatable and could belong to those early days when the fishermen were a law unto themselves. Heart's Content was there in 1610, so also Spread Eagle, and Cuper's Cove which soon turned into Cupids. There was no formality here to restrain the sailors' creative spirit.

In 1623 the king granted the south-west peninsula, that is almost an island, to Lord Baltimore (the same who was later to found Maryland) and, being romantically inclined, he called it Avalon. It still keeps the name adding a touch of Welsh mysticism to the strange mixture of themes and languages in the island where Englishmen first planted names overseas.

The first European name on the continental mainland is Labrador. It is probably even earlier than the discovery of the mainland of South America, and for the northern continent it is easily first. But there is an obscurity about its origin that has given rise to much discussion. The word, in Portuguese, means a farmer, or worker on the land (related to our 'labourer') and it was apparently the nickname of a man whom we see as a shadowy figure in contemporary records. In 1492 the king of Portugal granted a commission to Joao Fernandez Labrador to seek for new lands in the north-west ocean. We hear no more of that enterprise but ten years later, after Cabot's voyages, we find Joao Fernandez of the Azores (surely the same man) associated with several merchants of Bristol in a charter for a new voyage from there. Several early sources, mostly from Spain, state that the land of Labrador was discovered by the English, and one of them* says that they gave it that name 'because he who gave an indication of it to the king of England was a farmer [*lavrador*] from the Azores, when he [the king] sent on discovery Anthony Gabot, the father of Sebastian Gabot'. Whether or not the man called Labrador sailed with Cabot, his name was associated with that northern coast among the seamen of several nations. It is unlikely that it was given formally; Sebastian Cabot did not put it on his map, but from 1502 onwards it appears on some maps – though in variable positions – and while other names perished it survived.

The second earliest European name on the North American continent, and the first in what is now the United States, is Florida, and the giving of this is well recorded. On the evening of 2 April 1513 the distinguished Spaniard, Juan Ponce de Leon, who had formerly sailed with Columbus and was now exploring northwards from Puerto Rico, anchored off a low coast with lush vegetation. It was Easter time which in Spain is called the feast of flowers, *Pasque Florida*, and as he looked at the green land he thought there must be flowers there and named it Florida, the land of flowers.

* Alonzo de Santa Cruz.

Not very long after, in 1535, the name California came into being for that other long promontory on the other side of the continent. It is said to have been given by Cortez, who set out to explore that farther coast after his conquest of Mexico, and found only a parched land which he took to be an island. In his report to the king he called it Santa Cruz, a name that was already overworked in the New World, but he or members of his expedition seem also to have spoken of it by the fanciful name California, which they took from a Spanish romance about an island inhabited only by women. He was as wrong about the women as he was about its being an island, but the name has stood, and, like Florida, it is unique and euphonious and takes us back to the age of the conquistadores, who though they were harsh and violent had yet a vein of poetry in their composition.

It was not until 1584 that the English placed their first name upon the mainland, and this also was poetic and romantic: Virginia. In a letter of that year Sir Walter Raleigh tell us that the Queen herself called it so, but I cannot help thinking that he, the perfect courtier, must have made the first suggestion that the projected colony should be named in her honour, though the final form may have been her choice. They were both poets and scholars and between them made a name of charm and dignity. That first colony ended in disaster, but the name lived on.

Throughout all that colourful and exciting century hardly another English name was planted on the new-found continent. Around the Gulf of Mexico and down the coast of South America the Spanish and Portuguese were making and naming settlements, while in the north the Breton Jacques Cartier penetrated into Canada and began naming there. In the Arctic English seamen were groping through ice floes for a way round the land mass, but in more temperate zones the Elizabethan sea-captains, Drake, Grenville, Hawkins and the rest were too busy sacking Spanish ports and sinking Spanish ships to do much in the way of settlement or naming. Raleigh had made his one contribution and was then lost in his dreams of El Dorado which did not exist. Drake, ever practical, sailed right round to the far side of the continent and planted the name of Albion – literally on a wooden post – on the coast of what is now California. A superb gesture, but as no one followed it up it came to nothing. It was not until the first decade after 1600 that the true age of settlement began for English, French and Dutch. Then, almost at once, the spate of naming began.

Chapter 17

THE AMERICAN COLONIES

When an enormous spread of population across a continent creates new names in thousands, their chief requirement is diversity. This is present in abundance in America. There is also much repetition, but this is partly atoned for by the great variety that springs directly from the colourful history of the land.

An essential for such a rich mixture is the use of several languages. The charm and variety of English names owe much to Brittonic, Danish and Norman French, and far more languages have contributed to the place-names of America. First in seniority, although second to English in quantity, are the Indian names, and these alone are the products of many languages. For obvious reasons they cannot be treated fully here – a lifetime of study and a series of volumes would be needed for such a work – but neither can they be entirely omitted. Twenty-six of the fifty states have Indian names and many of the great rivers and cities. Their lively and distinctive character is an asset to the country. But although native in origin they owe much to European influence. Not only their prominence in the modern world, but the forms in which we know them and the significance we ascribe to them was in most cases given them by the white man.

Many names of Indian origin were simply words spoken at early encounters with little comprehension on either side and, perhaps, not place-names at all until the newcomers made them so. Chesapeake, for instance, is taken to have been the Algonquian phrase *chi sepi ook*, 'at the big river'. The last word corresponds with the preposition 'at', and seems to have been an indeterminate grunt, for the English settlers, hearing it at the end of many local expressions, rendered it in a great variety of spellings. *Sepi* is 'flowing water', and *chi* all that remains here of *michi*, 'big'. It was the first English colonists, left at Roanoke by Sir Richard Grenville in 1584, who heard an Indian village described in that way. They wrote it first as Chesepiook, and applied it to the big bay that was the chief feature of the neighbourhood, modifying the sound to suit themselves. But the Indians may have called the bay by another name.

The majority of Indian names that can be understood are simple descriptions of natural features. Massachusetts was arrived at from *mass adchu ut*, 'at the big hills', confused perhaps with *mass adchu seuk*, 'the big hills people'. It was Captain John Smith, leader of the first successful English colony, who heard these phrases as he explored the coast in 1616, and wrote them as one word in his report, adding an English plural to signify a tribe. Connecticut, first written as Quenticutt, meant 'at the river mouth', but the English soon began, when they settled there, to use it for the whole river, and later for their colony.

As well as many languages there were different dialects within each. In Algonquian, which was one of the most widely spoken, *michi* and *missi* and *mass* were all variants of the same word meaning 'big'. Mississippi is again 'big river'; in fact it is basically the same as Chesapeake. French explorers in the region of the Great Lakes were told by the Algonquian of a big river or *missi sepi* further west and set out to find it. If they had come from a different direction and heard what other tribes had to say about it, it might have become famous under another name. G.R.Stewart in his excellent book *Names on the Land* has given a dozen different Indian names for this river, ranging from Olsimochito to Mico, but it was the first recorded by the French that won through to fame.

We see that a large part was played by chance in determining which native words and phrases attained permanent places in world geography. Some Spanish explorers in the south were met by Indians who called out 'Teichas', meaning 'Friends'. Later the Spaniards used this word in speaking of that tribe and then applied it to their territory. And so came Texas, a fine name with a good meaning, but not an Indian place-name. Again, when Captain Cook landed on the north-west coast the Indians who gathered round him said something like 'Nootka' as they pointed to the bay. So he wrote that on his chart. But experts in the local language say that the only word it could have been means 'Go round'.

Many Indian names have no known meaning. Manhattan, which had been written on a chart by a nameless explorer before Henry Hudson sailed into the harbour there in 1609, is unexplained with any certainty except that it referred to a tribe. For Tennessee no origin is known; it named an Indian village before the English applied it to a river that rose nearby. So with many famous names. Since some tribes were nomadic it is not always known to what language a name first belonged; it might be old and already contracted before the white man heard it; and he frequently wrote it carelessly. Like the Celtic names of England, first recorded also by men of an alien race, many have gone beyond recall as regards meaning, though they have gained significance of other kinds.

We will come to Indian names again, and also to the Spanish names of the south. For the present our concern is with the first English settlers, for it is their language that has dominated subsequent naming throughout the country, and the ideas and decisions of their descendants that have chiefly influenced its character.

The first abortive settlement of Virginia left few names – beside that of the colony itself – and the only one in the English language, Cape Fear, is singularly inappropriate to the man who gave it, Sir Richard Grenville. His ship was nearly wrecked in the violent surf, his crew almost despairing, and having safely landed he recorded the danger-spot in this way. On the whole he and his cousin, Raleigh, who between them founded this unlucky venture, having launched their splendid, royal name for the whole colony, were content with native names for its detailed features. Indeed, their romantic natures seem to have relished the exotic words. And so Hatteras, an Indian word for a sheltered anchorage (later transferred to the headland that gave the shelter), and Roanoke, which, perhaps, meant a beach with white shells, were put on record. No doubt those first Virginians left hopefully at Roanoke named some of their surroundings with English words, but as they were never seen again their names died with them.

But when another century had begun, and hopes of more settlements were in the air, the new generation of Englishmen began the business of making names in their own language for the new continent. Queen Elizabeth was still on the throne though old and failing when Captain Bartholomew Gosnold, a Cornishman from Falmouth, sailed up the coast northwards from Virginia, noting the islands and inlets, and writing names on his chart. He was not the first to do so, but no one had taken notice of other people's names before, and now for the first time two names were to stick fast; one for an island where he saw wild vines and which he called Martha's Vineyard, thinking no doubt to please his daughter Martha with it when he got home; the other a long narrow promontory behind which he found a good anchorage. Here on 15 May 1602 he 'took great store of cod fish' and named it Cape Cod.

Five years later came the first permanent English settlement, named Jamestown for the new king. Now the great task of naming the continent had begun in earnest, though no one then could have realized its magnitude. As it developed in America, very distinct styles followed each other, overlapping and co-existing, forming an intricate pattern which may be sometimes flamboyant but is never dull.

The first style of naming to emerge strongly and one that merits the first place in every way is the royal style. It began with Virginia and continued with Jamestown and from then on was considered the proper way of naming any place that was intended from the start to be important. Virginia referred directly to the Queen – so called by the poets – and also was well suited to a virgin land with a suggestion that it was young, beautiful and desirable. Jamestown is a straight-forward expression of loyalty, as many others of the same sort would soon be.

The first settlers, having named their prospective town for the king, went on to christen the two capes at the entrance to their bay Henry and Charles in honour of his sons, the elder of whom was soon to die young, leaving Charles to inherit the throne. Prince Charles, consulted on the matter while still a boy, added the name of Ann to another cape to the north, in honour of his mother, Anne of Denmark, and would have had Cape James too for his father, but the one he picked, the most prominent of course, was the one that Captain Gosnold had named, and in this case the Cod stood firm against the king.

Later, as Charles I, he granted a charter for a separate colony to be called by a latinized version of his own name, Carolina.* It is formed from an adjective made feminine to agree with *terra* (understood), a natural procedure for educated men. But it was many years before this colony was actually founded and the town which became its principal centre as Charlestown (later contracted to Charleston) took its name from his son Charles II.

Whether Charles I himself was responsible for naming Carolina or whether it was politely suggested by his Attorney-General, Sir Robert Heath, to whom the grant was made, is not clear, but it is recorded that the king himself in less formal vein coined the endearing name of Maryland. In this case he had granted a charter to Lord Baltimore, a distinguished Irish peer who had already tried his hand at a colony in Newfoundland and had ideas of his own about new settlements and their names. Hoping that his new colony would grow fast he meant to suggest Crescentia as its name, but before he had come to the point the king forestalled him with the hope that this time the Queen's name might be honoured, and the noble lord could only acquiesce. This French princess is generally known by her full name, Henrietta Maria, but 'Maryland', suggested by the king, reveals what he liked to call her.

There are far too many royal names to enumerate in detail, particularly in those southern states founded by grants to the aristocracy. So too in the West Indies where other Englishmen were making settlements in the same loyal spirit. It was the time when nationalism was at its zenith and found ready expression in loyalty to the sovereign. And so, although a few royal names were – as we have seen – created by the kings themselves, the majority were a genuine reflection of the feelings of the colonists. When they called a new town Kingston they were happy to proclaim, 'We are the king of England's men.' The other colonizing countries did it too, but none to the same extent as the English. To the Spanish, for instance, the chief loyalty was to the Catholic church, and among their names in

* The first form was Carolana.

G

America there are at least twenty of religious character to one referring to their royal family.

The most important royal name in America is, of course, New York. In 1664, when England was at war with Holland, the king's brother, the Duke of York (later to be James II), who was then in command of the navy, sent a force to capture the Dutch settlement on the American coast. This was achieved without bloodshed, and, immediately, on the very day of the Dutch surrender, the English officer in charge of the operation, Colonel Richard Nicholls, proclaimed that New Amsterdam was henceforth New York. There is no record that he took much thought on the matter. The title of the royal person under whose orders he was acting was the orthodox choice. He was clearly not imaginative, and settled the business in the shortest and plainest manner. It was all in the day's work, like lowering one flag and running up another.

And so a great city was named. No one could claim that New York is euphonious (though less cumbersome than New Amsterdam), nor that the association with a singularly un-successful English king could be of the slightest credit or consequence to such a place. But great cities can rise above inappropriate names and this one has done so. If Americans ever give a thought to its original significance they tend to disregard the duke who failed so dismally as a king and think instead of that old grey city of the north with its walls and towers and ancient honour, from which so many English princes took their title, often succeeding to the throne though only second sons.

Most of the Dutch names in the neighbourhood remained as they were, but Colonel Nicholls made one further change. Fort Orange he felt expressed too plainly an allegiance that was ended. (This was of course some time before William of Orange came to the throne of England as William III, when the whole situation changed.) As the Duke of York was also Duke of Albany, the colonel used that title for the second Dutch town. It seems a pity that he did not leave Orange, which would now be valued as a link with the founders, and use Albany for the whole colony (formerly New Netherland), thereby avoiding the awkward repetition of New York for state and city. Although Albany is a Scottish title, there is no place of that name in

Britain. Its roots are deep in the past, for it is a northern variant of the ancient Albion (page 295).

The chief drawback to these royal names was that one family even with its attendant titles could hardly produce enough variety and a tendency to repetition soon appeared. The Restoration of Charles II produced a crop of Charlestowns including two in the West Indies. But the settlers in the Bahamas who had chosen this name changed theirs diplomatically to Nassau when William, Prince of Orange Nassau, became king of England. Williamsburg in Virginia, founded in 1699, was also named in his honour, appropriately using a Dutch ending. Annapolis in Maryland was coined for Anne, the last of the Stewart sovereigns, as a princess before she came to the throne. Whoever made this one showed good artistic feeling in putting the long ending, the Greek *polis* (a city), to compensate for the very short name. The result is a happy one and was copied later in Nova Scotia when Anne was an old queen.

Then came the Georges, and Georgetowns began to appear. The last state to have a royal name is Georgia, named in honour of George II in 1732. Several towns in the south were named for his son Frederick, who would have succeeded him had not a cricket ball ended his career, and for other relations male and female, Augusta, Caroline, and Cumberland, the last being the title of his most objectionable son.

The War of Independence brought this royal style of naming to an abrupt end in the colonies that broke away. Not so elsewhere. In loyal territories it continued vigorously, and years after the Declaration of Independence English sea-captains were naming features of the Alaskan coast after English royalties. Alaska has never been British, but the names remain.

But in the thirteen seceding colonies this source was cut off. What is truly remarkable is that in their anti-royal zeal the colonists did not change any of the names already given (as Colonel Nicholls had changed Orange). Even Georgia remained undisturbed though the name of King George was anathema. In this they showed good sense, and an admirable feeling for continuity and tradition. It is a loss when nations overthrow their names with their governments, and sacrifice old association to transitory politics. But the Americans in rejecting British rule did not reject the English language, and these names were now part of their speech. So they remain as links with kings and queens to whom Americans were once loyal, and though no more of that sort were coined, those that already existed were liked purely as names and repeated when new settlements were made, in commemoration of the earlier American towns. In this way there are Charlestons and Georgetowns even in the west but their significance is different.

This tendency to repeat names from other places brings us to the next style of English naming in America, which also started at the time of the first settlements, and proved the most prolific way of producing place-names, not new, but second-hand ones, even third- or fourth-hand, but serviceable none the less.

It began with that first leader among the colonists, Captain John Smith. It was he who first wrote on a map the words 'New England', transferring the name of his native land to the new hemisphere, and when he had explored that coast much in the same fashion as Captain Gosnold had done a few years earlier and noted a number of the Indian names he wrote a full account of it with a dedication to Prince Charles (later Charles I), humbly entreating that 'you would please to change their Barbarous names for such English, as Posterity may say Prince Charles was their God-father'. The prince, who was then sixteen years old, was very ready to oblige and replaced several Indian names with English ones. Only one of them remained to grow into a town, Plymouth, which he had changed from Accomack. This turned out an appropriate choice for, as everyone knows, the Pilgrim Fathers sailed from Plymouth in Devon. They landed first on the sandy windswept shore of Cape Cod, and when they found a better refuge across the bay the name of Plymouth was there before them.

This transference of names from the old homeland to the new has been so widely practised by all British settlers wherever they have gone that it seems a natural and obvious method of naming. But it is much less common in colonies of other nations and had never been done by the English as they spread about Britain. When the Pilgrim Fathers began it on a large scale it was a new phenomenon, and though their natural feelings of homesickness and affection for their native places will partly explain it, there were other causes at work too.

There was no love of royalty among the Puritans, and in their settlements no names were made from kings, courtiers or important people. Nor could saints' names – that great standby of Catholic colonizers – be even considered. Nor was there any enthusiasm for Indian names; they did well enough for natural features such as rivers and mountains which were wild in their nature, but a Christian community was a very different matter, and from the first the leaders of the Pilgrims set their minds against barbaric names for their townships. They were great disciplinarians these Puritan leaders; they had not left home to encourage freedom of thought, and on this point they were adamant. They did not even like newly made natural descriptions such as Sandy Bay or Mountainside, and when settlers in such places asked for recognition as townships, they were made to change the names. In this spirit, Trimountain, named from three hills, had to be changed to Boston. The authorities who made this order were no etymologists and did not know that in rejecting those innocent hills they were taking a saint into their midst. (For St Botolph see page 75.) Trimountain, shortened to Tremont, as it is in a main Boston street, would have been a fine, original name, but the Massachusetts General Court preferred conformity to originality.

And yet, with all these objections, names they must have, and the names of England offered an inexhaustible supply. And then again they helped to assuage those nostalgic feelings that the most heroic colonist must sometimes feel. In a new and savage land, where rocks, forests and swamps are obstacles to be overcome, descriptions of nature are less attractive than in civilized countries where bricks and mortar are more in evidence. Settlers in wild places are generally looking forward to making their surroundings more comfortable. They cannot have the roads and well-built houses, the church and market-place all at once, but they can have a name that suggests such things, and this is what they often choose.

The New England colonists set a fashion that was followed all across the continent. No doubt others would have done it, but not, perhaps, to the same extent. And later pioneers pressing westwards repeated the names of the towns they had come from, which were as often in New England as Old England, and so, in the end, there was too much repetition. No one could blame the pioneers for this. Distances were greater in those days, and when you had toiled five hundred miles with an ox wagon, you were fully entitled to call the place whatever you liked when at last you stopped.

Fortunately there was little tendency to preface these repeated names with 'New'; if there had been, the result would have been like an epidemic. Only in a few places did it seem necessary, and these were mostly large areas named by men who did not live in them, but spoke of them from a distance. Such a one was Captain John Mason of the Royal Navy to whom Charles i granted land in 1629 which he named New Hampshire after his home county. Another was Sir George Carteret, head of the principal family of Jersey, who made a gallant effort to hold his island for the king in the Civil War and was rewarded after the Restoration with some of the land captured from the Dutch, which he called New Jersey. In the same way Maine nearly became New Somerset, but the word Maine which had been used for this district for some time – first recorded in 1622 – was upheld against it. Nobody really knows how Maine arose and there is no reason to connect it with France. The most likely explanation is that seamen exploring the islands that fringe its coast referred to it as 'the main', meaning the mainland.* If this is so it is the only one of the American states where a natural English name grew up spontaneously, all the others having been deliberately chosen.

With English names in America it often happens that old spellings are preserved that have changed in England. Hartford for instance was spelt that way in its place of origin up to the seventeenth century, but has since settled as Hertford, though the pronunciation remains the same. In some cases whole syllables have survived only in America, as in Lexington (page 109). Sometimes where the spelling has remained the same, sounds that had been lost in England, even before the *Mayflower* sailed, have been restored in America under the influence of the written symbols, and to hear an American say

* In seventeenth-century records 'main' is used just as much for a big stretch of land as of sea. It may be noted here that this is also the meaning of Alaska, the 'mainland', in the language of the tribes of the Aleutian Islands.

'Chat-ham' giving value to every letter can startle an Englishman who never thought it could be anything but 'Chat'm'. But these are minor points. The sharing of names is one of the many signs of our common culture, and helps to make us feel at home in each other's countries even if pronunciation can sometimes take us unawares.

One would think that the Puritan colonists in America with their strong religious convictions and a new land before them would have produced a glut of biblical names, but though there are some well-known ones they never became very numerous. Within the first decade of settlement Salem was used in Massachusetts, and eventually it was copied in almost every state, always in the same form, the solemn full-length Jerusalem being consistently avoided. But that was the pattern with religious names, a repetition of one that had been tried and liked rather than venture on a new one. Bethlehem was not used until 1743 when a group of Germans of the Moravian church chose it for their village after singing hymns together in a stable on Christmas Eve, but the city that stands there now, noisy and wealthy with the production of steel, has little to do with their simple stable-and-manger piety. It was respect for such names that generally held the English settlers back. It seemed presumptuous to take such holy names, whereas there was no sinful pride in Ipswich or Falmouth. Such names were their birthright.

Moral abstraction seemed safer ground, and some early and distinguished examples were produced, most notably Concord, Providence and Philadelphia. Yet this class is also smaller than one would expect. The Puritan taste for giving moral names to their children, Faith, Hope and Charity, Temperance and Obedience, even Repentance, Reformation, Praise-God, Fear-Not and the like, might, one would have thought, have supplied place-names in hundreds. Here was a new line that might have developed in a big way; but it remained limited and restrained. It seems that the majority of settlers in a strange land prefer familiar names to new ones.

There must have been much talk among the earnest-minded in those days of 'God's providence', for Providence appeared as a name in several places at much the same time. In 1627 some

Puritan lords in England chose it for a settlement they had planned on an island near the coast of Honduras. It turned out anything but providential and the settlers who survived the first years did so as little better than pirates. In very different circumstances, a few years later, one Roger Williams, a free thinker and philosopher who was condemned in Massachusetts for his outspoken opinions – including the shocking theory that the land all rightfully belonged to the Indians – escaped into the forests and lived with a friendly tribe. He named the place where the Indians gave him shelter Providence, having as he wrote 'a sense of God's merciful providence to me in my distress', and here a fine city inheriting this inspired name has proved more worthy of it. The same name was given to the first important town of Maryland but later changed to Annapolis, the inhabitants apparently preferring royal to divine patronage, but more probably wanting, very sensibly, an individual name of their own. And it was used for the island of New Providence in the Bahamas, settled in 1664 as an outpost from Carolina.

Even before the naming of New Providence a group of settlers in the Bahamas had led the way in the use of Greek to express a high ideal. They came from Bermuda in 1647 and called the uninhabited island that they chose Eleuthera, which means 'free'. Their colony was not a great success and they mostly drifted elsewhere but the name remained.

A more notable example of the use of Greek for this type of name was Philadelphia, chosen by the Quaker leader Penn in 1682. He knew the name from his Bible, for there was a Greek city of that name in Asia Minor, abandoned in ancient times. Penn cared nothing for this city nor for the Emperor Attalus Philadelphus after whom it had been named; it was the meaning of the Greek words 'brotherly love' that attracted him, as expressing perfectly his hopes for his new foundation. A splendid name for a noble city whose early distinction has never been dimmed.

This type of name has continued throughout American history, producing a small but steady stream of towns and villages dedicated to Freedom, Friendship, Unity and so forth. The number of virtues called into play is limited, the three just mentioned being by far the most popular, but they are varied by the use of different languages, and by the attachment of different endings, producing such hybrids as Friendsville and Fredonia. But this kind of coinage belongs to the later period. In the early colonial days such names were linguistically pure.

The prolific source of place-names that consists of the surnames of prominent men other than royalties was hardly tapped at all in the first century of settlement and little used before the revolution. But there are exceptions, and a few early ones must be noted. First there are the names of those noblemen who had interests in the colonies and were so high in worldly estate as to rank near to royalty from the colonial point of view. Foremost among these was Lord de la Warr, who, as the first Governor of Virginia, was the representative of the king in the new untamed land. As early as 1610 a big bay was named for him, his title, which he wrote as three separate words, running together easily and melodiously as Delaware. After a little more exploration it followed naturally that the river that flowed into this bay was called by the same name, and then the tribe of Indians who inhabited its hinterland were spoken of by the settlers as the Delawares. Later, when this area was constituted as a separate state, the river-name was used for it. And so it came about that Thomas, Lord de la Warr, soldier and courtier, who had as a young man been knighted by Queen Elizabeth, had in the end a whole state to his credit, a great river and an Indian tribe.

Among the Lords Proprietor to whom charters were granted no family was more distinguished than that of the Calverts, the founders of Maryland, who bore for several generations the title of Lord Baltimore. This was taken from a small village in the south of Ireland (page 125) where they had once resided, and in due course it was used for one of the counties of the growing colony. It was not until 1729 that the town of Baltimore was founded, taking the name of the county of which it was to be the chief centre.

For the names of commoners to be deliberately given this sort of prominence was almost unknown in the early colonial period, but there is one well-known example of outstanding interest. The only non-royal individual, besides Lord de la Warr and George Washington, to have his name included in a state-name is William Penn, who, as a modest Quaker, was the very last person to want such an honour. Penn planned to call his

projected colony New Wales, but when he applied to Charles II
for his promised charter, the king – according to a generally
accepted account – dismissed this unoriginal idea and suggested the more poetic Sylvania, having heard that the land
was well wooded. Then in an ebullient mood he added 'Penn',
no doubt as a kindly gesture. The charter was signed, and Penn
obliged to accept it, but he was deeply embarrassed and could
only tolerate the name by saying that he took it as a tribute to
his father. The result is charmingly original.

But though in the deliberate naming of any place that might
become important there was no thought at first of thus immortalizing the common man, yet in a purely unofficial way
farms and other points of interest were spoken of by their
owners' names, and such spontaneous phrases as Harper's
Ferry and Bunker's Hill were numerous in common speech.
If and when such places were formally constituted as towns it
was probable that new names would be chosen, but not always.
Sometimes these colloquial names lasted into the later period
when this type had become more acceptable and then they
might grow into important places. As an example let us think
of Hyannis on Cape Cod, the very stronghold and centre of
conventional English place-names. The Pilgrim Fathers who
settled in this region had dealings with an Indian chief whose
name they wrote as Iyanough, a man 'personable, gentle,
courteous, and fair conditioned'. For over a hundred years his
lands on the south shore were spoken of as Iyanno's or Hyano's
and when at last a village grew up there it kept his name.

The capture of New Netherland by the British in 1684 led to
the adoption of many Dutch names in the territory which
became New York and New Jersey. The Dutch were not
imaginative namers. They liked, as the English did, to reproduce the names of their homeland, transporting such town-
names as Breukelyn and Haerlem (Brooklyn and Harlem) or
otherwise fell back on the plainest kind of natural description.
Dutch is a language so closely related to English that frequently
a very slight modification of sound and spelling is all that is
needed by way of translation. It was a Dutch skipper who
named Long Island (in 1614), leaving his own name Block to
another island, and many of the well-known features of New

The principal claims of the European powers in North America at the end of the 17th century.

- Hudson's Bay
- LABRADOR
- NEWFOUNDLAND
- RUPERTS LAND
- NEW FRANCE
- CANADA
- ACADIE
- NEW ALBION
- LOUISIANE
- Mississippi
- ENGLISH COLONIES
- NEW SPAIN
- FLORIDA
- CALIFORNIA
- MEXICO
- UNKNOWN

Land claimed by Britain

Land claimed by France

Land claimed by Spain

All names shown as then used

York, such as Broadway, Wall Street and the Bowery (a garden) remained almost exactly as the Dutch had spoken of them. They called the big river that flows into the splendid natural harbour simply the North River, having in mind the Delaware as the South River, or else they called it the Great River (*Groote Rivier*) making it a twin to the Rio Grande. But the English knew very well that it was an English seaman, Henry Hudson, who had discovered this harbour and river for the Dutch, and when they became masters of the colony they preferred to use his name. In all probability it was Dutch seamen who started the name Rhode Island on its course by calling it Roode Eyland, because of a reddish tinge in the earth, but who added the 'h' is unknown.

It was nearly a century after the capture of the Dutch colony that the Seven Years War against France ended in British victory and a rich reward of French territory in North America fell into British hands. The names that had been given by the French in these lands were for the most part accepted as part of the new acquisition and are still in vigorous use, though with very varied pronunciations.

In naming their new territories overseas the colonizing nations of Europe developed very different styles, the Spanish formal and religious, the Dutch plain, the English clinging to old names but also showing an original creative turn. The French names given in America have something in common with each of these, but something different too. As good Catholics they made use of saints' names and religious symbols, but far less than the Spanish. The St Croix river in Maine, named by their great explorer Champlain in 1609, is the French version of that favourite of Spanish name-givers, Santa Cruz, 'the holy cross'; and at the end of French colonization in America, when all their land was ceded to the British in 1763, a few French settlers moved across to the western bank of the Mississippi which they hoped was beyond British rule and there founded the city of St Louis, naming it in a way that proclaimed its French loyalty. But taking a broad view of French names one sees the religious element as only a small proportion.

Likewise they used royal names as the English did. Another of their colonial heroes, La Salle, he who first sailed right down the Mississippi from near the Great Lakes to the Gulf of

Mexico and took possession of the land around its mouth in the name of his king, Louis XIV, proclaimed the very name for it that one would expect, Louisiane, Like Carolina it has the ending of a feminine adjective as suited to a land, which the English colonists changed later from French to Latin. Some years after La Salle's great journey, when the principal city of this new French province was founded, it too received a royal name, Nouvelle Orleans, in honour of the Duke of Orleans, regent for the child Louis XV, and chief patron of the enterprise. It is the exact counterpart of New York, named also from the title of the prince closest to the throne, and only incidentally the name of a fine old city. As to the transporting of place-names from their homeland for their own sake, the French, unlike the English, hardly did it at all.

In general the French explorers, covering vast areas around and behind the English colonies, tended to call the principal landmarks by the simplest of descriptive terms, such as Terre Haute and Fond du Lac which are now large towns. But because their language is so different from ours, their words, though plain and practical in origin, often seem to have more distinction than our own equivalents would have. Lake Superior sounds grand and elegant, much more so than Upper Lake which is all that it literally means. Strange that the greatest lake in the world (unless we count the Caspian Sea) should have no better name than this, but the French must have been sated with great lakes by the time they reached this one. Detroit is simply the straits, a narrow passage from one lake to another; but the combination of French spelling with the most uncompromising English pronunciation has made a unique and effective city name. In noticing these very simple names we must remember that the Frenchmen who gave them were explorers rather than settlers. They were not consciously founding towns like the Pilgrim Fathers, but seeking out new territory and new converts for their faith and merely noting the strait or the high land or the end of the lake as strategic points on their journeys. It was English-speaking settlers who made them into towns.

But the great strength of French naming, in which they surpassed all the other colonists, was in the collecting and immortalizing of native names. They more than any others learned to know the Indian. Their missionary priests would often spend dangerous months and even years living with the Indians in the forests, learning their languages so that they might teach and influence the tribes, and when they travelled among the lakes and forests they had Indian guides from whom they learned the native names. It was a Frenchman who first heard of the Mississippi and when in 1672 a Jesuit father, the lovable Père Marquette, set out with his friend Louis Jolliet down this river they spoke between them at least six Indian languages. At every sign of habitation they strove to establish friendly contacts, holding up a peace pipe at the prow of the canoe; and that one adventurous journey enriched the map with Wisconsin, Iowa, Missouri, Omaha, Kansas, Arkansas, and other now familiar names. Nearly all were the names of tribes or of rivers or of both, and often it is impossible to say which took its name from the other. Most of these words were longer and more complicated when first written down, for the French like other colonials modified awkward native words to suit themselves, but, understanding them well, they were better able to drop prepositions and unimportant inflections than the Dutch or English, and their final products have on the whole more simplicity and grace.

Before that famous journey down the Mississippi the French were already familiar with the Ohio, whose name signified to the Seneca Indians on its banks 'a fine river' or 'fine road'. They also knew well the tribe who called themselves the Illinois, which is simply 'the men'. At first Lake Michigan was 'the lake of the Illinois', but when this tribe migrated elsewhere the French used instead another local term, *michi guma*, which was another way of saying 'big water', and their pronunciation made it Michigan. Near the southern end of this lake was the *milo aki* or 'good land', now Milwaukee, and at the very end where they used to portage their canoes across to the river that would take them southwards they passed a hollow where wild garlic grew which the Indians called *chicagou*, the onion place. Here stands Chicago.

Sometimes the French translated the Indian words into their own language, and some of these have been re-translated into English. The Rocky Mountains were earlier *les montaignes rocheuses*, and the French called them so before they had seen them, having heard them so described by Cree Indians from the west. But often such translations got no further than French. Baton Rouge, the red post, is the French version of the same words in the Choctaw language which described a post stuck up to mark the limit of the tribal hunting ground. Now they name a modern city. Such examples could be greatly multiplied.

English-speaking Americans taking over French names treated them in whatever way came easiest. Some were translated, some pronounced as if they were English, some more or less in the French manner, many with a compromise. In regard to Indian names one might think that it would not much signify which race had collected them, but it could make all the difference. The pronunciation of Illinois, for instance, has developed from that of the French. The English called the same tribe the Wellinis. And it is the difference between the two languages that has caused the state of Arkansas to be pronounced Arkansaw, although the river, along which English settlers made their home, is spoken as Arkánsas.

On the whole the settlers who spread and multiplied over former French territory swallowed the French names whole and with relish. But one important replacement took place even in the heat of the war. The Ohio river was a vital route through the Alleghennies, and here at a strategic point the French had built a stronghold that they called Fort Duquesne after their governor. Twice the English attacked it in force, but each time were repulsed with heavy losses, and when at last it fell to them in 1758 their commanding officer, Brigadier John Forbes, rejected the name Duquesne which had a bitter taste in British mouths, as associated with painful setbacks. He replaced the French governor with the English prime minister whose brilliant conduct of the war was producing victories on every side. But since 'Pitt' was too short and abrupt to make an impressive place-name, he added -burgh of which the original meaning is 'fort'. He was himself a Scot and therefore he spelt this addition as it is regularly spelt in Scotland, as in Edinburgh for instance, and no doubt he pronounced it with a fine rolling 'r', making it sound much more like the English 'borough', which is exactly the same word, than the Dutch or German 'burg' to which it has since been assimilated. But Pittsburgh, though it has been germanized in pronunciation, has remained true to its British origin in spelling, and the final 'h' still stands.

In all those frontier regions where English, French and Indians hunted, trapped, explored, manœuvred against each other, fought, and made peace the names are rich in history.

Chapter 18

THE UNITED STATES

The winning of their independence brought to Americans a new outlook towards naming. Up to that time they had regularly drawn on England for material, but now everything was changed, and instead of distant royalties and their ministers they began on a large scale to use the names of their own people. As to the bringing of place-names from England, which had proved such a stand-by in colonial days, it was so deep-rooted that it never really ceased. But in the first excitement of independence it received a considerable setback. England was out of favour, and pioneers of new settlements who wanted regular town-names rather than newly invented ones tended to look farther afield for them. They looked to Europe, to Asia, or back into the ancient world for something noble and inspiring; and so the little towns with their wooden clap-board houses that were springing up on all sides became – instead of Hartford and Birmingham – Paris, Berlin, Athens, Troy, Sparta, Cairo, Memphis, and felt themselves part of world history.

In their revulsion against England Americans turned particularly towards France, who had helped them actively in their struggle, though an enemy so short a time before. And now everything French was admired. Influences from other languages made their mark too, and Greek and Latin were used more freely. In fact, in the field of naming the chief results of gaining independence were both a much greater use of home products and an influx of imports from a far wider field. We must look at these points in more detail.

The use of men's surnames for places had been gaining ground slowly all through the eighteenth century, but those used belonged for the most part to English politicians or generals, such as Pitt or Amherst. Lord Amherst had commanded the British force in America in the Seven Years War, and as his title was in its nature a place-name it sounded well without any addition. A shorter name like Pitt needed building up (page 195). A few local men had also been honoured in this way but it was more often a spontaneous growth than a deliberate plan, as at Trenton in New Jersey, which began as 'Trent's town', having been laid out as a speculation by William Trent in 1714.

But now this personal style suddenly expanded into one of the principal methods of name-making. By this means every locality could pay its tribute to national heroes, and honour its own outstanding citizens. And so strongly has the style developed that any successful and popular American may hope one day to have his name on the map.

To begin with, Washington was the obvious choice for the splendid capital that was to be built. No dissident voice was raised for it had every advantage. It honoured the leader of the nation, and was fortunately a dignified word of sufficient weight for such an important assignment. A fine name if only the Americans could have left it respectfully to stand alone. But in their love for the man and their democratic freedom to name their land as they please, they have made it one of the commonest place-names in the country.

A special survey, made in 1932, the bicentenary of Washington's birth, lists 121 centres of population in the States bearing the name of Washington. Some of these are very small or suburbs of other cities; *The Times World Atlas* gives a mere twenty-five towns and cities, and nine other features, but that is more than enough. The crowning error was to allow a state to take this name. This really does cause confusion, especially outside America. As New York is in New York State, many people expect the same relationship between the Washingtons.* Americans must reconcile themselves to qualifying their capital as Washington, DC. They are, of course,

* I speak from experience, having a son in Washington State. I grow tired of explaining that it is nowhere near the city.

accustomed to adding Minn., Miss., Pa., Va., and so forth to a great many of their names, even in conversation, but they might have managed for their capital to have a name that could stand unqualified.

Americans are a warm-hearted race who love to honour their great men, and George Washington was not the only one to receive such a nationwide tribute. That man of many parts, Benjamin Franklin, who worked with him in creating the new nation, even appears to surpass his score in numbers, but a few of the twenty-seven of the towns so named commemorate other men. All the early presidents are well represented, Jefferson, Madison, Monroe and Jackson all having over twenty to their credit, including such variations as Jacksonville. Of these four men Jackson has the highest total. It is a common surname and some of the places were probably named for other Jacksons, but there is no doubt that Andrew Jackson, popular hero of the south and west, is responsible for most. Lincoln also has a good score, as one would expect, of about twenty-four towns and villages. But if one treats these numbers as a gauge of popularity, one must keep in mind that the earlier ones have a big advantage, since any name that is launched in America is apt to be reproduced over and over in the course of time.

Not only political leaders but men of all sorts have been honoured in this way. Kit Carson, adventurous scout of the western frontier, has his city (a state capital too), and a minor Indian chief, called See-yat or something like it, and described by those who knew him as a scamp and a villain though a likeable one, has his name (in one of its variable forms) preserved in the city of Seattle. Many towns were named for the business men whose money helped to develop them. And some hoped to attract capital by the bait of a personal place-name. Such a one was the little town of Twin Forks in Washington State. Its leading inhabitants, wishing to expand the place, looked round for a wealthy man whose interest might be secured. They picked out George D. Pullman, of sleeping-car fame, and wrote to him saying that they were naming their town in his honour, with a hint that they were in need of funds. Mr Pullman sent them $50. A disappointment, but the town became Pullman. Sometimes the approach was the other way round. A Mr Bicknell who wished to see his name on the map advertised that he would present his handsome library to the first locality who would oblige him. Hence Bicknell in Utah. But these last two examples are not, I believe, typical; in general it was genuine admiration that prompted the choice.

In their thirst for more heroes for name-making Americans looked back into the past, and soon after the Revolution it dawned on them that Christopher Columbus, though revered as the discoverer of the New World, had been entirely neglected in this respect. His compatriot, Amerigo Vespucci, who had followed in his wake, had been honoured out of all proportion to his merit, but Columbus had not so much as a bay or a rock. Here was a name to make much of, a sonorous one too, that could stand with dignity as it was or be turned into Columbia if one liked to think of a city or a land as feminine. In this latter form it narrowly missed naming the whole nation, but the American people failed to seize this chance. Again it was almost chosen for a state – in 1853 – and should have been so chosen, for the principal river of the territory in question had already been named Columbia; this would have continued a tradition of naming states from their chief rivers. But Washington was preferred. However, the name was not wasted. Over thirty cities and towns in the States are called after Columbus, and though his name missed the highest honour it has been accorded a special place in the heart of the nation. In this book there is no room to consider the very local names that must run into millions, but if we could do so we should find the towns of America filled with countless streets, squares, avenues and other features named for Columbus.

A good many foreign celebrities may be found among American place-names, but a far greater number commemorate Americans. And since the majority of these, even to the present day, have family-names that originated in the British Isles, the character of American naming has remained very largely British. The deliberate importation of place-names from England had greatly decreased in number since the Revolution, but the use of so many surnames still supplied much of the same material. A large proportion of English and Scottish surnames consist of the names of towns and villages, and so although the significance was now different, personal rather than local, the result could be just the same. Lincoln owes its use in America largely to a great man, but it is an English city too (page 29). Denver, Houston and Dallas are all just cities to the average American. If he thinks back a little in his own history he may know that they were men. James Denver, soldier and administrator on the western frontier; Sam Houston, tough hero of Texas; George Dallas, a vice-president; but, farther back still, they were small villages where the ancestors of these men once lived, and we must go even farther into the past to reach the time when the names were formed. Denver, in Norfolk, was *Dena faer*, the 'crossing place of the Danes' in the marshy land close to the Great Ouse; Houston is a village to the west of Glasgow, the *tūn* or enclosure near 'the house'; Dallas, also Scottish, is in Morayshire, and means the meadow by the wood.

The interval between the creation of the original village-name in Britain and the secondary name in some far distant country to which it has been carried by a family is seldom less than a thousand years, but the names are none the worse for that, having had time to mature and lose rough edges.

Among the surnames that have provided such a rich store of naming material for all the new countries, those that are derived from place-names have been particularly congenial. It is true that Americans would not hesitate to use a surname of any kind when they wanted to honour a particular man – the number of Jacksons is proof of that – but when there was a question of choosing between two or three possible men, the one whose name sounded like a place had a big advantage. When a city was being planned on the shores of Lake Erie in 1796 Moses Cleaveland, one of several gentlemen who had invested money in the district, took part in the original survey. He was a retired general of moderate distinction; if his name had been Smith or Brown the planners might have turned elsewhere, but Cleaveland sounded well and looked good too (though a little better without the 'a' as the editor of the first local newspaper decided). It is the name of a hilly district in Yorkshire, literally 'the cliff land', but they gave no thought to etymology, and just as well, for Cleveland, Ohio, lies low and flat. They simply liked the name.

One more example from a large field. In 1865 those in charge of the founding of a university town on the Pacific coast chose – after deliberating on it for more than a year – the name of Berkeley. Their immediate motive was to honour Bishop Berkeley, the famous philosopher, who as a young man had been an active pioneer of American education, and whose poem beginning 'Westward the course of empire takes its way' was felt to be particularly suited to the situation. They named it for the man, but they themselves, being men of scholarship, did think of the derivation too. They knew that Berkeley was an English village with an ancient castle, and that the name meant a meadow or clearing among birch trees, and though they had no birch trees around their selected site they thought it a pleasant concept, and a fitting name. So in one way and another English place-names continued to spread across America.

When the wave of admiration for France was at its height English-speaking Americans began making place-names for themselves out of French materials, but these are quite a different matter from the genuine ones bequeathed to the land by French colonials. Enthusiasm for the language was not always matched by a sound knowledge of it, and the results were sometimes more American than French. Not that it matters; they were made for American use. One of the first of this sort was Vermont, which was meant to signify green mountains. When its inhabitants applied for statehood under this name there were plenty of people ready to point out that a Frenchman would say *monts verts*, and that although it was reasonable to drop the final letters, which are in any case silent, the word-order was essential to the French character. But the inhabitants of those green mountains liked it that way, and stood firm, and now it seems to be exactly right.

In 1780 Louisville was named in honour of the king of France, just ten years before his life was ended by the guillotine. And the Marquis de La Fayette who had come in person to help Americans fight for their independence received his tribute from a number of places, some adopting his full name, some shortening it to Fayette, and some adding the newly fashionable ending to make Fayetteville.

So we come to that typical feature of American naming, *ville*, that was taken up with avidity when the nation was young, and used – as many would say – to excess. There are far more towns in America ending with *ville* than in France, and it has been combined with every kind of word, however incongruous. To those who have much feeling for the niceties of language such names as Higginsville seem discordant. Not that any English-speaking person should criticize the borrowing and use of a foreign word, but *ville* was never properly borrowed, never taken into the language for ordinary use, as many other French words such as 'cascade' and 'prairie' were. It remains unmistakably French, and, as such, seems an awkward companion for such a very English name as Higgins. It is even worse when added to a name that already contains its meaning. Washingtonville is a case in point.

But though *ville* has provoked adverse comments, a more generous view is possible. Americans spread so fast and created so many new centres of human life that their need for words signifying a settlement was enormous. The English 'town', whether in full or contracted to 'ton', had been much used in the colonial period, and to a lesser degree 'borough', generally reduced to 'boro', or later preferred in its German or Dutch form 'burg'. But still these were not enough. The Greek *polis* which had been used to make Annapolis before 1700 was now brought much more into play, but for a small place it sounded pompous, and on the whole this was realized and some moderation observed. 'City' came into use a little later, a word which, unless it is to lose its meaning entirely, should be reserved for the great towns. There are 'cities' in the west which consist of little more than shacks and trailers. But the ordinary American pioneers had, generally, too much sense for this kind of pretentious naming. They only needed a simple little word – or rather several of them to give a choice – indicating a settlement, and *ville* was one that suited them well.

A point in its favour is that *ville* as pronounced in the States is lighter and easier to say than 'town' with its long vowel or 'boro' with two syllables, and Americans have always had an ear for a well-sounding name, caring more for that than for linguistics. Washingtonville is still a mouthful, likewise Jeffersonville, but Knoxville and Nashville (localizing two heroes of the Revolution) are good names. Centerville says what it means in a style that is purely American; Beaverville and Elkville, closely related to the natural scene, are charming.

Towards the end of the nineteenth century, when in most of the country the roughest pioneering work was done and life for many was both comfortable and prosperous, a wave of romanticism became widespread. Literary influences had been at work before, but mostly of a classical sort. Troy and Ithaca owed their attraction to the part they played in Greek legend, but now a taste for books of a more recent and popular sort began to have its effect. Scott was much read, and so Waverley, Montrose, Woodstock and Ivanhoe made their appearance, several times each. From Shakespeare Belmont is easily the favourite, largely owing to its pleasant and obvious meaning, well suited to a hilltop site, but Elsinore with its gloomy associations may be found too in sunny California and in Utah. Poetry was much enjoyed and though no one can have wanted their new settlement to become a Deserted Village, the line 'Sweet Auburn, loveliest village of the plain' was irresistible. *The Times World Atlas* shows Auburns in sixteen states.

Naturally Americans idolized their own poet, Longfellow, and Hiawatha became the name of at least two towns. But more remarkable was the fate of that hero's love, the gentle Minnehaha. In the Sioux language *minne* is 'water'* and *haha* a waterfall. In 1852 the inhabitants of a settlement near falls of this name thought they might use it with a suitable suffix for their growing town. At a public meeting they considered Minnehahapolis, and some pruning was wisely agreed on. Among all the thousands of hybrids that descendants of the English have concocted in different parts of the world the marriage of Red Indian with classical Greek is one of the strangest. But how effective. Minneapolis is a beautiful name, melodious, original, and expressive of the feelings of its founders. Perhaps rather too imposing if the place had remained small, but it has grown into a great city to match its name.

It was literary association and the very real desire for something beautiful that led to the adoption of such names as Arcadia, Aurora, Flora, Panacea, Belvidere, Bijou and so on, words being taken freely from any language or period in the search for something poetical. The great Mr Jefferson used Italian to name his home, Monticello, 'the little mountain'. His choice was, naturally, apt; others not always so. Among the

* Minnesota, originally a river-name, means 'cloudy water'.

less sophisticated the quest for beauty could end in mere prettiness – Sunbeam, Rosebud, Fairylawn.

Another symptom of the romantic feeling of the time was the enthusiasm for archaic words as place-name material. The forming of new names on the English pattern was no novelty. A name like Watertown, for instance, was no importation but freshly made to fit the circumstances, and very successfully. But now there came over the land a scattering of such names as Avonlea, Meadowvale, Glendale and Sunnyhurst, using old-fashioned terms that Americans knew from the language of poetry, but had never uttered in their everyday speech. They are still being coined and are extremely popular.

A more important manifestation of the romantic movement was the growing enthusiasm for Indian names. In the early colonial period many of these had been adopted only because they were there, and the general aim was to replace them with something more civilized. But later, even while his land was being taken from him more and more rapidly, there came admiration for 'the noble savage' and some recognition that his names for his ancient homelands were more fitting than anything that the white men could invent. After Independence this point of view grew stronger, and from that time the great majority of territories admitted to statehood were given names derived from Indian words. The first of these was Kentucky, *kenta ke* or 'grass land' in the Iroquois tongue, and this was followed soon after by a series named from their chief rivers, Tennessee, Ohio, Alabama, Mississippi, Missouri, all Indian in origin.

As the nineteenth century advanced the romantic view of Indians was voiced by many writers, and whenever a new territory or state needed a name the public demand for an Indian one was so strong that if no suitable one was readily available something was searched for or artificially constructed out of Indian materials. In the district that became Nebraska the chief river was the Platte, so named by the French because it flowed over a flat plain, but some enthusiast found that the Indians had called it *ni bthasca*, of which Platte was a translation, and this was freely remodelled to suit the public taste. Wyoming meant a flat place in the Delaware language and was first used for a small settlement in a valley which suffered a massacre by Indians. This incident inspired the English poet, Thomas Campbell, to write a sentimental poem, *Gertrude of Wyoming*, which helped to popularize the name and head it for statehood. Arizona too had a small beginning but was extended gradually over a wide region. Recorded at an early date by Spanish explorers, it meant 'the little spring'; then it was used by a mining company which brought it into public notice, and its splendid sound did the rest. Oklahoma consists of the words 'red man', put together by a Choctaw chief in 1866 when asked to suggest a name for land allotted to his tribe. Idaho was said by some to mean 'Gem of the Mountains', but this was an example of popular etymology at its most fanciful and its real origin is quite uncertain.

In naming states the final decision lay with Congress, the general policy being to settle on a name already in use locally and to concur with the wishes of the inhabitants. An exception was made when the Mormons found their promised land by the Great Salt Lake and wished to name it Deseret, a symbolic word in the Book of Mormon. This was unacceptable as a state-name, belonging as it did to a religion of which most of the nation disapproved, so the native river-name, Utah, was substituted. (The Mormons then renamed the river Jordan.) But on the whole these Indian state-names, which outnumber those of any one other language, were an expression of local feeling and became greatly and even fiercely loved from the moment of their inception. When it became clear that two states instead of one were to be made out of the plains where the Dakota tribe ranged, the white settlers in each part stood so firmly for the name Dakota, refusing any other, that North and South Dakota were created. This had obvious disadvantages, but the love of the name outweighed them.

Oregon is one of the state-names that has no known meaning, but what it lacks in etymology it makes up in history. While the French were still the chief explorers to the west they heard tales from Indians of a river beyond the great mountains that flowed into a western sea, and a name that was something like Oregon, though very variable in its early forms, was copied from an old French map and used by the men who strove to reach this almost legendary goal. When at last the Pacific coast was reached overland, the river down which the explorers made their final stages was already named by an American ship's captain, Robert Grey, who had discovered its mouth not long before, and named it Columbia after his ship. So the great river of the west which many had spoken of as Oregon never needed that name and it was given instead to the territory that lay beside it. This land too was something of a legend to many who desired to get there, a promised land which could only be reached by incredible effort over the famous Oregon trail. If ever a name was forged out of endurance and achievement it was Oregon.

Thus the Indian languages have carried the main burden of naming states, but in thinking of these native words that have been given special importance we must not omit to mention the thousands of lesser Indian names scattered all over the country. Some are little changed from their originals; some have become unrecognizable through English influence. Some are barbaric in sound, such as Oshkosh, the name of an Indian chief; but many have a musical rhythm that is very pleasing – Saratoga, Tallahassie, Tuscalosa. Some are amusing, or so they seem at the first hearing – Weewahitchka, Withawccopa, Sopchoppy. Every country should have some comical names – there are plenty in England – it adds to the pleasures of travel.

We have been thinking for the most part of names that were deliberately chosen, but all the time the natural names were growing beside them. In the newer countries these spontaneous names are often in danger of being jettisoned in favour of something more impressive or fashionable when development takes place, but nonetheless a great number of them manage to survive. Americans tend to be faithful to names that have once become identified with their homes, especially if any stirring incident has taken place to add an emotional association. Such names as Valley Forge, however humble in origin, are safe from change. Sometimes when a fine name was chosen for a town that was rising in importance the older natural name persisted in spite of it. When Little Rock became the state capital of Arkansas there was a move to rename it Arkopolis, but Little Rock stood firm, and long may it do so, a splendidly simple name that takes one right back to the first encampment on the spot. There cannot have been much there when a little rock was a landmark.

Many names of this type are harsh and inhospitable as the land was (Rattlesnake Buttes, Mud Lake, Deadman Gap, Stinking Water) and it is not surprising that they belong more often to natural features than to towns. And when one finds a town whose name has unpleasant associations an inquiry will often reveal that it belonged first to a stream or valley where settlers came later, accepting the name that was there. One would hardly choose Troublesome or War for one's home-town, but they exist. Each originally named a creek, one of which gave trouble by flooding, the other the scene of warfare with the Indians.

Names describing a milder setting have grown into use for towns and cities in large numbers: Pine Bluff, Rock Springs, Twin Falls, Three Forks, South Bend. In England, where practically all the names are of this type, farms grew into villages, and villages grew bigger so gradually that no one ever thought whether a name was suitable for a town or not. Liverpool means much the same as Mud Lake but no one ever questioned it. American pioneers were much more conscious of the future and could see a city in their minds while looking at mud or boulders. Consequently they often added this word to the natural description, as at Salt Lake City, but the basic physical truth remains.

These names have a freshness springing from reality that no manufactured name can quite equal. The simplest, where one word is enough, are perhaps the best, but they have to be a little unusual to avoid repetition. Flagstaff is a fine example. One can visualize it so plainly, that landmark in a wild land. Anchorage is good too. The same statement has been made in many countries and many languages, Le Havre, Porto, Poole, Wick. In hundreds of other cases something more has been added to these basic words, but these have needed nothing.

Wild beasts and birds have played a notable part in this natural naming. The elk and the beaver lead the way, each having well over forty places in the United States listed in *The Times World Atlas*, well ahead of George Washington with his thirty-four. Of course, far more places with these names could be found in more detailed maps, but the big atlas serves for a comparison. A great many of the animal names belong to creeks and other natural features, but many that began in that way have grown into towns. We have Beaver City, Beaverville, Eagletown, Elkton, Elk City, and many more fine names, lively and original. The big city of Buffalo began as Buffalo Creek; it was named from an Indian, but his name came from the animal, and how right the inhabitants were, when their town began to grow, just to drop 'Creek' instead of changing it to 'City'. Buffalo is strong and striking, better without trimmings.

It was not until the middle of the nineteenth century that the large regions of the south and west that had been colonized by Spain were incorporated in the United States. Then, to what was already a linguistic mixture, a great mass of Spanish names was added. They were romantic sounding names, many of them dating from the sixteenth and seventeenth centuries, including the oldest of European origin in the whole country (page 174); and Americans adopted them enthusiastically, changing only a very few.

The names that the Spaniards gave in their overseas possessions are very distinctive in character, formal, dignified and intensely religious. Their style, far removed from that of the English, reflects the different mentality of these two great nations. The Spanish loved religious symbolism, naming places Santa Cruz (the holy cross), Corpus Christi (the body of Christ), Sacramento (the holy Sacrament) and Conception over and over again, names of a type that is never found in England although it was fully named long before the Reformation. The Spanish also loved saints. This is paralleled to some extent in the Celtic parts of the British Isles, but in England few towns have saints' names, and in America they have been consistently avoided by English settlers. St Louis, St Paul, St Joseph and other well-known examples were named by Frenchmen.

So much Spanish exploration was accomplished by Jesuit and Franciscan friars toiling heroically over scorching deserts and inhospitable mountains, and so often the first settlement consisted of a white adobe mission church built to save souls, that it was natural that the dedication of the church should also serve to name the settlement that followed. But even when the first building was a fort, as at San Agostino (now St Augustine) in Florida, so named in 1565 by the cruel Don Pedro Menendes, or just a bay to be noted as useful harbour, as San Diego, written on an explorer's chart in 1602, a saint was chosen because the place was discovered on his day, a practice that many other explorers have followed. San Diego was a medieval Spanish friar who had not long been canonized when his name was placed on the Pacific coast.

The Spanish, following in the style that Columbus had initiated, delighted in long grandiose names. Santa Fe in California was founded and named in 1598 by Don Carlos Onate, who called it *La Villa Real de la Santa Fe de San Francisco*, the Royal Town of the Holy Faith of St Francis. Time did not alter Spanish verbosity, for nearly two centuries later another town nearer the coast was christened *El Pueblo de la Reina de los Angeles de la Porciúncula*.* The last word is the name of the little church at Assisi, built on land that was called literally 'the little portion' by St Francis. This system of lengthy naming worked out better in practice than one might expect, for the local inhabitants, who clearly could not repeat all that, could pick out the words that were most convenient for practical use. Both these places were really named in honour of St Francis, but Santa Fe and Los Angeles are completely different names, and the straightforward San Francisco was still available for a big bay further up the coast.

Of course the Spaniards, like everyone else, spoke of their discoveries in natural words, and did not always make up elaborate names to replace them. No name could be more natural than Rio Grande, the big river, or El Paso, the crossing place. Las Vegas is only 'the plains', Sierra† Nevada 'the snow-covered range', and Colorado with its glorious rolling syllables simply 'red'. No one who has seen this great river flowing through its canyon of red sandstone cliffs will need to ask why it is called the red river. And how much finer it sounds in Spanish.

American place-names have been created by Indians, English

* The town of the Queen of the Angels of the little portion.
† *Sierra*, used for a range of jagged peaks, means literally 'a saw'.

sovereigns, Spanish grandees, French Jesuits, seamen, explorers, hunters, trappers, mountain men, businessmen, Congressmen, and a host of ordinary settlers of both sexes; in fact, one might say, by representatives of the entire population, but especially by those who have shown enterprise, energy and an adventurous spirit.

The first pioneers were often unlettered people who could choose a name without knowing how to spell it. A group who settled in Missouri wanted to call their new home Raleigh, after the town in North Carolina from which they had set out, but they wrote it Rolla. So it remains, and so it has been repeated farther west. In contrast to them were the men of education who could produce classical names such as Phoenix, for a town to be built on the site of a burnt-out Indian village, or Akron (Greek, 'summit') for the highest point of a projected canal route.

Many place-names were chosen by vote at town meetings and other local gatherings, and there too names given by the first arrivals were discussed and often rejected as too uncivilized for a later taste. In this way Whiskey Hill and Mosquito Gulch, both in California, were changed by their residents to Freedom and Glencoe. Decisions were not always easily reached and in one place in Kentucky the matter was so hotly disputed that the only name that could be agreed on was Disputanta. In 1950 the inhabitants of a town with the factual name of Hot Springs were persuaded to change it to 'Truth or Consequences' by the promoters of a radio programme of that name, who offered practical inducements. A general vote of the inhabitants was just in favour of the remarkable change.

It fell to the lot of certain individuals to give many names. Explorers naturally are in this class, though some (like Drake, for instance) have given none that have lasted. A notable journey in the history of American naming was that led by Captain Lewis and his assistant, Captain Clark, in 1804. The expedition was sent out by President Jefferson to follow the Missouri to its source and find a way across the mountains to the Pacific coast. By the end of the following year the party had reached their goal, having charted hundreds of miles of rugged country, and given a name to every landmark of importance.

The instructions given the two captains by Jefferson had probably included advice about names, for those that they gave were all of a high standard, straightforward and truthful while avoiding repetition. A rough hillside where they held a council with some Indians became Council Bluffs; a river with cloudy water 'of a peculiar whiteness', the Milk River; and when Lewis discovered the great falls of the Missouri he was so struck with 'the sublime spectacle of this stupendous object' that he only wrote Great Falls on his map, letting the truth speak for itself. In their party they had some French trappers who knew of names given or recorded by their own countrymen as far as they had penetrated, and also some Indians, including a squaw with a papoose on her back, who turned out to be the best guide of them all, knowing the worst part of the mountains as her homeland. So they were able to record and keep many earlier names besides those they gave themselves. Of course they honoured Jefferson with a fine river, and most of the members of the party had their names given to some rock or creek or chasm. Even the papoose, whom they nicknamed Pompey, lives on in Pompeys Pillar, a rocky pinnacle in Yellowstone Park (which itself translates the Indian name). Eventually, when all was satisfactorily concluded an admiring nation named two towns in the newly opened-up region Lewiston and Clarkston, and other parts of the country followed with variations on the theme.

Other men, though of less individual fame, whose work led to much name-giving, were surveyors for roads and railways and officials of the Post Office. A general instruction, in the late nineteenth century, that no new Post Office could be registered under a name that already existed in the same state meant that names chosen by local people could be rejected; if they could produce no new ideas the department would supply something. Sometimes the local population was almost non-existent, or too widely scattered to consult. The store-keeper who looked after the post might scratch his head in vain, with no help but that of a few illiterate cronies who tended to crack jokes. It was this kind of situation that produced names like Wynot in Nebraska and Difficult in Tennessee. A last resort when a chosen name had been rejected was to spell it backwards, the origin of Tesnus in Texas. But perhaps it was even worse to admit defeat and write to the Post Office Department for a ready-made name to be sent by return. Better a local joke, however weak, than a soulless thing picked out by a clerk in an office hundreds of miles away.

But difficulty in finding names is anything but typical of the American people, and if I were to select any one general impression of their name-giving it would be that as a race they are highly creative in this respect, with a special feeling for a sonorous rhythm. They have used the Latin ending -a or -ia widely, and more because they like the sound of it than for any great love of the classics. When a name was needed for the terminus of the Western and Atlantic Railroad in 1845, the constructor of the line suggested Atlanta and the directors accepted it with enthusiasm. When 'Indian Territory' seemed a bulky phrase, a sure instinct reduced it to Indiana. The names of nearly all the later-constituted states were chosen for euphony rather than meaning. If Colorado and Nevada had been translated into English, would they have been considered for a moment? Red and Snowy? It was their romantic sounds that won them statehood.

Of course there are ugly names too, plenty of them, and absurd ones, especially for smaller places where the racy local speech has produced such jocular expressions as Rabbit Hash and Possumtrot, Hardscrabble and Knuckles. Then there are the border names consisting of half each of two adjoining states, Texico, Calexico, Mexicali. There is every kind. 'A terrible mix-up,' an American friend remarked. A 'mix-up', certainly. That is what it had to be.

Chapter 19

CANADA

Much that has been written about the place-names of the United States applies also to those of Canada, and along their three thousand miles of frontier hundreds of names are held in common. But there are marked differences. The Spanish element, so strong in parts of the United States, is lacking in Canada, where a sprinkling of Portuguese names on the eastern coasts is the sole legacy of the great wave of exploration that set out from the Iberian Peninsula. On the other hand, French names, which in the States are only a legacy from the colonial period, play a far more dominant part in Canada, where French remains a living language in which new names are still being coined.

As to the antiquity of its naming, Canada has a decided lead over its neighbour. The first recorded name in the United States is Florida, given in 1513, when the names Labrador and Newfoundland had already been in use for a decade, and several places on the Newfoundland coast were known to cartographers by their present names. And in the summer of 1534, the year before Cortez set out for California, when Drake and Raleigh were unborn and Elizabeth Tudor a baby, the Breton sea-captain, Jacques Cartier, rounded the northern point of Newfoundland and entered the great gulf which is the gateway to Canada, and along whose shores he gave and recorded many names.

The original journals of Cartier's voyages still exist, the first written apparently by himself, and the second by one of his ship's company, so we can share his wonder and delight in all that he saw. Like many French explorers he displayed a lively interest not only in the beauty of the scene but also in the native inhabitants and was quick to establish friendly relations with every group of them he met.

Near the entrance of the gulf he mentions names – Belle Isle, for instance, from which the straits take their name, and Blanc Sablon, the 'white sands' on the northern shore – as if they were already known, a sign that other French seamen had been there. But once he was well inside the gulf the names were all his own or what he learned from Indians. He gave them in a straightforward seamanlike way, describing what he saw or felt as each new bay or headland came in sight, and remembering the saints on their appropriate days. From that first voyage only a few of them have survived, among them La Baie de Chaleur, or Chaleur Bay as the English call it, where the water shimmered in the heat haze of July, one of many names that sound much better in French. Heat Bay would be insupportable. Full of hope that he would find a way to the East Indies, he called the point on its southern side Cap D'Esperance. This was remembered by later comers, although located a little differently on a headland across the bay, now officially Cap D'Espoir. English sailors, sticking closer to the sound than the sense, call it Cape Despair.

In the following summer he came again and penetrated farther. On 9 August the wind, veering round against him, forced him to seek shelter in a little bay on the northern coast, and as it was St Lawrence's day he heard mass and named it *la baie Saint Laurens*. He had given many names along that shore and could not guess that, while others would be little known or forgotten altogether, this one would emerge from its bay – where it is no longer to be found – and extend itself over a thousand miles of seaway. The bay was opposite Anticosti Island (an Indian name oddly contracted) and later seamen may have called the passage between them by the name of the bay, from which it spread farther. Whatever the cause, it was one of those names that grow far beyond the imagination of their begetters. Well into the next century official French maps showed the great seaway only as La Grande Rivière de Canada, but the saint's name must have been slowly gaining in use among the seamen and *habitants* of the gulf until eventually it became the accepted title of one of the great rivers of the world.

The very next day an even greater name was recorded in Cartier's journal. At the end of his first voyage he had taken two Indians back to France with him, and now had them with him as guides and interpreters. They told him of three 'kingdoms', the lands of their kindred and allies, which he would find further upstream – Saguenay, Canada and Hochelaga. The first lay along the banks of the river that is still called the Saguenay. The second, Canada, written on that day in 1535 exactly as it is today, comprised the region a little further upstream, where the Indians had a village called Stadacona (later known by another Indian word, Quebec). When Cartier put Canada on his chart he had no conception of its future.

On 3 October his ship anchored close to the third 'kingdom', the large encampment of Hochelaga. The Indian inhabitants received him joyfully, and after a feast of welcome led him up to the summit of a steep, nearby hill which gave a view far to the west. Cartier was much struck by the beauty of what he saw – '*La terre, la plus belle qu'il soit possible de voir*' – but there was disappointment too. Instead of the hoped-for, distant ocean lay only unending hills and forests, brilliant in autumn colouring, and the river as glimpsed among them, foaming in fearful rapids. This was his furthest point westwards, and realizing the significance of the occasion he named the hill on which he stood Mont Royal, thinking of his king, Francis I, who had sent him on this quest.

Mont Royal, long since contracted to Montreal, is the oldest recorded name of any city on the American mainland north of Mexico. However, there was no permanent habitation in that place for a full century after Cartier's visit. The next we hear of it is when Champlain came there in 1603. The Indian village had gone, and though he realized the strategic importance of the place as the farthest navigable point up the great river, he began no settlement. The chief interest to him lay in the rapids or falls that barred the way, for which he used the French word *sault* or 'leap'. He called them the Sault St Louis, and this might well have become the name of the city, making a pair with Sault Ste Marie, named fifty years later and five hundred miles farther west. But in 1642 the Catholic missionaries, who were never more than one step behind the first explorers, founded a religious house on the flat land between Cartier's *mont* and Champlain's *sault*. It was dedicated to the Virgin, and as a town began to grow around it, became known as Ville Marie. If the British had not won Canada, its biggest city today might be Villemarie, but they came into possession in 1763 and, as they had never much cared for names with a 'popish' sound, they preferred the older name that was still current for the mount. Because it had existed so long – over two hundred years – chiefly in the colloquial speech of the French Canadians, it had been contracted naturally into one word and somewhat changed in pronunciation according to the local usage – just as names were in England in early times – and it was in this popular form that it became official, Montreal.

If we have lingered over Cartier's names – and we could easily stay much longer – it is because beginnings are always important. Columbus's long-winded religious style foreshadowed the manner of Spanish naming in the New World for centuries to come, and Cartier's much more simple and varied manner was typical of the French.

Throughout the seventeenth century French pioneers from Champlain onwards explored and named the vast area drained by the St Lawrence. They were soldiers, missionaries, fur traders, *coureurs de bois*, aristocrats and farmers; they endured incredible adventures in rivers, lakes and forests, travelling and living with Indians, sometimes dying of their tortures. Some of the lands that they named became later part of the States, and their style of naming has been discussed on pages 192–5. It is chiefly characterized by a pleasing variety and spontaneity closely related to the natural scene. They used saints' names, but not to excess; they paid tribute to their king and other notabilities – Champlain for instance named the Richelieu River for the great cardinal who at that time dominated France – but such names were given sparingly. Far more often they were content simply to state the nature of the place, as at Trois Rivières, an important junction of canoe routes, or to describe it with a swift touch of imagery. The River Chaudière (cauldron) seemed to boil; the Rideau (curtain) was named from falls that hung smooth and shining as silk; Fort Qu'Appelle (Who calls?) guarded a rocky defile where voices echoed strangely; the village of Gran'Mere was close to a rock that

217

looked like an old woman. They could laugh at each other in their new surroundings too. When the Sieur de la Salle (he who later voyaged right down the Mississippi) built himself a farm above the Sault St Louis in 1671 it was mockingly called La Chine (China) because that was where he was hoping to get to. It is still Lachine, a busy suburb of Montreal.

But perhaps their greatest gift to the naming of Canada is their recording of Indian words, now known to all the world. For their principal settlement, Quebec, founded in 1608, they proclaimed no grand religious or royal name as the Spaniards or English would have done but were content with the native word which meant the narrows. It was a significant word, for here, for the first time, the great river is penned in between high cliffs, making an obvious defensive point, the key to Canada in later days. And how right they were to keep this name, for it is unique in the world and, rooted in local truth, a name that many cities might envy.

The exploration of Canada was accomplished largely by water and this is fully reflected in its best-known Indian names. The provinces Ontario, Manitoba, Yukon and Saskatchewan all take their names from lakes and rivers. The last means 'swift flowing', Yukon simply 'the river', and Manitoba is the water of the great spirit Manito. Ottawa also was the name of a river long before it was chosen for a city. But primarily it was the name of the tribe who inhabited its banks, and whose braves arranged their hair elaborately high on their heads, though otherwise they went stark naked.

To French exploration we owe all the names of the Great Lakes, whether their origins were French or Indian. Superior and Michigan, being largely in the States, have been mentioned on page 193. Ontario means simply fine or beautiful lake (the ending 'io' being a term of commendation as in Ohio). There remain Erie and Huron, both called from their dominant Indian tribes, but both in their final forms owing more to French than to Indian speech. Around Erie lived a tribe who called themselves the panthers. The French called it *le lac des chats*, but they used the native word too, which at first was written down as Yenris but later simplified to Erie. Huron is a French word implying a likeness to a wild boar. In France it was used for peasants because of their rough, bristling hair and as applied to these Indians it referred to the way they forced their hair to stand up in a sort of crest, somewhat in the style of the Ottawas. The French had many dealings with the Hurons or 'boar-heads' that were generally but not always friendly.

One of the most famous names in North America, Niagara, is also one of the most obscure. The falls were not discovered very early, because in that wild land where lakes and rivers were the only highways cascades on a grand scale were thought of rather as obstacles than as beauty spots to be visited. When Indians told of high falls ahead, the keen explorer looked for a different route. It is not known for certain who was the first white man to see Niagara, possibly Ettienne Brulé, who made several journeys alone, before being killed and eaten by the Hurons, in about 1632. Some ten years later the name begins to appear in the accounts of Jesuit missionaries, but scarcely recognizable, as Ongniaahra. Like the rocks in the falls it was gradually whittled down to something smoother, and the fanciful etymology 'thunder of the water' developed. It is now agreed that the name is derived from Iroquois words which did not describe the falls directly, but the neck of land between two lakes that the Niagara river cuts through. 'Land cut in two' is one attempt at translation. But it has created a significance of its own that is known throughout the world, and its final form has a wild, vigorous sound that suits it well.

The French had been exploring, settling and naming the vast territory that they called New France for over two centuries before it was conquered by England in the Seven Years War, and even then another twenty years were to pass before a large body of English settlers came to share it with them. These were the Loyalists who came as refugees from the American states in 1783. It is from that date that the naming of Canada by the British began on a large scale.

But long before then a few outposts of this northern land had been settled or at least explored by British enterprise, and we must look back to them for the first English-Canadian names. First in the field was Cabot who left no recognizable name. But contemporary with his voyages and closely allied with them there arose the natural name Newfoundland (page 172), which he must have heard and used often as he talked with his crew or his English patrons.

Next came the names on Newfoundland itself which began to grow from that time onwards. Something has been said of these on page 173. They consist of a charming and lively mixture of Indian, Portuguese, French and English, many of the most inexplicable (Quidi Vidi, Goobles, Renews, and so forth), being corruptions of other people's names made by illiterate sailors. Even the Indian names such as the Annieopsquosh Mountains seem to have a more humorous character than elsewhere.

Just across the water from Newfoundland, where the continental coast jutted out towards it, the British planted another lasting name of a very different sort at an early date, Nova Scotia. This was concocted by Sir William Alexander, a Scottish poet and courtier who came into England with James I as tutor to his sons. The theme, New Scotland, was as pleasing to the king as to himself, and it was as natural as breathing to these two scholars to put it into Latin. It was in 1621 that the king gave Sir William a charter granting him 'jurisdiction over Nova Scotia'. The fact that the French were in occupation of that region (which they called by the native name Acadie) was ignored, but proved a difficulty. During the following century several attempts to plant settlers had no success, and no permanent name was established by the British until 1710 when the French Port Royal was finally captured and renamed Annapolis in honour of Queen Anne. Three years later, by the Treaty of Utrecht, Acadie was ceded to Britain and Nova Scotia, coined long before, became something more than a name. (See map on p. 191.)

For another forty years Annapolis remained an English stronghold in a land peopled by French and Indians, but in 1749 Parliament decided on a serious attempt at colonization, and sent out over three thousand English settlers to build a town for a new capital. It was named Halifax, after the Marquis of Halifax, President of the Board of Trade, who had been active in the affair, and who is called on his monument in Westminster Abbey 'the Father of the Colonies'. This type of name-giving was to be much used all round the Empire in the following century.

But now we must turn to another early outpost – one that is still remote from all the busy centres of population, but which received permanent English names even before King James's charter for Nova Scotia. This is the ice-bound region where English seamen sought for the North-West Passage from the reign of Queen Elizabeth. There was no rivalry here from other nations to displace their names; and because each of the sea-captains was glad to profit by the others' experience, the seas and coasts they charted became known from the time they were first seen by the names of those who found them. They are all there still: Frobisher Bay, discovered by Martin Frobisher in 1576, Davis Straits, where John Davis sailed in 1585, Baffin Bay and Baffin Island, first charted by William Baffin in 1616, and many others down to Sir John Franklin, who was lost in a northern expedition in 1847 and whose name is now written across a thousand miles of Arctic territory. And since then more still.

Of the early explorers the greatest was Henry Hudson, and no large geographical feature in the world has the name of its discoverer more dramatically stamped upon it than Hudson Bay. Here in 1610 his hopes soared in the belief that he had at last reached the open ocean on which he could sail to China and Japan, only to be dashed months later as the farther shores of the enormous bay barred his progress endlessly. Here, when he refused to turn back in spite of approaching winter, his mutinous crew set him adrift in a small open boat with his son and left them to their death among the ice-floes. After this dreadful event – admitted by the mutineers when they reached England – this bay was never spoken of by any name but his.

But hope continued and the next year an expedition set out under Thomas Button to sail to Japan by way of 'Hudson, his Bay'. He wintered in the Bay and finding no way westwards came safely back having left his name in Button Bay where he had sheltered. While he was there his navigator, Master Nelson, died and Button named a large river in honour of this honest seaman. A few years later Thomas James explored the southernmost waters of Hudson Bay, and from him James Bay is named, not from the king as one might suppose. By this time Charles 1 was on the throne and Captain James's ship was

H*

called after the queen, Henrietta Maria, a name that he left on a prominent cape.

It was not till the reign of Charles II that the great Hudson Bay Company was founded, the oldest trading company in the world. Its first chairman of directors was the king's cousin, Prince Rupert, who had won fame in the Civil War, and the charter given by the king granting a large, vaguely defined territory to the Company (kings never hesitated to give away unknown lands) named it Rupertsland. This name lasted until the middle of the nineteenth century when a new arrangement of territories squeezed it out; but Rupert's name survives in that region on a river, a bay and a trading post. And far away on the Pacific when a name was wanted for a new coastal town, and a public competition organized to find one, the choice fell on 'Prince Rupert'. So the gallant prince is not forgotten in Canada.

Two other forts built on Hudson Bay as trading posts were called York and Albany (the latter also naming a fine river) from the titles of the king's brother, soon to be James II. These may be compared with New York and Albany, USA, named after the same unfortunate prince a few years earlier. And another of the distinguished chairmen of directors at about the same time, John Churchill, later Duke of Marlborough, also had a river and a fort. Many people glancing at the map of Canada and seeing the names of Nelson and Churchill side by side on the shores of Hudson Bay must think that they are of modern origin commemorating the two great men who come first to our minds today. But they are personal links with Charles II's reign.

From these first English names on the fringes of what is now Canada we return to the time just after the War of Independence when the loyalists from America came to settle in the northern land which remained British (though it had been so only a short time) and where other Scots and English colonists soon joined them. And before going further we must stress the important part played by the Scots in the peopling of Canada. This was partly due to the fact that whole Highland regiments which had been used in the American war were disbanded and compensated with Canadian land. But more important was the

poverty and distress in the Highlands at that time which
caused many Scots to seek a livelihood elsewhere. Thus came
not only a flow of individuals but large organized migrations
such as that of the Catholic Macdonalds of Glengarry who came
in a body in 1802, led by their hereditary chief who became
also their bishop, to settle on the upper shores of the St Lawrence,
and the large project launched by the Earl of Selkirk in 1811 to
plant Highlanders on the Red River. These and other settlements brought the bagpipes and the Gaelic tongue to Canada
from its first beginnings as a British country, and a race of
hardy Scottish pioneers whose names are now scattered widely
over it.

In all the young countries settled overseas by people of
British stock certain regular types of name have been given by
them, which may be briefly classified as royal names, names of
distinguished men, ready-made place-names imported from the
British Isles, romantic and literary names, and natural un-
planned ones arising from local conditions. We see all these in
Canada corresponding very closely to those in the United
States, but in each class there is a difference that comes from
historic causes, and though the same styles are apparent, there
is remarkably little repetition between the two countries.

It is with tributes to royalty that loyal colonists are inclined
to begin: in America, Jamestown; in French Canada, Port
Royal; and in British Canada, as soon as the United Empire
Loyalists had established themselves just over the border, they
expressed their feelings with the name of Kingston. This
theme, which had come to a sudden halt in the newly formed
United States, was now carried forward enthusiastically by its
neighbour.

These royal names are easily identifiable and only a few
need be mentioned. New Brunswick, constituted out of part of
Nova Scotia in 1784, honoured the German prince who had
married George III's eldest sister, and its capital Fredericton
(formerly St Annes) was named for the king's second son, later
Duke of York. Prince Edward Island had been St John's
Island, but there were far too many St Johns in that region and
in 1798 it was changed as a compliment to the king's fourth
son who was then resident in Quebec as commander of the
army. He was shortly to be made Duke of Kent and then to

223

attain a greater claim to fame as the father of Queen Victoria. The capital of this island, Charlottetown, had been named for his mother thirty years earlier (replacing the charming Port la Joie). Skating rapidly over Victoria's large family we will mention only Lake Louise, named for her fourth daughter who was then the wife of the Governor-General, and Port Arthur on Lake Superior which commemorates the visit of her third son in 1866, later the Duke of Connaught.

It was typical that Victoria's influence ensured that the largest area available should be attached to the name of her beloved Albert, tastefully latinized as Alberta. At the same date (1882) a name was required for the capital of the adjoining province, Saskatchewan, and a general wish expressed that it should honour the Queen. As Victoria was already in use for a fine new city growing on the Pacific coast, a variation was achieved (at the suggestion of Princess Louise) by using the Latin word, Regina.

From the names of royalties we pass naturally to those of other individuals of distinction; and Canada is to be commended in having honoured in this way chiefly those most closely connected with her own history. There is indeed a sprinkling of English statesmen who were admired from a distance: we noted, for instance, the name of Halifax among its first English settlements, and, in the same region, Shelburne was named not long after for the current prime minister. But as time went on more and more places were named from men personally connected with the country, and conversely those who served her outstandingly have nearly all their place.

From a great number in this class we can pick out only a few. First, Sir Guy Carleton, a great governor and soldier whose gallant defence of Quebec against the Americans in 1775-6 was the chief factor in saving Canada for Britain. Afterwards, as Commander in Chief of the British forces in America, he became the rallying point for the loyalists and was foremost in organizing their settlement in Canada. Guysborough, in Nova Scotia, was named for him, its first inhabitants being mainly his disbanded soldiers. Both his surname and his title – he became Lord Dorchester – are preserved in towns of the Maritime Provinces.

Then there was John Simcoe, first governor of Upper

Canada, from whom Lake Simcoe is named, and General Sherbrooke who had distinguished himself in the Peninsular War under Wellington and became Governor-General in 1816; the pleasant town of Sherbrooke south of Quebec being his memorial. His successor, Charles Lennox, Duke of Richmond, had also been with Wellington (it was his wife who had given the famous ball in Brussels on the eve of Waterloo). His term in office was not long for he died suddenly from the bite of a fox, but the names of Richmond and Lennoxville date from it. Another Scottish nobleman, and one who played a vigorous part in Canadian history, was the idealistic Earl of Selkirk who founded the Red River settlement and himself fought in a pitched battle against its rivals. He has a fine range of peaks, the Selkirk Mountains, and his family name, Douglas, occurs in many places. Inevitably James Wolfe, who won Canada for Britain in 1759 and died in the moment of victory, is on the map too, at Wolfe in Ontario for instance. But in Quebec, the scene of his triumph, the inhabitants are largely French, and for them the spot where he landed below the cliffs – Wolfe's Cove to the English – still keeps its French name, Anse au Foulon.

Those who have been best honoured with place-names, and appropriately so, are explorers. Sometimes this was a belated act of recognition, as in those few places christened Cabot and Cartier in the nineteenth century; but in many other cases the name dates from the time of discovery. Earlier in this chapter we noted some of the men who left their names in the icy north from the sixteenth century onwards, and the practice continued throughout the opening up of the west. Alexander Mackenzie, after his epic journey of 1789 down the great river two thousand miles in length that is second only to the Mississippi in North America, was inclined to name it Disappointment River, because instead of emerging into the Pacific, as he had hoped, it turned obstinately northwards and carried him into the Arctic Ocean, but to those who had sent him out and to the nation at large it became the Mackenzie, and later a great range of mountains and vast District were added to his honours. Soon after the turn of the century two more hardy Scots, David Thompson and Simon Fraser, successively crossed the Rockies and explored rivers which did bring them to the Pacific and which now bear their names.

Probably the sea-captain whose name has made the most impact in Canada, apart from Hudson, was George Vancouver, an Englishman in spite of his Dutch name, who surveyed the west coast in an English ship in 1792. He had been there fourteen years earlier serving under Captain Cook, who was in fact the real discoverer of the island that would later bear the name of his midshipman. But Vancouver when he came again as a captain was the first to chart it in detail and prove that it was an island. Nearly a century later the city that had grown up opposite the island also received his name, an unusual, and impressive one; Cook was by far the greater man, but his one short syllable was uninspiring, and on that coast it remained only on an Alaskan inlet.

Many of the principal towns of Canada, especially in the west, began as fortified trading posts, where Indians brought their furs to the agent of one of the great trading companies, and sometimes the man in charge, known familiarly by his first name, has left it there for posterity. One such place is Fort William on Lake Superior, which sounds like a royal name. It belonged, however, to William MacGillivray, who established the fort for the North Western Company in 1802. Another is Jasper, which immortalizes Jasper Hawes, who manned the post there in 1817. These names have their roots in reality.

And the pioneers who built their log cabins in virgin land are also represented. Hamilton in Ontario is not named from a duke of that title, as one might guess, but from plain George Hamilton who started a farm there in 1812. Peterborough in the same province was inspired by the first name of Colonel Peter Robinson, the official leader of a party of Irish emigrants, who settled there in 1825.

The name of Peterborough brings us to that strong tendency of the British overseas to reproduce the names of their native land. In this case the place was named after a man, but that form was chosen because it sounded like an English town. This British habit has been practised enthusiastically in Canada and there is no more confident and complete piece of naming in this class, to be found anywhere, than in Ontario, where London in the county of Middlesex stands on the river Thames. Many Canadians feel pride and satisfaction in this London that is all their own; others are aware that, to the world at large, it must always be 'London, Ontario' and the necessity for a qualification is a weakness.

To my mind results have been better when the names of smaller towns and villages from the British Isles, not famous themselves – and there are thousands of them – have been given a new life overseas. I think of Calgary, for instance, a little inlet on the sparsely populated island of Mull, with a few grey cottages and one big house, then of the rich and vigorous city of the prairies, teaming with life, at least a thousand times as big as its parent, if measured by population. This is a happy relationship. If the people of Calgary, Alberta, ever think of the origin of their name they have the kindest feelings for that little Hebridean bay, while the few inhabitants there feel a glow of pride in their large offspring. As to the meaning of the name, that is something remote and obscure. It was probably given by Norsemen, for all those islands were once part of a Viking kingdom, and it may have meant an enclosure for calves, which would not be at all amiss for the scene of Alberta's great rodeo. But Colonel MacLeod, who named the Canadian town in 1876 – it having formerly borne his own name as Fort McLeod – was not thinking of etymology, only of his boyhood home.

This was the spirit in which hundreds of British names were given right across Canada. One settler taking up land called it after his English school, Haileybury, others remembered a farm or house, or a whole region such as Cornwall. They speak for themselves.

Every type of place-name that people of British stock have given in the United States can be found also in Canada, the moral abstraction (Fort Resolution, for example, and Unity); the classical (Arcadia, Neptune, Marathon); the romantic-historical (Albion, Plantagenet, Viking) the fanciful-poetical (Moonbeam) and the literary. This last class includes many of the same favourites that are found south of the border, such as Auburn and Waverley, but Canada had her own way of honouring literary genius: a large town named Stratford on the river Avon complete with a Shakespeare Theatre.

On the whole there is a lower proportion in Canada of what we may call 'fanciful' names, and in most of the classes mentioned above examples are not numerous. There is also much less use of Latin and Greek endings than in the States. The real strength of Canadian naming lies in something much more spontaneous and closer to reality, the natural names that have sprung from local facts. All countries have this type of name, and those of Canada, the English as well as the French, are particularly vigorous and lively. They show us the country as it really is: Swift Current, Maple Creek, Smoky Lake, Caribou Mountains, Red Deer, Goose Bay, Great Bear Lake, White Horse, named from the white-foaming rapids in the river, and Moose Jaw, which is not clearly explained but perhaps a landmark on a trapper's trail. Many reflect contact with Indians and often translate their words. On the Great Slave Lake one tribe kept prisoners from another in subjection; on the Peace River warring tribes had made peace; Medicine Hat is a translation of the Indian name and the exact explanation is controversial; two or three rival stories exist, concerned with the hat of a medicine man that was either stolen or captured in a fight or stuck up on a pole. Thunder Bay echoes a tribal legend of the dreaded Thunderbird that swooped with dark wings over the sea. Sioux Lookout explains itself.

Natural naming goes steadily on in modern times. Telegraph Creek, Port Radium, Uranium City are the real thing – how far removed from Arcadia and Moonbeam. But all kinds are needed to give variety and all kinds are there. Canadians have called some of their rivers Severn, Thames and Avon, but they also have the Red River, the Rat, the Moose and the Beaver, and these are more truly their own.

It has happened in Canada that place-names have been more subject to change than in almost any other British community. This is a direct result of her very stormy early history, in which Europeans were pitted against Indians, French against English, Canadians (French, Indian and English together) against Americans, and one great fur-trading company against the other. In this constant warfare names became symbols of supremacy, and changed back and forth with the fortunes of the opposing powers.

We have seen how Acadie fell a prey to the more pompous Nova Scotia, and the historic Rupertsland to the duller North West Territory; some other changes of importance must be noted. The French had honoured their greatest governor, the Comte de Frontenac, by giving his name to a strategic fort and the lake on which it stood. One of the first acts of the English Loyalists when they came into possession was to change Fort Frontenac to Kingston, and to revive the native Ontario for the lake. The former change is – in my opinion – regrettable. There are many Kingstons, and Frontenac would have been unique. It has a fine sound, and was a link with a great man worthy of generous treatment.

On the same lake the French had another fort that they called Fort Rouillé, after their colonial minister. The English – again more patriotic than original – renamed it Fort York, which already existed on Hudson Bay. The French continued to prefer their own name, and ten years later, when a large town was founded on this spot, the difficulty was resolved by reviving the native name Toronto. Its meaning is obscure – probably something to do with logs floating in the water – but that did not matter. It was individual, belonged to that place, and offended no susceptibilities. From this kind of experience the authorities grew wiser and when it came to naming the capital city to be built for the whole country, they chose after consultation with the Queen the Indian Ottawa (page 218).

Another city with a history of change is Winnipeg. It stands on the Red River which had been named by the French, and it appears first in the records as Fort Rouge. It lay in the untamed no-man's-land that the Hudson Bay Company claimed as its own, and early in the nineteenth century when Lord Selkirk, one of its chief directors, established his Scottish colony here it was renamed Fort Douglas, from his family name. But the North-Western Company of Montreal, which was also activated largely by Scottish enterprise, built a rival fort a short way up the river that they called Fort Gibraltar (implying that it would never yield) and fierce battles were fought between them. By 1836 a compromise was reached and a great stone fortress built, which was called Fort Garry, a Highland name with which the Scots on both sides had associations. It stood at the centre of canoe routes and wagon trails from all directions, and around it drifted a population of half-breed blood, Indian, French and Scottish – fur-trappers, buffalo-hunters, and adventurers of many kinds. For forty years, the name Fort Garry

229

epitomized the most romantic elements of the west. Then in the 1860s came administrative changes, extension of law and order, and a fashion for admiring Indian names. In the general reorganization the town around Fort Garry was given the name of the large nearby lake, Winnipeg. Its meaning is 'muddy water'. Those who want to make the best of it translate the adjective as 'cloudy' but its early translations include 'dirty' and 'stinking'. It is not known why this is so, for the lake seems clear. There is nothing against Winnipeg as a name, but it already existed on a lake and a river; Fort Garry, which had survived a tough period and grown colourful in the process, deserved to go on to city honours and not be relegated to a suburban position. All the cities of Britain that end in -burgh, -borough or -bury began as forts. If they had all changed their names when they became large towns, how great the loss would be.

Change is sometimes necessary. Some original names really will not do, and, in all the newer countries, natural names are liable to fall victims to civic pride. One can sympathize with the inhabitants of Mud Creek in Nova Scotia who, after seventy years, changed their name to Wolfeville. One can see too that some people might not care for Rat Portage and yet it is sad that it should have to go, exchanged for the mild sounding Kenora. Every portage where pioneers carried their canoes, sweating and toiling to reach navigable water, was rich in adventure. Many have held their place on the map and none should be lightly let go.

The trouble about changing names is that when you have done it once, you may be tempted to do it again. There was a settlement in Ontario known as Sandhills, then it went in for improvement and called itself Mount Pleasant. For a time it was also known as Ebytown from a leading local man. But something more impressive was wished for, and as it had a good many German residents it became Berlin and remained so for ninety years. In 1914 this proved an unfortunate choice, and was changed to Kitchener. Let us hope it is now stabilized.

Many of the early changes came from French and English rivalry, and in the Eastern Provinces the coexistence of the two languages still causes variability and strange effects. Where English settlers have taken over French names there may be a translation, often a poor one or merely a rough approximation of the sound, but these being produced by simple unpretentious people have often more charm than a correct translation could achieve. Lake Sally, for Lac Salé, is much better than Muddy Lake, and Passenjammers more entertaining than Passage à Mer. Where the French have taken over from the English – and as their rate of increase is much higher, this has been happening in several areas in recent times – they have tended to retain the English name for official use, but to add something of their own to it, generally the dedication of their church. This has resulted in such curious mixtures as St Jacques de Leeds, L'Ascension d'Inverness and Sacré Coeur de Jésus de Crabtree Mills.

This precarious balance between French and English, so clearly mirrored in names, belongs only to the province of Quebec. Elsewhere, in spite of much immigration from other European countries, English, Scottish and native names share the honours. From Victoria in the south to Old Crow on the Porcupine River in the Arctic, the full range of typical British naming can be found from 'royal-respectful' to 'local-natural' with native words to make variety. There is much less repetition in Canada than in the States, and the only cause for regret is that so many historic names have been changed. In spite of that, hundreds of original names – both French and English – do remain from the earliest settlements, and Canada's place-names are as full of exciting history as those of any country in the world.

Chapter 20

SOUTHERN AFRICA

The first knowledge that the English had of Africa was in the fifteenth century when their ships began to adventure down its Atlantic coast in the wake of the Portuguese. We know that they were there, for in 1481 the king of Portugal asked Edward IV of England to restrain his subjects from encroaching on 'the seignurie of Guinea'. How much they were restrained is doubtful. Their dealings with Guinea continued sporadically and profitably, and they brought back its name to England with the significance of high-quality gold. Meanwhile they picked up other African names and some that the Portuguese had given, such as Sierra Leone, the lion mountains, so named because the sound of thunder among the peaks was like roaring; and they scattered a few words of their own along that huge mysterious shore, simple words such as Gold Coast, which lasted for four hundred years but is gone now, replaced by the African Ghana.

In more modern times the establishment of British colonies brought more English names to this coast. Some have gone but several notable ones remain – at the time of writing – as relics of a period of service that did something to atone for earlier depredations. There is Freetown in Sierra Leone, founded as a settlement for liberated slaves, Bathurst in Gambia, and Port Harcourt in Nigeria, both named for English colonial ministers. However, all that north-western coast is now so African in character and the surviving English names so few that we pass it quickly, going on to South Africa where English settlers have given names in large numbers that are still in secure use among their descendants.

With a large territory to be named, it is a tremendous asset, as previously noticed, to have the use of several languages, and in this respect South Africa is certainly not lacking, having the variety given by Portuguese, Dutch, English, and a number of native tongues. Of the European languages Portuguese has left the fewest names, but they include the oldest and some of the most famous.

In May 1488, four years before Columbus's first voyage, the Portuguese seaman, Bartholomew Diàz, seeking a way to India, passed a headland and found the coast at last turning eastwards. Because of the rough weather he was meeting he named it Cabo Tormentoso, the cape of storms, but on his return King John of Portugal, rejoicing that the way seemed now open to the Indies, as indeed it was, named it Boa Esperanca or Good Hope. This became so famous a name and its meaning so well understood in all European countries that many nations still speak of it in their own words, while the common noun that signified that literal turning-point in world exploration, the *Cabo, Cavo, Cap, Kaap*, or Cape, has alone named South Africa's oldest province and most historic town. No city in the world has a simpler or more natural name than Cape Town, or Kaapstad.

It was fifteen years after Diàz's voyage that another Portuguese captain, Antonio de Saldanha, landed in the bay sheltered by this cape and climbed and named the mountain that rises behind it. Its flat top with the white cloud hanging over it like a cloth suggested the obvious metaphor, in his language *Mesa*, but carried on by the Dutch and English as *Taafel* and Table. At first the bay was known as Agoada de Saldanha ('Saldanha's watering place') but being dominated by Table Mountain it became Table Bay, and Saldanha's name was transferred to the next opening to the north.

Meanwhile on Christmas Day, 1497, Vasco da Gama, the first European to reach India by sea, had named another stretch of coast farther eastwards, using the Portuguese word for Christmas, *Natale*. This method of naming places by dates has been employed by explorers all over the world producing a good variety of names – Dominica (Sunday), Ascension Island, Easter Island, Christmas Island and many others. The advantages of their different languages is apparent; Natal has

233

always been a distinctive name, its origin almost forgotten in its strong, individual African character.

Since the Portuguese made no attempt to settle at the Cape their names there are coastal only. Algoa Bay (lagoon) and Santa Cruz Island ('holy cross', now called Sainte Croix) were named by Diàz. Cape Algulhas on the southernmost point of Africa means 'the needles', because of its sharp rocks, reminiscent of the Isle of Wight in name but very different in physical character.

It was not until 1652 that the Dutch made their first permanent settlement at the Cape, having regarded it hitherto, as the Portuguese also did, chiefly as an obstruction to be got round on the way to India. For the next hundred and fifty years they had as much of it as they wanted to themselves except for the Hottentots who were gradually driven away or subjugated. They showed no interest in Hottentot names, but named the land in their own way as they spread over it, and when – after the Napoleonic Wars – it came under British rule they still kept on moving outwards, farther and farther, occupying new lands and naming in their own language.

The British in their turn when they came into possession changed a few Dutch names, but the vast majority remained, and now those given by the two races are so intermingled that both seem equally the heritage of the modern South African. This feeling is aided by the close relation and likeness between the languages, many place-names such as the Fish River, the Sand River, and the Salt River being so similar that they may be felt to belong to either language. Besides this, the names given by the British were to some extent influenced by those of the Dutch and vice versa; therefore we must think of them all as part of the same story.

At the first glance the names of Dutch origin are simple and straightforward, abounding in natural description, as in Rondesbosch, the round wood, and Modderfontein, the muddy spring. Because it was a hot, dry land a supply of water made a focal point for a new settlement; hence, the frequent occurrence of 'fontein' which means a natural spring, though to the English ear it suggests something more elaborate. Bloemfontein was probably a spring among flowers, though there is a school of thought that claims that it once belonged to a farmer named Jan Bloem.

But Dutch naming at the Cape had more imagination in it than is sometimes said. The district called the Paarl (Pearl) took its name in the first few years of the settlement from the smooth, round boulders, set high on a ridge and shining like pearls in the sunlight; while the Drakensberg (Dragon Mountain) was dark and formidable. And at the time of the Great Trek when the Boers, as the Dutch farmers had come to be known, set out with all their families to find themselves new lands, their adventures and emotions were faithfully reflected in their naming; Weenen (weeping) commemorates the massacre of a large party of *trekkers*, with all their women and children, by the treacherous Zulu chief Dingaan in 1838; Blood River records their revenge later in the same year when they killed three thousand Zulus in one battle. Their passion for independence is expressed in the town-names Vryheit (freedom) and Vryburg (free town).

Independence was the essence of their character from the start, and, unlike the English, they showed very little tendency to import names from their mother country, preferring to make their own. The Orange River was so named by an Englishman, a Colonel Gordon, employed by the Dutch East India Company to make a survey in 1779. He chose the family name of the Staat-holders of Holland as being the most suitable, and probably did not realize that he was naming in a typically English-colonial style. Hitherto, the Boers had been content to speak of it as the *Groot Rivier*, exactly as they had done of the Hudson in America. Their own river-names are simply descriptive; two with less obvious meanings to the English are the Vaal (yellow or tawny-coloured) and the Mooi (beautiful).

They liked to honour their own leaders and this included those governors sent out from Holland who really identified themselves with the new land and the outlook of the settlers. The first to be put in charge, Jan van Riebeek, was remembered in the name of the mountain Riebeek's Casteel, but the one that made the most impact was Simon van der Stel who ruled the little colony for the last twenty years of the seventeenth century, retiring then to the farm he had built on the slopes of Table Mountain, and leaving the governorship to his son. His name lives in Stellenbosch, which he founded in 1679, and more familiarly in Simons Bay and Simonstown, and his wife's name in his farm Constantia, named by himself and much loved, the home of his last years. His vineyards there prospered and the name was copied in other wine-producing districts.

All the principal Voortrekkers have their memorials in town-names. A notable example is Pietermaritzburg which consists of a combination of Peter Retief and Gerhard Maritz. The first of these was the leader of those murdered by Dingaan and avenged at the Blood River; the second, his friend and companion, lived to reach Natal but died there soon after from the hardships of the journey, in the same year that his fellow *trekkers* founded their new capital. And the chief leader of this epic journey, Andries Pretorius, was later honoured in the great city of the Transvaal, Pretoria.

Pietermaritzburg was not the first of the composite place-names that became a feature of South African naming. In 1745 the Governor Hendrik Swellengrebel founded a new town in the west of the colony which he named Swellendam from a combination of part of his own name with that of his wife, Engela ten Damme. In honouring his lady he was following the style begun by Van der Stel, and this kindly and courteous method of placing her name on an equality with his own was also to be repeated. In 1785, when the arrival of a new governor, Cornelius Van der Graaf and his wife, coincided with the founding of a new settlement, it was named Graaf Reinet to compliment them both, Reinet being her Christian name.

This style of combining names and also of honouring the wives of public men was taken up by the English. In 1820, when the first officially organized party of English settlers were landed in Algoa Bay, and the laying out of what must clearly become an important seaport town begun, the acting-governor, Sir Rufane Donkin, had no hesitation in giving it the name of his wife, Elizabeth. Lady Grey and Lady Frere, both large villages in the Cape Province, preserve the formal titles of two more governors' ladies, while in the cases of Ladysmith and Ladybrand the words have been combined to better (if rather odd) effect. The most famous of this group, Ladysmith, commemorates the gay, spirited Spanish wife of a popular governor, hero of many military exploits, Sir Harry Smith. Her first name, Juana, was more suited to her romantic character than the stiff English title, but the chances of war were to give it glamour. And as they were a devoted couple it is appropriate that her husband's name, telescoped into Harrismith, has also its place on the map not far from hers.

Not only governors' ladies were immortalized in this way. An engineer laying out an early railway called an important junction by his wife's complete maiden name Alicedale, and a private landowner establishing the first beginnings of a town on his farm-land where a beautiful willow grew combined the tree with his wife's family-name to make Willowmore.

In other young countries, when a town has been called after a man, one of his names has generally been thought quite enough, but the Boers tended to use both, as in the town of Louis Trichart in the Transvaal, and thought nothing of making a name like Piet Potgietersrust (*rust* means resting place or settlement) referring to another famous *trekker*. This lengthy style seems also to have had some effect on the English when they began to establish their own towns. King William's Town seems a very laborious statement, and it is not surprising that in local usage it is generally reduced to King. Many of the Boer names too have been shortened in use: Pietermaritzburg is called Maritzburg, Piet Potgeiter has lost his first name, Springbokfontein has become Springbok, and the ambitiously named Pretoria Philadelphia has proved more practical without its long tag.

Pretoria is unusual among Boer names in its formal dignity and classic form, their most general characteristic being a simple factual quality. This natural style is exemplified in the name of the great modern city of Johannesburg (generally abbreviated to Jo'burg) which was evolved in such a casual, unpremeditated way in the confusion and excitement of the newly discovered gold fields that no reason for it was recorded; and although the founding of this city – now of over a million inhabitants – took place just within living memory (1886) it is not known for certain which of several men called Johannes is thus immortalized. According to the historical notes in the *Official Guide* to the city, the honour should probably go to the Acting Mining Commissioner, Johannes Meyer, who established his camp on the windy ridge among many others and wielded

237

what authority there was among the hopeful throngs of diverse races who flocked to the scene. But there are other claimants, among them Johannes Rissik, the Government Surveyor, whose son has confidently asserted that the city was named for his father.

Whoever it was, the fact that the man's first name was used shows that it was no solemn choice of officialdom but rather the spoken words of his companions on the spot. In England and other old countries many cities are called by the names of early leaders of whom we know nothing, like Beorma of Birmingham, but for so young a city this kind of obscurity is almost unique.

In the first decade of the nineteenth century the Cape became a British possession and from then onwards English names were given to new settlements in increasing numbers. Like the Boers the English made much of the names of their governors and other leading personalities on the spot, but there the likeness ends, and the general character of naming as practised by these two races is sharply contrasted.

The Boers' strongest love was for land of their own to farm and freedom to do what they chose on it without interference or advice from any one. They had lost their links with Holland without regret and wanted no others. In this they were much more like the Anglo-Saxons than the English colonists of their own time, and their names are of that early style, referring directly to the land and to their own occupation of it. The British colonists also gave names that expressed their feelings, and the strongest of these, as reflected in their choice, were love and loyalty to England. The names and titles of English royalties, ministers of state, and other representatives of the homeland appear on all sides, and English place-names were reproduced not with any interest in their original meanings, which would seldom have been appropriate, but for the personal and historic associations of later times.

The very first name given by the English at the Cape was the standard, true-to-type George Town named for the king in 1811. It was quickly abbreviated to George, and fortunately so, for since there were Georges on the throne for more than a century – during a time of great colonial expansion – so it follows that the number of Georgetowns in the world is excessive.

The Times World Atlas gives twenty-nine of them, including the capitals of Guyana, Gambia and three West Indian Islands. Other royal names followed, easily recognizable and needing no further comment.

It became the fashion in the colonies of the nineteenth century to name more from people than from places. What British colonists really hankered after were familiar names from their homeland, but as most prominent men had titles, and titles were generally derived from places, this desirable result could be obtained and the gentleman honoured in one stroke. The first governor, Lord Caledon, had as title the name of a small Irish town which was used for a village at the Cape that the Boers had called Zwartberg. The second, Lord Charles Somerset, became a regular fount of names for new settlements, several of them now large towns. Somerset East and Somerset West, over three hundred miles apart, made an unnecessary piece of repetition; Fort Beaufort and Beaufort East are derived from the dukedom of Lord Charles's father; and Worcester from his eldest brother's earldom. In the same spirit a later governor, Sir Lowry Cole, named Malmesbury after his father-in-law, Lord Malmesbury, who was foreign secretary for a short while.

A very different type of personal name was provided by Sir Benjamin D'Urban, a distinguished officer who had seen action in the British army in many parts of the world before becoming governor of the Cape in 1834. When a new village site, behind mangrove swamps in an almost land-locked bay, was laid out under his name, it may not have seemed destined for a specially notable future. But there is an element of chance in these matters, and Sir Benjamin had drawn a lucky card. The swamps were drained, and now Durban, which shed its apostrophe after some decades, is the third city of South Africa, a great and beautiful seaport city, and its unusual name (of Huguenot origin) is one of its assets.

A little further down the coast we come to Port Shepstone, which preserves a name well deserved to be remembered. Sir Theophilus Shepstone, who became Agent for Native Affairs in Natal, and later, Administrator of Zululand, made greater efforts to understand the natives and to treat them fairly than any who had come before him. The Zulus called him Somtseu, the Mighty Hunter, and mourned his death as the loss of a brother.

Further south again we come to the large port of East London, a piece of uninspired repetition, which the qualification East (South would have been more to the point) does little to improve. There is a strange background to this name, connected with the mysterious George Rex, who was generally understood to be the illegitimate son of George III, born before his marriage to Queen Charlotte. This gentleman, who had ample means, came out to the Cape in its early years as a British colony, and was treated with respect. He and his son, John Rex, played active parts in opening up this harbour to shipping, and it became known very naturally by their name as Port Rex; a short, crisp name in a land where many are unwieldy. But in 1847 an official announcement by the governor changed it to the present one. We can only infer that it had been found embarrassing. Whatever the cause, the name was replaced with something respectable, if dull.

Not far distant is Grahamstown where the name of another early pioneer has remained safely in possession. Colonel John Graham, an enterprising Scottish officer, had taken the chief part in its foundation in the first few years of the colony, and the name has a natural and genuine character. Very different are the names taken from distant notabilities who had never seen the places that honoured them. South Africa, like Australia and New Zealand, has too many of these. Bathurst, Newcastle, Carnarvon and Kimberley are all the titles of Colonial Secretaries, some of whom, like Lord Bathurst, have namesake-towns in several continents. These men did, of course, exercise great influence on colonial policy, and local governors, who often had the task of choosing names, were very much aware of their powers, but to the ordinary colonist they meant nothing more than acceptable place-names.

Let us think for a moment of Kimberley. First a Boer farm called Voorsicht (Foresight) where a child was found playing with sparkling pebbles that proved to be diamonds; then a mining town mushrooming all around it, and referred to by the speculators who crowded there, and all who spoke of it for several years, as the New Rush. This might have remained as it was, or been slightly remodelled as Rush Town or Rushton, or

New Rushton, but as it grew rapidly larger such natural names were felt inadequate, and the title of the Colonial Secretary was officially conferred on it. Kimberley, which is the name of a village in Norfolk mentioned in Domesday Book, is Anglo-Saxon in origin. It was 'Cyneburg's lea', an open glade belonging to a woman, named Cyneburg. Kimberley is more euphonius than New Rush, but in this new situation is lacking true significance.

The Boers had always despised the natives, whether Bushman, Hottentot, Zulu or of any other race, and made no effort to record their names which survive in the Cape district in very few places, and those chiefly wastelands such as the Karoo ('dry place' in Hottentot); and the English settlers, for many years, were more intent on filling the land with gracious and familiar-sounding English names than on seeking out the local ones. But during the nineteenth century a wave of liberal and romantic feeling (as we noted earlier in America) produced the movement that brought about the abolition of slavery, and the great expansion of missionary work. We see it expressed in the enormous public interest in the travels of explorers, and in the popularity of exotic adventure stories, such as those of Rider Haggard, who had himself travelled about South Africa as secretary to a governor, and saw Zulu warriors as exciting characters capable of nobility as well as cruelty.

All of this had its effect on naming, and towards the end of the century there was much more tendency to find out and preserve the native names in South Africa than there had ever been before. The modern seaside resorts of Amanzimtoti ('sweet waters') and Uvongo ('rumbling') both bear Zulu river-names, in contrast to the ultra-English Margate and Ramsgate a little farther down the coast. But this development came late and half-heartedly as compared with the respect given to Indian names in North America; South Africa has nothing to compare with the native-named cities of Chicago, Quebec and Ottawa.

However, when we go on to consider the countries that lie to the north of South Africa, territories that were brought to the knowledge of the world by British exploration in the nineteenth century, and opened up to civilizing influences by British

241

enterprise, a glance over the map shows the change of outlook in the matter of names since the century began. In these newly found and savage lands some few English names were bestowed; the great explorers of the age, such as Speke, Baker and Livingstone, finding magnificent lakes and waterfalls, felt that such superb phenomena merited the noblest names that could be given them and so, as patriots, called them after the Queen, her husband and her son (Lakes Victoria, Albert and Edward); but the same men took intense interest in the native names – Tanganyika, Nyasa and so forth – committed them to writing for the first time and brought them to the attention of the world. And in these central African countries that were colonized by the British within the last hundred years, for the vast majority of towns, villages and natural features the native names were preserved. This was so even before the present African governments began to reject the few English names they had.

Even in Rhodesia, the most English country in Africa, the white settlers have on the whole preferred the native names to importations of their own. The chief exceptions are the names of the country (page 309) and that of the capital city, named in 1890 for Lord Salisbury, the Prime Minister (page 26). The second largest city, Bulawayo, keeps its old name, or most of it. It was Gubulawayo, 'the place of killing', and it was probably well earned. The Victoria Falls still bear the old queen's name, and an impressive name it is, well suited to magnificent scenery, but the native name, Mosiatunya, 'smoke that thunders', is still well-known. There are, of course, many minor English names in Rhodesia, as there must be in any English-speaking country – for their homes, residential suburbs and so on, the English settlers have shown much the same tastes as their counterparts elsewhere – but for whole towns, villages and the features of the land the predominant note is African.

Zambia, formerly Northern Rhodesia, has shed a few English names but never had many. Its capital, Livingstone, still retains the name of the great Scottish explorer, who more than any other deserves to be remembered in this region. May it never change, for no man was ever a better friend to the black African or stood more manfully against his exploitation. By the time Kenya was established as a British colony early in the present century the preference for native names, even among the enthusiasts for making it 'a white man's country', was so strong that the newly founded capital received the Swahili name for the area where it was built, Nairobi, 'the swamp'. But in the modern African Kenya, as in Tanzania and Uganda, there remains that sprinkling of English names that must be found wherever British colonists have made their homes, and the great lakes Victoria, Albert and Edward retain – for the present – their royal names.

But these countries are barely on the fringe of our subject and even now are engaged in withdrawing themselves farther from it. As to the future, it would be rash to attempt any prediction about so unstable a continent, or even about those parts that were once British, but one fact that stands out is the importance of the English language. These young independent African states may choose to jettison certain English place-names but they cannot reject the speech that is their only means of communication with each other and with the rest of the world. That is perhaps the greatest gift of the British to Africa (and the same applies to India), and as long as some of the people are talking English there will be some English names.

Chapter 21

AUSTRALIA

Nobody knows who was the first white man to see Australia; but the first recorded sighting was in 1605 when the ship *Duyfken*, sent out by the Dutch East India Company to seek for more spice-bearing islands, ran aground on the east coast of what is now Cape York. The skipper, Willem Jansz, took this to be part of New Guinea – which had been visited earlier by the Portuguese – and, having got his ship clear, explored a little way down the coast; but not liking the look of it he headed back for the Dutch base at Batavia. His chart still exists, and one name that he wrote on it remains in use for the cape where he turned, Keer Weer, which means 'turn round'.

This name, the oldest in Australia, is typical of the Dutch reaction to the large, bare land they had found. During the rest of the seventeenth century their ships from time to time explored its northern and western coasts, but finding nothing to tempt them they made no settlement and eventually gave up looking any further. However, they were sufficiently possessive to write 'New Holland' across it on their charts, and to give names to the various points that they had visited, several of which have survived to the present day.

The chief of these early Dutch names may be briefly mentioned. There is Dirk Hartog's Island, named from a seacaptain who was there in 1616 and left his name on a metal plate to prove it. Six years later a ship named the *Leeuwin* (Lioness) reached the south-west corner of the continent, and soon after that a skipper called Pieter Nuyts rounded the bend and saw the easternmost part of the southern coast; Cape Leeuwin and Cape Nuyts, both preserving the Dutch spelling, are relics of these voyages. Meanwhile, in 1624, far in the north, another skipper, Joosten van Colster, gave the name of his ship, the *Arnhem* (called after the town of that name), to a cape in tropical waters, and from there it has spread to include the whole of Arnhem Land, a territory much bigger than Holland. And it must have been at that time that the great Gulf of Carpentaria was named, for the governor of the Dutch East Indies at that date was General Pieter Carpentier.

It was a successor of his, Anthony van Diemen, who dispatched in 1642 the most famous of Dutch explorers, Abel Janzoon Tasman, to seek new lands that might be profitable. Setting out from Mauritius on an easterly course, he passed the south-west corner of New Holland, the farthest point that his compatriots had reached, and continued without sight of land until he came to the island now known as Tasmania, but which he called dutifully Anthony van Diemen's Land in honour of his patron. Cruising round its southern coasts, and going only once ashore himself and then no farther than the beach, he gave several names that are still there, such as Schouten Island (from another patron), Maria's Island (from the governor's wife), and Storm Bay, which is almost identical in Dutch and English. But he never knew if this land was an island or what lay to the north of it, and seeing no signs of wealth he sailed on eastwards over another thousand miles of stormy sea.

This sea also bears his name and rightly since he was the first white man to see it and probably the first human being to sail across it; for the Australian aborigines were not a seafaring people, and the Maoris who were had approached New Zealand from the north. He saw New Zealand but was driven off by the Maoris and turned away northwards back to the Dutch East Indies.

Instead of provoking more exploration Tasman's voyages were followed by a lull, but in the last decade of the century there were two notable events. Another Dutch captain, Willem van Vlamingh, searching down the west coast of New Holland for a missing ship, turned into a good anchorage and seeing to his amazement black swans with scarlet beaks named the Black Swan River on the spot. To him the essence of the name was 'black', but since Australians take black swans for granted

I

and like short names, they reduced their English version to Swan River.

And in the very last year of the century there came – as far as we know – the first Englishman to step ashore on the Australian mainland. This was the one-time pirate, William Dampier, who, after many adventures in strange company, had turned respectable, published a travel book and persuaded the authorities in England to send him on a voyage of discovery. He landed in the bay sheltered by Dirk Hartog's Island, where he had been once before; and this time he gave it a name, a plain, factual one, Shark Bay, the first English name in Australia. But he disliked the arid coast as much as the Dutch had done, thinking the natives whom he saw 'the miserablest people in the world', and soon sailed away.

To the British settlement of Australia these early voyages form only the curtain-raiser. They ended with the seventeenth century, and after that came a long interval before the curtain rose again on the main performance.

If we look for the chief name-givers of world history, Captain James Cook, self-taught son of a Yorkshire farm labourer, must certainly rank among the first of them. None can compare with him in the magnitude and diversity of the regions, ranging from the Southern Ocean to the Arctic in which he gave a name to every notable natural feature visible from the sea.

His principal voyages, which added so vastly to man's knowledge of the world, filled the years between 1768 when he was sent officially to Tahiti to observe the transit of Venus and afterwards to search for 'the Southern Continent' (which did not mean New Holland but something further south), and 1779 when he fell on a Hawaiian beach, hacked to pieces by savages; and among his achievements were the charting of the whole of New Zealand, the east coast of Australia, the west coast of Canada and Alaska, and more islands than anyone would care to count.

With so much scope for his creative talents (ten thousand miles of hitherto unknown coastline would be a moderate estimate) he might have stamped his personality more obviously on the world than he did, but he was a reserved and modest man, disliking any form of ostentation, and his style of name-giving moved more in accordance with the accepted practice of his day than towards flights of fancy. Therefore, since naming places from people had lately become the fashion in the colonies, he used his great opportunity largely to express his gratitude and respect to those who had most helped him in his career or earned his admiration. But he did make original names too, and those we will come to later.

Before he set eyes on Australia he had spent some time in the Pacific, where he had named the Society Islands, not from the sociable nature of their inhabitants which would apply very aptly, but as a tribute to the Royal Society who were the chief instigators of his voyage. He had then charted New Zealand, placing a number of names of admirals and other officials on its coastline so that when another land came in sight on 13 April 1770 he had already worked off a fair amount of his gratitude.

Some of the distinguished names he used again, varying the geographic details; Admiral Hawke, who had a bay in New Zealand, received a cape in Australia, and the two chief secretaries at the Admiralty who had been active in the arrangements for the voyage, Sir Philip Stephen and Sir George Jackson, who had been given capes in New Zealand, were now further honoured with what seemed good harbours. Cook had no time to sail his ship into every opening in the cliffs, and never knew that Port Jackson would one day be called 'the finest harbour in the world'. So he sailed on north-wards, charting and naming. After naval men his thoughts turned next to royal dukes and politicians: Cumberland, Gloucester, Rockingham, Halifax, Grafton, and so on, placed on capes, bays and islands, sound only like English places, but are all named for men. Grafton was Prime Minister when Cook left England, Rockingham his rival in office.

Modern Australians complain that too many places are called after Englishmen who never saw Australia. But at that date no one had seen it, except Cook and his companions, and of course the Aborigines, with whom he failed to establish any verbal communication, though he tried hard to do so. Of his ship's company he used names only rarely. The first man to sight land was his First Lieutenant, Zachary Hicks, who received his reward in Point Hicks; and when soon after the first landing a seaman from the Orkneys, named Sutherland, died of consumption and was buried ashore, the site of this first British grave became Sutherland, now a suburb of Sydney.

But Cook's names were not all personal by any means. As a cartographer himself, he knew well the importance of variety in place-names, and soon evolved a style of his own, in which he expressed the truth of what he saw in plain words, but wishing to find distinctive names for all the bays and headlands that came into view day after day, he avoided repeating the simplest terms, such as Sandy Cape, and sought constantly for new descriptions that would be at once true and original.

So it was that the first place where they went ashore received a name that everyone remembers. At first he wrote it in his journal as Stingray Harbour, but when the two scientific gentlemen who travelled with him came back to the ship excited by the new specimens of plant life that they had found, he changed it to Botanist's Bay, and then as a final touch perfected Botany Bay. His changes show that he was not lacking in artistry; the sound as well as the sense must be right, and in this case the result caught the public fancy and became in later years a by-word in England for the convict settlement, which was in fact never placed there.

His names on this coast based on his observation and experience include Broken Bay, Cape Dromedary (from its two humps), Cape Manifold (from more humps), Smoky Cape (where native fires could be seen), Bustard Bay, Thirsty Sound (where they found no water) and Cape Upstart. All went well until they reached the Great Barrier Reef; then came Cape Tribulation, 'where began all our troubles', Weary Bay, and Cape Flattery, where 'we judged ourselves to be clear of all danger, but soon found otherwise'. After running on to the reef one dark night he managed to get off again and having at last reached a safe anchorage on the coast for much needed repairs he called it by the name of his ship, Endeavour River. The ship had given him good service and when he had rounded the northernmost promontory, which he called Cape York 'in honour of his late Royal Highness', and found a passage to the west (a little to the south of the one the Spaniard Torres had taken long before) he used its name again for Endeavour Strait.

If we look at the large quantity of Cook's names we see many that are original, while others are too standard in type to be of great interest. He was at his best when easy and relaxed, but unfortunately the more important the occasion seemed the more formal he became, and in his wish to produce something dignified became merely dull. This is what happened when he took possession of the whole coast and called it New South Wales. Cook felt that he was naming a new British land with a great future, and that is why it turned out heavy.

His own name has no great geographical prominence in Australia, as it has in New Zealand, and for this apparent lack of recognition we can only blame its plain, serviceable, un-melodious nature, for he is held in high esteem. If, on his return to England, he had been given a title, based on a locality as they usually are, Whitby perhaps, where he was apprenticed to the sea, whatever name had been chosen would have been given an honourable place on the map; but his life was cut short before so much as a knighthood had come his way, and Australia can show no greater local memorial than the little town of Cooktown on the spot where he repaired his ship after his adventures on the reef. A find of gold once sent its population up to 30,000 but now it has fallen to a few hundred.

Captain Cook was only the first of a series of naval officers on whom the early naming of these two southern lands devolved. Since they could only be reached by long sea voyages their control depended on the navy and when, after a long interval, it was decided to confirm Cook's annexation of New South Wales, and much later and very unwillingly to take responsi-bility for New Zealand too, the first two governors to be sent out in each case were naval captains. When more detailed surveys were needed, these were tasks for the navy, too.

As we should expect from a service with such strong tradi-tions, these officers all gave names in much the same style. Like Cook, they could make original names that were simple and effective. Captain Phillip, for instance, first governor of New South Wales, on being struck by the 'manly' bearing of some natives who waded into the surf to stare at his boat, named the beach on which they stood so fearlessly, Manly Cove. But the strongest loyalty of these naval men was to their superior officers, to whom they felt an unquestioning duty, and when it seemed likely that a place would be important they tended to choose the names or title of those in authority over them. Junior officers might give the names of governors, but the governors themselves turned their thoughts loyally to England, to the Admiralty Lords or Ministers of State from whom they took their orders.

So it was that when Captain Phillip had taken the decision that Botany Bay was unsuited to the penal colony that he was supposed to plant there, and had found a far better site, a superb one only a few miles distant, he 'honoured it with the name of Sydney Cove'. It was on 26 January 1770 that this name was given at a simple ceremony on the beach, where the flag was hoisted and a toast to the royal family drunk. Phillip was a man of vision who realized that he was founding something more than a convict settlement. That he thought of calling it Albion indicates his patriotic feeling and sense of history, however he put this aside and made a conventional choice, the title of the Minister of State responsible for the enterprise. But he was wrong when he said deferentially that he honoured the cove. Lord Sydney, known irreverently as Tommy Townshend before he got his title, was a lesser man than Captain Phillip. As Secretary of State for Home and the Colonies he held great power for a short time, but 'his abilities, though respectable never rose above mediocrity'.* Time has shown the honour to be the other way round.

And yet what was Phillip to do? He could not name it after himself, and he had enough sense not to create yet another Georgetown after the king. At least Sydney has the great advantage that it is not a well-known English place-name, being probably a contraction of 'St Denys' brought to England as the surname of a Norman family, therefore its local significance is pre-eminently Australian; and it is pleasant in sound. Captain Phillip did not do badly after all.

After him came other naval men. Only the east coast of Australia had been charted by Cook, and in the early years of the colony his work was continued by a series of young officers eager to discover its size and shape and relation to the coasts

---

* Sir N. Wraxall. *Historical Memoirs of my own Time.* 1815.

that the Dutch had visited, two thousand miles to the west. George Vancouver, who had been a midshipman on Cook's last voyage, gave somewhat uninspired names of the regular sort; it was careless of him, for instance, to name a Cape Howe, from the Admiral, on the south coast when Cook had already named one on the east. His own name was to attain more geographical prominence than those of any of the officers he sailed with, but on a distant Canadian coast. James Grant in 1800 also stuck to naval tradition, naming Cape Nelson and Mount Gambier from contemporary admirals, and Portland Bay from the duke who had succeeded Lord Sydney in office. Lieutenant Murray, finding a large landlocked harbour in 1801, called it Port King after the governor at that time, but the latter generously changed it to Port Phillip in honour of his first predecessor. But by far the most important of this group and one whose character and abilities would have brought him more fame had not his life been ruined by misfortune was Matthew Flinders, whose voyage in the *Investigator*, begun in 1801, added almost as many names to Australia as Cook himself had given.

Flinders's names are just like Cook's. He had the same happy knack for the natural name and the same sense of duty that produced the formal ones. As he generally noted the reason for his choice in his journal we can see very clearly the alternation between his actual circumstances – 'Anxious Bay, from the night we passed in it' – and formality – 'Spencer's Gulph, in honour of the respectable nobleman who presided at the Board of Admiralty when the voyage was planned'. Close to this gulf he found another where he named many features around the later site of Adelaide. This gulf he named after Lord St Vincent, better known as Sir John Jervis, who had taken his title from his victory at Cape St Vincent, and succeeded Lord Spencer at the Admiralty, 'and had continued to the voyage that countenance and protection of which Earl Spencer had set the example'. This was generous, for last minute interference from the Admiralty had caused delays and disappointments. At the entrance to these two inlets Flinders and his men explored a large island and made a great slaughter of kangaroos which produced an excellent soup 'and as much steaks for both officers and men as they could consume by day and by night. In gratitude for so seasonable a supply I named this southern land Kangaroo Island.' Rightly the native creature was commemorated here among the distant earls.

The unlucky loss of one of his boats with all its crew gave rise to several other genuine names in which formality was forgotten, Cape Catastrophe, Memory Cove, and Thistle Island, the last named from Mr Thistle, who had been in charge of the missing boat. Soon after, when a French ship came in sight 'and we cleared our decks for action', he named the place – where fortunately no shots were fired – Encounter Bay. Meanwhile the French ship *La Geographe* with her companion *La Naturaliste* passed on and left their names on the south-west coast not far from the cape named from the Dutch *Lioness*.

It was Flinders who gave the name of his close friend and sometime shipmate, George Bass, to the strait that divides Tasmania from the mainland which Bass had explored adventurously in an open boat. This was well given, but only too often – as we have seen – he joined in the regular chorus of respect to the Admiralty Lords. For their part the Admiralty, who had little idea of what was going on in the remoter colonies, repaid his devoted service with neglect and parsimony. While he languished for six years in French captivity in Mauritius (having put in there for help after a shipwreck on his way home, not knowing that war had broken out again) his wife and child were left in penury. On his return his health was broken and he died soon after, but not before he had completed his account of his voyage that proved New Holland and New South Wales to be one land, for which he suggested the name Australia.

Too often the story is repeated in colonial history of energy, enterprise and loyalty out on the perimeter answered by apathy and ineptitude at the centre, and this was particularly true of the first twenty-five years of colonial Australia. English politicians of this time were not without great qualities, but they were busy with other matters, and little interested in the southern hemisphere. The American colonies had proved a sad disappointment, and they had no wish to replace them with others even further off. A small colony had been founded in New South Wales for a particular purpose but they did not wish it to grow.

This attitude was opposed by the Colonial Reformers, who succeeded in changing it by the late 1830s. In 1854 a separate minister was appointed for the colonies, which previously had been looked after by the Secretary for War, when he had time to spare them. But even these Colonial Secretaries had little knowledge of colonial needs, and followed each other in such rapid succession that they never had time to learn. However, this did not check the loyalty of the colonists and as they spread out and established new settlements largely on their own initiative they continued to express their sense of duty to the home government in their choice of names. Australia has a particularly strong line in Colonial Secretaries. Hobart, Bathurst, Glenelg, Newcastle, Normanby, Carnarvon and Kimberley are all the titles of lords who held this office, the first three combining it with War. Lord Goulburn, who appears on the Australian map in several places, was an under secretary in the same ministry.

And not only towns but natural features were named in this political style, the most notable example being that of Australia's greatest river. The first white man to see any part of it was the explorer Alexander Hume, in 1824, and his own name does remain on the part he saw, now a reservoir; but the man who revealed its whole extent by navigating it in a boat that he had carried laboriously overland and struggling back upstream on short rations, the gallant Captain Sturt, named his 'broad and noble river' after yet another Colonial Secretary, Sir George Murray. To its greatest tributary he gave the name of the governor who had encouraged the enterprise, Darling, and the latter should have returned the compliment, but the great river remains the Murray, its saving grace being an easy-flowing sound which consorts well with the largest of its tributaries to retain its native name, the Murrumbidgee. Sturt may have acquired wisdom from this experience, for in his later expeditions he was more inclined to give natural names such as the Barrier Range and the Great Stony Desert.

Sir George Murray, a retired general, who had been governor of Canada, was now MP for Perth. One act of his as Colonial Secretary is worthy of memory though little noticed at the time; he was the first to enunciate in Parliament the principle that British subjects in all parts of the world have

1*

equal rights regardless of the colour of their skins, a statement
that was received with applause from all present. His honours
in Australia did not end with the river, for in the same year
(1829) a new and separate colony was being founded far in the
west. The newly appointed governor, Captain James Stirling
(later Sir James and an admiral), had chosen a beautiful site for
its capital, and being a Scot himself was keen to honour the
Scottish statesman in charge in London, but instead of just
taking his surname, he chose instead his constituency, Perth. To
its port he gave the name of Freemantle, the surname of the
captain who had sailed out ahead of him to make the first
survey and proclaim the annexation.

The obsession with colonial ministers faded only gradually
as a new generation of Australians widened their scope to
include other prominent contemporaries and even local men as
subjects for name-giving. For the new settlement in the south-
east some bold spirits even put forward the name of its enterprising founder, John Batman, but 'Batmania' was not a happy
suggestion; more orthodox views prevailed, and the title of the
Prime Minister, Lord Melbourne, was preferred. Then for the
next city to be planned, in 1836, the name of the Queen was
chosen, Adelaide. William IV reigned for only seven years and
his shy gentle wife is little known, but her name has served well
for a city that seems to have something of feminine grace about
it.

About the same time a Polish gentleman, a rare phenomenon
in such a predominantly British colony, climbed the highest
peak in the land; and, by virtue of his achievement, named it
after the Polish national hero, Kosciusko. This at least struck a
new and original note though with little relation to Australia.

Meanwhile, another naval survey ship, the *Beagle*, was
exploring the bays and inlets of the torrid north, and its captain
giving names in the customary naval style; Point Torment
referred to the mosquitoes, but most of the names were for
royalties or naval officers, and by way of a change he named one
harbour Darwin for the young naturalist who had been on that
ship on its previous voyage, 'in memory of an old shipmate and
friend'. Darwin, back in England, was as yet unknown, and his
great work when eventually published did not bring him
instant acclaim. So when a town began to grow in Port Darwin

it was at first given the more impressive name of Palmerston, from the Prime Minister; and it was not until 1911 that the name of the great scientist was revived for it.

By the middle of the century Australians were learning to use the names of their own leading men, and eventually all the early governors – a memorable set of men – and all the chief explorers were accommodated on the map. Such names as the Darling Downs, the Lachlan and the Macquarie Rivers (from the two names of one Governor) the Stirling Range and Gippsland tell the real story of the country or part of it. Flinders's name was placed on a range of hills that he had sighted from his ship; Sturt's on a desert over which he had toiled, and also on several minor rivers and other features as if to atone for the one that should have borne his name; Lake Eyre is named for the first white man to see it and to reach the western settlements by an overland route; while Burke who crossed the continent from south to north but died in trying to return is commemorated at Burketown.

When Queensland was opened up in the fifties the name of one of the early governors of New South Wales, Sir Thomas Brisbane, was thought good enough for its capital; other towns took the names of still more local men, Cairns for one of the first governors of the new province, and Townsville from a successful cotton grower Richard Towns. And as the style of naming grew more local and more informal so the ladies began to be included in the compliments. The Mary River was named for Lady Mary Fitzroy (a governor's lady) and Maryborough grew on its banks; another river was called Katherine by the explorer, J.M.Stuart, after a young lady of his acquaintance; and when in 1872 Sir Charles Todd established a base for a telegraph line in the very centre of the continent, he named it Alice Springs after his wife. Modern Australians have shortened it to Alice and matched it with other names of wives and sweethearts. So naming became more popular, but still nearly always personal.

Of course, Australia has its natural names that have either arisen spontaneously or been chosen by men of good judgement expressing what they saw. Some of the simplest are best: the Blue Mountains, the Great Barrier Reef, the Granites. But there are not as many of these 'real' names as one would like to see, and hardly any for towns.

Not enough has been made of the wonderful wild life, unique to Australia, which could provide so many colourful and distinctive names. Americans and Canadians have not hesitated to accord full city honours to the buffalo, the beaver, the elk, the moose and other animals as well as birds and trees, but Australian creatures have had little recognition in this way. Early explorers had a more natural approach to this matter; the Dutchman Vlamingh named the Swan River from the evidence of his eyes, and Dampier's one contribution refers to the shark, which still plays its ominous part in the same waters; Flinders too, though caught up in the nineteenth-century web of custom, gave the kangaroo – that symbol of Australia – its most prominent placing on the map.

True there are many little-known names that are as natural as one could wish – Kangaroo Bluff, Emu Creek, Blue Gum Gully, and so on – but when a regular township has been established in such a place, it has generally been felt necessary to give it a more formal name. In such cases new settlers, not long out from Britain, have often chosen the name of the place they have come from, not because their new surroundings remind them of it in any way, but for the reverse reason, that everything is so different, and the familiar name more valued than it ever was at home. But even more often, especially when a name was wanted for a town likely to be important, Australians have followed their established custom of naming from people, thus scattering the continent with surnames.

Does this mass of British names – whether local or personal – make for too much uniformity? Fortunately there are several factors that have prevented this. The first is the rich variety of British place-names, created out of several languages over a long period of time. Certain famous ones have been repeated too often and recur in every English-speaking land, but the huge number of tiny villages, hamlets and farms in the British Isles that are unknown to the world but remembered by individuals, form a source of supply that can never be exhausted.

Even greater, perhaps, is the variety of British surnames. No one has ever been able to calculate how many different ones exist but certainly there are over a hundred thousand. Some are very common, but these on the whole have been avoided in Australia, the man with the more unusual name being generally preferred for local immortality. And looking round the principal cities one is struck more by their diversity than by any suggestion of sameness.

Australians have named from men but also with a feeling for sound. For important towns two or three syllables have generally been preferred, and this has come hard on the men with plain, short names like Cook. At least twelve prime ministers of England received good placings in the first century of Australia's history, but the greatest of them, William Pitt the Younger, has nothing more notable than Pitt Street, Sydney, a vital scene of activity certainly, but not ranking with a whole town. If Lord Melbourne had been a second son without a title (as Pitt was) and only William Lamb he would hardly have had a great city to his credit ('Lamb' would be absurd in Australia); as it was, his title, derived from a village in Derbyshire where his family had its seat, had a gracious sound and has made an admirable name. Brisbane, an Anglo-Norman nickname for a tough type (*Brise ban* or 'Break bone'); Freemantle (see page 100); Hobart, a rare early variation of the Christian name Robert; Darwin, an Anglo-Saxon man's name; Darling, an endearment, used as a nickname since before the Conquest; and Bunbury, originally a tiny village in Cheshire – all these are rare English surnames, and there are Scottish and Irish ones contrasting with them. Wherever you look, the variety is there. You might say there has been some luck in this, but there has been some selection too.

But the fact remains that there are too many surnames, and too often they have displaced others that belong more genuinely to the living scene. Think of the shanty town that grew in a northern bay on the Timor Sea where pearl diving flourished, and luggers came from many harbours bringing trade. They called it Port of Pearls. But then it grew rich and was renamed in 1883 after Sir Frederick Broome, Governor of Western Australia. There is nothing wrong with Broome as a name, except that it displaced something better.

In the second half of the nineteenth century a new influence appeared on the scene that did much to enliven the established pattern of naming. This was the discovery of gold and later of other valuable metals. The miners who flocked first to the diggings at Ballarat came from California and other countries but were mostly English-speaking, and they brought with them a new vigour of speech that was to affect Australians so strongly that since then they have accepted the term 'Digger' as a national label.

Moving from one find to another, with a cheerful disregard of hardships, they named their camps, some of which grew into permanent towns, in a free and easy style that owed nothing to convention. Some names they brought with them, such as Eureka ('I have found it') which had been a favourite in California; some they would carry elsewhere, such as Broken Hill which began in the stony Barrier Range that Sturt had found, and was carried on to Northern Rhodesia, now Zambia. They might name from the cheerful facts, Golden Ridge, Silverton, Iron Knob, or merely from hope, Utopia and Paradise. Marble Bar shows a nice mixture of the two for it was inspired by an unusual slab of rock, but has a suggestion of luxury drinks.

When they named a mining camp from a person, it was someone they knew well. Bendigo, said to be an attempt at Abednego, was the nickname of a local prize-fighter. When this grew into a respectable town there was a move to call it Sandhurst, which fortunately failed. Mount Morgan belonged to three Morgan brothers who worked it together. Mount Isa was named for its discoverer's sister, Isabel. If they happened to hear a native name with a rolling rhythm that took their fancy the miners often kept it and so such names as Coolgardie and Kalgoorlie leapt to fame, but their own invention never failed. Two prospectors who found their way across difficult country with the help of the stars called their lucky strike Southern Cross, and when it grew into a town they named the streets from constellations.

The modern Australian miner has changed his technique and is more of an engineer than a digger, but he still makes names that are rich and racy and without inhibitions; names like Rum Jungle and Humpty Doo.

But the chief element in Australian place-names that saves them from the accusation of dullness is the presence of so many

Aboriginal names. In the early days of settlement when there was more contact with the natives in their own habitat, quite a number of names had been preserved, simply because they were heard and used with little thought. It was only very gradually that any appreciation of them grew, and only in this century that serious study of the native languages has begun.

The first Aboriginal name to be recorded and rescued from extinction is Paramatta, which owes its life to Governor Phillip. Having explored up river from Sydney and found a pleasant site for a second settlement, he was going to name it Rose Hill, but hearing that the natives called it Paramatta he showed his good sense by preferring that. But he was a man ahead of his time, and most English settlers at that time liked their own names better.

I have written in other chapters of the wave of humanitarian feeling for primitive races that surged up among the English-speaking people in the nineteenth century. As there had never been slavery in Australia so it followed that the strongest emotions on behalf of the black man were never roused there, but the difference in attitude from the early nineteenth century when the natives of Tasmania were exterminated, and the present time when much is being done on behalf of those who survive on the mainland, is very great. By the middle of the last century native names were already becoming popular; their strong rhythms and repetitive syllables were thought entertaining; and many were preserved for their sound without knowledge of their sense. Now, when much more careful attention is given them, it is often too late to recapture the lost meaning. Because the native peoples were very primitive and scattered widely over great distances, they had a great many different languages – as many as five hundred, it is said – some bearing hardly any resemblance to others, and this adds greatly to the difficulty.

Therefore it must be accepted that meanings of Aboriginal names are very uncertain. Paramatta has been translated 'the dark forest', 'the head of the river', and 'the place where eels lie down'. Woolloomoolo, which everyone likes, is something to do with a kangaroo or alternatively an Aborigine's attempt to say 'windmill'. Those that can be understood are mostly very simple natural statements, such as one finds in every primitive language; Murrumbidgee is 'big water' like Mississippi; Yarra, 'running water' or 'river'; Kalgoorlie is the name of a native shrub; Geelong, a swampy plain; Ballarat, a camp in a swamp; and Woomera the name of the throwing stick that is one of the Aborigine's few possessions.

It was a great triumph for the native language, or one of them, when an Aboriginal name was chosen for the Federal capital in 1913. A century earlier colonial leaders selecting a site for a capital city would hardly have considered this possibility. If they had happened to hear its native name they might have preserved it for a suburb or park but would never have given it the chief honour. What Canberra means is less important than the fact of its choice; several theories have been put forward including 'a meeting place', but this is far from certain.

As one travels about Australia one finds plenty of lively names, especially for the smaller places in regions recently developed, and this augurs well for the future; it is the more important names that are most open to the criticism of dullness, the worst offenders being among the names of the states. The larger a place, the harder it is to name, as Cook found when he toiled over 'New South Wales'. The other eastern state-names are more successful. Victoria and Queensland, two ways of expressing the same loyalty, are none the worse for that, since the sentiment was sincere and the two names pleasant in sound and different from each other; Tasmania, changed from Van Diemen's Land in 1855, is apt and original; but there inspiration ended, and the three remaining divisions of the country are still virtually unnamed. When the Swan River settlement was founded the governor, Captain Stirling, proposed Hesperia, 'western land', which would have matched perfectly with Australia; but perhaps it was thought 'high-faluting'; in any case, more cautious counsels prevailed as they have elsewhere, and so Western Australia, South Australia and Northern Territory are still waiting for something better.

This reluctance to fabricate new names, and the corresponding preference for statements of fact, are of course very much in the Old English tradition; but the Anglo-Saxons would soon have reduced such statements to briefer and more manageable forms. Western Australia would have automatically become

Westralia, and perhaps some such solution will be found. Anything is better than initials, the dreariest device yet invented for speaking of one's homeland. SA is particularly bad, as it may also be used for South Africa and South America.

If the variety in Australian place-names is less than that found in some of the other British-founded countries it must be attributed partly to the lack of violence and racial rivalry that has characterized its history. No country in the world has been more free of war, and if it has no Battle Creek or Blood River, and no mass of picturesque names in a third or fourth language, that is a small price to pay for such immunity. Australia's battles have been against natural forces, and it is the land itself that might be better represented in its names.

Chapter 22

NEW ZEALAND

The credit for discovering New Zealand is generally given to the Dutch navigator, Tasman, but of course the Maoris had discovered it many centuries before he did, after voyages just as great and much more hazardous. Their legends tell of a great leader, Kupe, who reached this remote land in about the tenth century, the date being calculated by generations, and returned to tell his people how to get there. All their genealogies go back to ancestors who made the journey in one or another of the giant canoes, whose names are still recited and held in honour.

These epic voyages to New Zealand were only part of a great migratory movement in which the Polynesian race spread all across the Pacific, colonizing islands many thousands of miles apart. In all these islands they retain the same background of mythology, and they know that they came long ago from an ancient homeland called Hawaiiki. This was not in South America as Thor Heyerdahl tried to prove; there is no question that the general direction was eastwards from Asia, fanning out to the north and south as far as Hawaii and New Zealand.*

Like British colonists at a later date they cherished the names of their former homes, and repeated the same place-names from island to island, one of the many proofs that link their journeys together and help to tell their history, and the name Hawaiiki, in the varying forms of different dialects, recurs in many island groups. It is best known as Hawaii and may be found also (as Havai'i) in the Cook Islands. It was from the latter group and from the Society Islands that are not far distant that the Maori

---

* Exactly how and when the Maoris discovered New Zealand is still controversial, but not the direction from which they came.

canoes set out on the last long lap to New Zealand, as is shown by the place-names from these islands repeated in the southern land.

Hawaiiki itself is not found as a place-name in New Zealand but recurs constantly in Maori legends. And another name that links New Zealand with Hawaii four thousand miles away is that of Maui, the Polynesian demi-god, who stole fire from the underworld, snared the sun and forced it to travel at a regular speed, and failed only to conquer death. One of the Hawaiian islands is called Maui and as every child in New Zealand knows the North Island is really Te Ika a Maui, 'Maui's fish', for it was he who hauled it up out of the sea.

Since New Zealand was big enough for the Maoris to spread and multiply, they lost the urge to seek for more islands, ceased to make their great ocean-crossing canoes, and for many centuries lived in complete isolation. On 13 December 1642 Tasman's two ships suddenly appeared before them. No direct account of what they thought of it has been preserved, but we do know that when Captain Cook's ship came, more than a century later, they were sure it was manned by goblins; and their ideas about the earlier visitation were probably similar.

Being by nature fierce and courageous they went out in their canoes to intercept the small boat that was pulling away from one of the larger ones; they killed four Dutchmen in the ensuing skirmish, and Tasman, surprised by this sudden attack, drew off without any further attempt to land. He sailed northward charting the coast from a safe distance, and marked on his map the place where the fight had occurred as *Moordenaars Baai*. This remained on world charts for over a century, but white New Zealanders have not cherished it. Their sympathies lie closer to the Maoris, defending their land, than to those Dutch sailors who saw it only to turn away from it. They respect Tasman and have named a noble mountain range, a peak and a glacier after him, but 'Murderers' is a hard word and they prefer to speak of this place as Golden Bay, describing its golden sands.

Tasman gave only one lasting name in New Zealand. At the extreme north, before he parted from the land, he named the last cape that he could see Maria van Diemen, in honour of the wife of the governor of the Dutch East Indies who had sent him out to explore. This lady, whom we can picture in a starched ruff as she might have been painted by her contemporary Rembrandt, secured three permanent placings in savage lands, for she has an island off the torrid Northern Australian coast and another near Tasmania as well as this New Zealand cape. In this last situation she is in strange company, for the adjoining headland, which stretches even a little farther out, still keeps its Maori name of Reinga, 'the leaping place of spirits'. Every Maori, wherever he was, believed that when he died his spirit must make the long journey to this cape, there cast itself into the sea, and so return to his long-lost home, Hawaiiki. Close by is the Bay of Spirits, and the whole promontory is held sacred to the Maori dead.

Just beyond this 'land's end', one of the most dramatic in the world, Tasman saw and named Three Kings Islands, since the date was the Epiphany; then he set his course for the Dutch East Indies and the brief link between Holland and New Zealand ended, except for the name of the whole country which must be considered later.

When Tasman had gone New Zealand's isolation was again unbroken for more than a century, until on 7 October 1769 Lieutenant James Cook (later Captain) (page 246) sighted its eastern coast. This was his first important discovery and he must have been a happy man during the next six months, which he devoted to charting the islands in detail, taking his ship skilfully around them in a figure of eight, and naming capes, bays, islands and mountains that no white man had seen before. Here it was that he developed his most characteristic style, using the incidents of shipboard life to supply him with ideas.

So it is that the coastline of New Zealand still echoes the story of that famous voyage. At Poverty Bay (now a prosperous place) he made his first landing. He had hoped to replenish his water and other stores but obtained 'no one thing that we wanted', owing to an unlucky affray with the Maoris. At Cape Kidnappers some of them tried to carry off one of his crew in their canoe; at Cape Turnagain he decided to go about and explore in the opposite direction; at Cape Runaway some threatening Maoris were put to flight; in the Bay of Plenty he saw many villages with cultivation around them and his dealings with the natives were more successful; in Mercury Bay he waited to observe the transit of Mercury; near Bream Head his crew enjoyed good fishing; in Ship Cove he careened his ship; and he would not go into Doubtful Sound because the mountains rose so steeply on all sides that he doubted if he would ever have enough breeze there to bring him out again. The very first name that he gave, the first English name in New Zealand, is Young Nick's Head, named from the boy, Nicholas Young, who sighted the land from the masthead; and the last is Cape Farewell.

Other names recall the weather or time of day when he saw the places, Cloudy Bay, Twilight Bay, Dusky Sound and Cape Foulwind; or particular fancies that came into his head as he sailed among rocky islands of strange shapes, Hen and Chickens, Mayor Island with the Aldermen close by, the Poor Knights, which reminded him of two armed knights on one horse, and the Brothers, close together in Cook's Straits. Nearly all that he gave have been remembered, even those that are not in general use. For instance, the snow-capped mountains that stand along the north-east coast of the South Island are always called the Kaikouras, but most New Zealanders know that Cook called them 'The Lookers On'.

In sharp contrast are the names of the distinguished men, nearly all naval, who had influenced his life. Now was his chance to pay his tribute. His first choice was old Admiral Hawke, First Lord of the Admiralty, under whose orders he sailed, the victor of several naval engagements. Cook gave his name to a large bay which in turn has named a province, Hawkes Bay. The Admiralty as a whole was honoured in Admiralty Bay, while two officers under whom Cook had served in Canadian waters, Captain Lord Colville and Sir Hugh Palliser, each of whom had recommended him for promotion, received tributes of Capes and Bays.

Hawke's predecessor at the Admiralty had been Lord Egmont. It is unlikely that Cook knew the derivation of his title from the Norman-French *aigre mont* meaning a pointed hill, but he must have known that the ending *mont* was suited to a mountain, and when a perfect, snow-capped cone came in sight, rising to nearly nine thousand feet close to the sea, he called it Mount Egmont. Fortunately, the native name Taranaki has not been lost, but is used for the surrounding province.

Of course, as a patriot, he used royal names too, but sparingly. One of the few that he gave in New Zealand was to the deep inlet where he spent three weeks overhauling his ship. Here he ran up the flag, proclaimed British sovereignty over the South Island, and ended the ceremony with a toast to the Queen, naming the inlet Queen Charlottes Sound. A few years later he gave exactly the same name again on the west coast of Canada – the distance must have seemed to him great enough to warrant the repetition. It may truly be said that his royal names are widely spaced for they stretch from South Georgia near the Antarctic Circle to Cape Prince of Wales in Alaska.

His own name is prominent in this land where his personality still haunts the coast. Pressed by his officers and his distinguished passenger, the botanist Joseph Banks (later Sir Joseph), he agreed that the Strait he had discovered between the two main islands should bear his own name, shortly afterwards retaliating by placing Banks's name on the volcanic peninsula, which he took to be an island, that juts out dramatically from the middle of the South Island. And in the next century, when the land was surveyed in more detail, the highest peak of the great range of mountains which he had named the Southern Alps was called after him. It is unlucky that his plain, blunt, honest English surname is so unpoetic. This beautiful peak, rising to over twelve thousand feet, was known to the Maoris as Aorangi (page 278). Feelings are somewhat torn on this matter. It seems so right that Cook and Tasman should stand as they do, side by side, Cook slightly the greater, but Aorangi is dear to New Zealand hearts, too, and in no danger of being forgotten.

After Cook's voyages another long interval – nearly seventy years – was to pass before the pressure of events forced the British Government 'with extreme reluctance' as officially stated, to annex New Zealand. But during that period, the existence of the country being known, there had been nothing to prevent adventurous characters from sailing there, to hunt whales, trade with the Maoris, and evade authority. There were also missionaries, courageous men who should be better represented in local names than they are. English-speaking settlements – all strictly unofficial – began to grow here and there, and with them a few English names, though since their very existence depended on friendly relations with the Maoris, most of the settlers learned a little of the language and tended to use the native names.

The largest of these early settlements in the lawless period was in the Bay of Islands where 'the very refuse of society' (according to Charles Darwin) had washed up in a natural paradise, and here the Maori name Kororareka was used. But farther south where there were fewer Maoris some English names became established in a haphazard way, and a few of them have survived. These include Port Nicholson which was discovered by James Herd, captain of a whaling ship, and named after his friend the harbour-master of Sydney; and Milford Sound, named by an adventurous Welshman, hunting seals in the first decade of the century. He named it after his native Milford Haven, but there is no resemblance between the gentle Welsh harbour and this dramatic southern fiord.

But the chief early haunt of the whalers was down in the south, where the blunt headland that faces out towards the South Pole was known to them as Old Man Bluff as early as 1803, and behind it in what shelter they could get they made their summer base. Bluff – which may be the oldest white settlement in the country – has also one of its simplest and most natural names.

Captain Cook had thought Stewart Island to be part of the mainland and had called it only Cape South. Its name comes from a William Stewart, of whom very little is known. In 1809 he was first officer of the *Pegasus*, a survey ship in these waters commanded by Captain Chase, and he may have been there earlier as a whaler, which could explain why the whole island was called after him and only a small bay after the Captain.

Several of the ships that came to this 'no man's land' have left their names on its coast. The *Pegasus* has given Pegasus Bay and Port Pegasus on Stewart Island; the *Coromandel*, a small naval vessel that visited the north-east coast in 1820, brought a name from India; and just before the annexation the brig *Pelorus*, patrolling through the straits, gave its name to

Pelorus Sound, three romantic names that make a welcome note of variety among the many places called after British personalities.

French navigators were looking around these islands too while they were still available to any enterprising nation. D'Urville Island, Cape Souci, and French Pass in the Straits are relics of their voyages – while De Vauchelles and French Bay on Banks Peninsula mark the one French settlement in New Zealand, slight relics one may say, but in a country that is so remote from outside influence any name that is not British or Maori in origin is a point of unusual interest.

Time may be measured by change and events as well as by years. In England the first few years of the nineteenth century seem comparatively recent, and a place-name coined at that time is classed as modern. In New Zealand at the same date the Maoris were still cannibals and the pioneering age hardly begun; the period has an aura about it comparable to what the English feel for the age of Drake and Raleigh.

When Captain William Hobson RN arrived in 1840 to take charge officially of the strangely assorted community in which the missionaries were trying to prevent the whalers from demoralizing the cannibals, one of his first acts was to rename the disreputable Korarareka to make it more suitable for a colonial capital. In selecting a name he followed the precedent set by Captain Phillip at Sydney and took that of the Minister of State for the Colonies, Lord John Russell.

But Russell had hardly enjoyed its new status for a year when Hobson realized the disadvantages of its position, and decided to move his infant capital farther south to the spacious double harbour which Kipling was later to call 'last, loneliest, loveliest, exquisite, apart', and which others at the time called 'Hobson's choice'. A superb site, but now he had to think of another name, and, having honoured the Colonial Secretary, he decided to repay a personal debt of gratitude. A few years earlier the friendly intervention of Lord Auckland, as First Lord of the Admiralty, had saved him from the retired list and assured his promotion. By this time Lord Auckland was Governor-General of India, but not a very notable one. Like Lord Sydney he was well-intentioned, but his policy was far from successful.

Neither would be remembered today, outside the detailed study of political history, if these two great Pacific harbours did not keep their names alive.

Lord Auckland's connection with New Zealand is less than Lord Sydney's with Australia. The latter was the responsible minister in London at the time that the convict settlement was founded and did authorize arrangements for its dispatch; Lord Auckland's contribution was only to Captain Hobson's career, which did not turn out very brilliant. In a difficult situation with few resources he did his best, but his health soon failed and he died after only two years in office, his chief contribution to the young colony being the site of Auckland and its name. No clear meaning can be given to it. The first syllable is pre-English, perhaps derived from a Celtic river-name. Before the Conquest it named a district not far from Durham and later was used for a group of villages all differentiated by additional words – among them Bishop Auckland which is now a large town; in England it is not used alone, and its unqualified form is unique to this place. New Zealanders take it for granted, and their city, sprawling unrestrainedly around its blue bays, has given it a character that is all its own.

In the same year that Auckland was founded the planning of more settlements for New Zealand was well under way. The government might lack enthusiasm but there were other leading men in England with new ideas and high hopes on the subject of colonization, notably Edward Gibbon Wakefield. These idealists formed the New Zealand Company and in one decade dispatched five complete colonies, whose names, like everything else about them, were the subject of earnest thought and discussion even before the ships left England.

For the first of them Wakefield chose Wellington, title of the Iron Duke, Prime Minister and Grand Old Man of England, which was readily agreed to. The old soldier and statesman was not then in office, but still active and gave the project his blessing. The title comes from the village in Somerset and as there are also other places of this name in England (page 69) it is less distinctive than Auckland, but belongs to that typical style of Old English place-name that distant colonists have always liked. In this case the first shiploads had already reached their hill-girt harbour before Governor Hobson had made his decision about Auckland, and were claiming that their colony should be the capital, but it was not until 1865 that they gained their point.

At the same time two other branches of the same society were making their plans. One of these met in Plymouth under the patronage of the mayor and the Earl of Devon, and it followed naturally that their settlement was to be called New Plymouth; like the Pilgrim Fathers they sailed directly from the old Plymouth to the new. The other group whose colony sailed in the same year (1841) chose the name of Nelson to match Wellington. It may have seemed to some less suitable, not being a place-name in origin, as most English titles are, but a surname of a patronymic sort; however, the custom of using men's names for places regardless of their nature was rapidly becoming widespread at this date, and the greatness of the man outweighed other considerations. When the settlers arrived after a particularly trying voyage – in one of their four ships sixty-four children died during the three-month journey – they began at once to follow out their theme, naming their streets and public places, as they laid them out, from Nelson's ships, officers and battles.

Two more schemes, put into action in the South Island, sprang from even more serious and high-minded motives that were largely religious in nature. Indeed, there had been nothing like it anywhere since the settlements of Pennsylvania and Maryland. The first in the extreme south was organized by the Scottish Free Church, and here in a land that is not unlike parts of Scotland, with its bare hills, bright skies and a nip in the air, a group of Scottish settlers gave names that helped to recreate the home from which they had travelled farther than any settlers before them. First they wanted Edinburgh, but not as a mere repetition, and so they took its old Gaelic form Dunedin, an inspired choice that gave them a name that was at once old and new; and in the same spirit they chose Clutha, the ancient name of the Clyde, for the big, rushing river that cascades through the hills behind the town, while Balclutha named a settlement on its banks. For the whole colony they preserved the Maori name Otago (slightly mispronounced – it should be Otaku – but all credit to them for keeping it) and scattered it with the names that were dear to them, Water of

Leith, Ben Nevis, Roslyn, Bannockburn and so on. Mosgiel was named after Robert Burns's farm in Ayrshire by the poet's great nephew who was one of the leaders of the enterprise and, for their other leader, Captain William Cargill, they concocted Invercargill by adding a Gaelic prefix. The Scottish influence has never ceased to function in this region, and the southern-most township in the British Commonwealth, a little holiday resort on Stewart Island, bears the simple Gaelic name of Oban, literally 'little bay'.

The other South Island settlement, most thoughtfully planned of all, was sponsored by the Church of England and supported by a group of distinguished intellectuals. The President of the Association formed to organize the scheme was the Archbishop of Canterbury, and from the start it was decided that the new province should be called Canterbury in honour of the mother church, and that one of its towns should bear the archbishop's own name, Sumner. The chairman of the management committee, Lord Lyttelton, gave generous finan-cial support and his title was used for the harbour. The actual leader on the spot was John Robert Godley, an enthusiastic product of the Oxford Movement; it was he who chose the name of the Oxford College, Christ Church, for the principal settlement, ' . . . and I hope my old College will be obliged to me', he wrote to a friend. It was an unusual choice; the British have never been much inclined to use religious names for towns, and many of the settlers thought this one too sacred for secular use and petitioned that Lyttelton should be the capital; but Godley carried his point. Lyttelton, Sumner and Christchurch were laid out as he planned, with their streets named from Church of England bishoprics. His own name remains on a headland.

Another early decision was that the river on which the chief town was to be sited must be the Shakespeare. But when the advance party arrived, they found a Scottish family already living on its banks, the brothers John and William Dean, in a homestead that they had built themselves without any sponsors or committees. They had named it Riccarton, from their Scottish birthplace, which remains as a suburb of Christchurch, and had called the river the Avon, from their old home too – there are Avons in all parts of Britain. Godley did his best to

make it the Shakespeare, but human nature was against him.
The Deans were respected as pioneers, and soon the new settlers
building their shacks along the winding stream were all saying
'Avon'. To Englishmen anywhere it is a word that sounds like a
river, which 'Shakespeare' does not.

As the new colony's territory included plains that stretched
for two hundred miles backed by high mountains, there was
plenty of scope for naming, and the chief surveyor, wishing to
gratify the distinguished gentlemen who had subscribed to the
enterprise, placed their names on the principal features. The
Ashley River is named for the great philanthropist, better
known as Lord Shaftesbury, who achieved so much in bettering
the working conditions of the poor in England; Lake Ellesmere
and the Ashburton River for two other noble supporters of the
scheme; but the two largest rivers that cut across the plains
north and south of Christchurch, the Waimakariri and the
Rakaia, threw off the lordly titles of Courtenay and
Cholmondeley as if they were so much driftwood, reverting to
their Maori names.

In the dealing out of nominal honours in this way there must
always be inequality and omissions, and those whose service has
been greatest may receive least reward. The courageous
missionaries of the early period had received scant recognition
of this sort, and now in the phase of rapid development, the
man who was the true founder, more than any other, of
Wellington, Nelson, New Plymouth, Dunedin and Christchurch
– Edward Gibbon Wakefield – was himself ignored when
names were being given. Because of the wild escapades of his
youth, which included the abduction of an heiress and a
consequent spell in Newgate, his long years of dedicated service
to colonial expansion were always under a cloud. Politicians
sought his advice and used his ideas but did not brandish his
name. Still a controversial figure, he must always stand high in
New Zealand history. It was he who brought it to the attention
of Parliament in 1836 as 'the fittest country in the world for
colonizing', he who formed the association that founded the five
colonies on the principles he had devised. No long-range
idealist, he went out to New Zealand with his two brothers, who
acted as practical leaders at Wellington and Nelson, and
remained there for the rest of his life. And yet the only

'Wakefield' of any note in New Zealand is the little township that commemorates his brother Arthur, who was killed nearby in a skirmish with a Maori chief.

When settlement is proceeding fast and many future towns need names there is often a tendency to follow fashions. Wellington not only suggested Nelson, but started a whole series of successful generals. Picton was named from Sir Thomas Picton, one of Wellington's senior officers who was killed at Waterloo, Napier from Sir Charles Napier of Indian fame, Havelock and the larger Havelock North (in quite a different region) from Sir Henry Havelock, the saviour of Lucknow. It happened that the district round Hawkes Bay was just being settled at the time of the Indian Mutiny, and the choice, not only of Havelock but of Hastings (for Warren Hastings) and Clive, resulted from a wave of spontaneous feeling about British India; but the fashion for military heroes was carried too far when a whole province was named for the great Duke of Marlborough, and its chief town for his victory at Blenheim in 1704. Otago countered this with two townships named for Cromwell and his victory at Naseby. Fortunately, after that enthusiasm for old battles dwindled.

As the colonists began to feel themselves growing into a nation they gradually shook off the tendency to name their places from people on the other side of the world and to use the names of their own leaders instead. Their one really great governor in their first half-century, Sir George Grey, was not neglected, Greytown in the North Island and the Grey River in the South being named from him. Greymouth on the coast followed automatically and shows how quickly a name is identified with a natural feature and its origin forgotten, for if one thinks of Grey as a man, Greymouth is an odd combination. Sir George had distinguished himself as an explorer, scholar and administrator in South Africa and Australia as well as New Zealand and has geographical honours in all three that are well deserved.

Other men who have themselves given many names and also had their own prominently placed are the official surveyors. Captain John Stokes, later an Admiral, who surveyed much of New Zealand at the time of the Canterbury Settlement, was the man who named Mount Cook, and also Mount Peel from the current Prime Minister, and his own name (not an inspiring one) remains on another peak. For a country so very much addicted to naming places from people New Zealand has been unlucky in the actual nature of the surnames presented to it by fate.

When it came to surveying the interior, the task passed from naval officers to explorers on foot, especially in the mountainous South Island, much of which is too rugged for horses. One of the most notable was Thomas Brunner, an adventurous young man who vanished into the west-coast forests for over eighteen months and returned after many discoveries but prematurely aged. His name lives in Lake Brunner and a nearby township.

Even official surveyors had to be mountaineers, bushmen, and good swimmers. One who was ready to 'rough it' was Julius von Haast, a German by birth and a distinguished geologist, who became Surveyor-General for Canterbury in 1861. His efforts opened up new mountain regions, and his European tastes and background provided some exotic names that seem not unsuited to the wild romantic scenery. The Franz Joseph Glacier, from the Emperor of Austria, Malte Brun and Elie de Beaumont (two high peaks) from a Danish geographer and a French geologist were among those of his choice. As a new road has recently been opened along the Haast Valley, which he first explored, his own name is now coming to public notice more than ever before.

In contrast to these foreign names, Arthur's Pass has a pleasant touch of informality. In the first decade of the Canterbury Settlement when the Alps made an almost insuperable barrier to the west it was the goal of many adventurous young men to find a practical way through. Samuel Butler was one who tried, and failed, and the title of the book he wrote about his attempt (turned into fantasy) now names a high sheep station Erewhon. But in 1864 young Arthur Dudley Dobson was more successful, and a few years later when his father, as Provincial Engineer, was given the task of putting a road of some sort through to the west coast, the latter remarked to his colleagues, 'I believe that Arthur's pass will prove the best.' From that time it had its name.

The task of surveying the South Island is still incomplete. There are still peaks unclimbed and unnamed and in the wild south-west the bush-covered heights intersected by chasms still in places defy penetration. In the North Island where most of the Maoris lived, preferring the warmer climate, all the mountains and rivers have known native names and most of these have been retained, but in the South, where the 'high country' was uninhabited, the task of naming it has fallen chiefly on the white settlers. Since 1946 the Geographic Board has stipulated that 'only persons who have climbed or traversed on mountain features have the right to submit names for them', but this is no new policy: since the early days, the explorers have also been the name-givers.

Those who have themselves battled with mountain conditions have more feeling for the peaks they have conquered than have public officials, who have only looked from a distance, and there are more imaginative names in the Southern Alps than anywhere else in New Zealand; some are very frank, even banal, but at least genuine – Aspiring, Stargazer, Headlong, Awful, Soaker, Pollux, Ajax, The Thumbs, Sword, Coronet, Sentinel, Amazon, Pinnacle, Misery and so on. They are mixed with the surnames of men – but mostly of those who have earned their right to be there.

The discovery of gold brought an influx of men to previously uninhabited districts, whose style of naming was rough and direct. The first strike was at Gabriel's Gully in Otago and other camps soon bore popular names such as Gentle Annie and Roaring Meg. However, such names are apt to be rejected sooner or later by the forces of convention, and the miners' names that have become permanent are their less lively efforts. Even so, Arrowtown, named from the river, which was so called because it ran so fast, and Reefton, from its gold-bearing reefs, are original names that sprang from facts.

In many respects New Zealand place-names have run parallel with those of Australia, and the chief complaint to be made against them is similar too, that not enough of them relate directly to the land. Why do so few of them refer to the wild life or the trees, or tell of hot pools, fountains of steam, rumbling rocks and other wonders? A New Zealander might answer that such things are contained in the native names, but surely the white inhabitants could coin names from them in their own words too. Too many place-names are still borrowed.

But I believe a trend towards more naturalism is already apparent.

Maori place-names are numerous, especially in the north, much liked, and better preserved than the native names of most of the other lands where the British have settled in numbers. One reason for this is to be found in the nature of the language itself; for the great strength of Maori is that it is a single language, in contrast to the hundreds of different tongues of the American Indians, African tribes, and Australian aborigines. Maori was not only spoken throughout New Zealand, with slight variations between north and south, but was also a part of the great Polynesian language of the Pacific. When Cook reached this land which had been isolated from the rest of mankind for perhaps four centuries he had with him a boy named Tupia who had been taken on at Tahiti, and it was a strange, historic moment when Tupia called to the Maoris who stood threateningly on the sea shore, and was answered in words that he understood. A link that had been broken for centuries was joined again.

Through Tupia Cook was able to talk to the Maoris, and showed great interest in them throughout his voyage, learning all that he could from them about their land. He took pains to collect their own names for their two main islands, writing them carefully on his finished map. Unfortunately, those who came after him found it much easier just to say the North and the South Island, and these prosaic names have become too firmly established to be dislodged.

The other important factor in preserving the native names was the zeal of the first missionaries, who learned Maori themselves long before the British annexation, and were there ready to act as interpreters when at last the officials came. Even more important. Thomas Kendall, one of the earliest of them, had the foresight to arrange for a leading chief, the great Hongi, to go to England and spend some months at Cambridge with a distinguished linguist, Professor S. Lee, who learned Maori from him, devised a phonetic system of spelling, and wrote a grammar and vocabulary. This was in 1820. What Hongi thought of Cambridge has not been reported. Unfortunately, though quick and clever, he was at heart a bloodthirsty savage, and he used his great opportunity to acquire a supply of guns for his return home; once there he led his tribe so armed against others, who still used Stone Age weapons, and in a few years reduced his own race by many thousands. The missionary's experiment, carried out at his own expense, had mixed results; but at least we can thank him that all Maori names (except for some half dozen or so that were established at a very early date) are written accurately, instead of having their identities lost through ignorant corruption as has happened to native words in so many other places. It cannot be said that white New Zealanders pronounce them well, but at least the spelling shows what they should be.

Maori is a simple language in sound and structure, though the thought expressed is often subtle. It has only fifteen different sounds, and these include no sibilants or anything harsh. When they first heard English spoken, it seemed to Maoris like hissing and scratching; when we hear Maori, it is clear and liquid like notes of music. English visitors are sometimes disconcerted by the many names beginning with 'Ng', but this may be pronounced as 'N'; in a medial position it should be like the 'ng' in 'singer', and never hard as in 'finger'. Every vowel should be clearly sounded, including a final 'e'.

These native place-names are of great interest because, though many consist of straightforward description, a large number are concerned with history and mythology. To take some simple ones first: by far the commonest element is *wai* (pronounced, generally, to rhyme with 'sky') and this is natural, as it means 'water'; and no land in the world has a greater profusion of rushing rivers. Waikato is the strong water; Waimakiriri, snow-cold water; Waitangi, water of weeping; Waitaki, the same thing in the South Island dialect; Waimate, dead water, a still pool; Wairau, many waters.

A few more well-known names with natural meanings include Wanganui, big harbour; Whangaroa, long harbour; Rotorua, two lakes; Rotoiti, small lake; Tauranga, sheltered harbour. *Waka* is a canoe, or a long, narrow trough. Wakatipu, a long, deep lake among mountains, is the *waka* of a goblin.

The majority are not so easy. Maori is a poetic language and many of its words have metaphorical meanings besides their common ones, which throws interpretation into doubt.

K

Aorangi, the native name of Mount Cook, is a case in point. *Ao* is a cloud, a bright cloud (there is another word for a dark one), but it may also be a land or a world. *Rangi* is the sky. The popular English translation, 'Cloud Piercer', is not at all accurate. Literally it is either 'bright cloud in the sky' or perhaps 'world in the sky'. To complicate matters it is an ancient name, brought by the Maoris from an earlier homeland and found also on peaks in Tahiti and the Cook Islands. When they gave it to the great southern mountain it was just like the settlers in Otago reproducing Ben Nevis, and people do not always know the significance of their own old names, however much they love them. *Ao* is also the first word in the Maori name for New Zealand, *Aotearoa* which is generally translated 'the long White Cloud', but could equally be 'the long bright land'.

Rangi is another word with several meanings. Literally 'sky' it can also mean 'light', and so 'day'. In this sense it occurs in many place-names, for the Maoris were great recounters of their own history and remembered many places chiefly by events that had happened there. Rangitoto, the conical island in Auckland Harbour, means 'the day of blood', and refers to the wounding there of an early hero, Tama te Kapua, whose story can be told in length. The same name occurs elsewhere, where the blood of other chiefs was shed. The Rangitata River means 'day of black clouds' or 'sky with black clouds' and in either case refers to some special event that took place there under a lowering sky.

Because Maori names often recall whole stories they tend to be very long.* They generally have a short version for practical use but as this consists of only a word or two out of a long phrase it often makes little sense without its context. For instance, the full name of Kaikoura is *Te ahi kai koura a Tama-ki-te-Rangi* which means 'the fire where Tama-ki-te-Rangi cooked crayfish'. *Kai koura* is literally only 'cooked crayfish', but Tama was a great hero and his stopping to eat at this place was a significant part of his adventures. The name belonged originally to the site of the township of Kaikoura on the sea,

* Reputedly the longest place-name in the world is the Maori name of a hill in the Hawkes Bay district, which is generally shortened to its beginning, Taumata. It has slight variations of form. The best known of them, which just surpasses the Welsh name given on page 155 means 'the brow of the hill where Tamatea, who had sailed all round the land, played his nose flute to his beloved one'.

but now includes the mountain range behind. Again Taupo (the name of New Zealand's largest lake) is the word for a feather cloak such as is worn by chiefs. In full it is *Taupo nui a Tia*, the big cloak of Tia, and only a poetical metaphor can explain it. Manapouri (another lake) means 'the anxious heart' and of course there is a story behind it.

Tongariro, the name of the central volcano of the thermal region, is made up of *tonga*, 'south wind' and *riro*, 'carried'. It is part of the myth that tells how one of the heroes who had come by canoe from Hawaiiki climbed this mountain and being nearly dead with cold called out for help, and how 'the south wind carried' his words to his sisters in his homeland who sent a magical fire to burst out of the mountain and warm him.

I know of no other people who have such fanciful names as the Polynesians. White New Zealanders have done well to keep so many of them; but they have the one disadvantage that their limited number of sounds produces similarities that can be confusing to those who know little of the language. Visitors tend to get muddled between the many *Whanga*s and *Waka*s and *Wai*s. Therefore the great variety given by English and Scottish names with their many ingredients is essential to the growing community. But as time goes on there should be fewer reproductions from elsewhere, and more fresh creations by the local people, in whatever words come most naturally to them, English, Scottish or Maori, or a combination of any two. Glentui, for instance, is a charming name. There is enough Scottish blood in New Zealand for 'glen' to be used reasonably for a wooded valley, and the native songbird gives a unique character. But there are too few such names as yet.

Chapter 23

LOOKING ROUND THE WORLD

In trying to follow the naming activities of the English-speaking peoples, it has been necessary to concentrate on those countries where they have settled in the largest numbers and where the character of their place-names can be observed in bulk. To regions that show a slighter scattering of English names, only a cursory glance can be given.

In India, for instance, although the influence of Britain was formerly paramount, its effect on place-names has been minimal. The growth of British power in the East was a very different matter from the settlement of such sparsely inhabited lands as North America or Australia. The English merchants who came first to India and found it rich and civilized, teeming with people, and packed with its own historic names, had no need or wish to invent others, except for their own special establishments, such as Fort St George in Madras, which still names a part of the city. Here and there some centre of commerce organized by British administration still records the fact, as at English Bazaar in West Bengal or at Lyallpur – named after Sir Alfred Lyall, a governor of the North West Provinces; here and there the modern form of a name, now generally accepted, is the result of English misspelling, as at Cawnpore, where the ending should be the Hindi *pur*, 'a village', but such cases are rarities among the mass of native names. However, England's greatest gift to India of a common language, indispensable if its people are to understand each other, means that expressions such as New Delhi, Grand Trunk Road and so forth are more likely to increase than to disappear.

Probably the best known English name in Asia is Mount Everest, named after Sir George Everest, Surveyor-General of India, who completed the first official survey of this region in 1841. How lucky it was that he had such a good surname, unusual, poetical in sound, and with a suggestion of eternity about it. Its origin is actually a corruption of Evreux, the name of a little town in Normandy, brought to England as the surname of a family and better preserved in the form of Devereux. Going even further back, it is not French in origin, but an early Celtic name, Evorac – the place of yew trees – identical with our York (page 6). But that is very remote from the mountain; it was called after a man, and even he is generally forgotten in the unique quality that the mountain has given to his name. The Tibetans called it Chomo Lungma, an old name whose meaning is uncertain.

Then we must think briefly of the Pacific. From the eighteenth century onwards British sea-captains have sailed about it, confidently naming what they found, and the Admiralty in London, while entering the new names on official charts, often added the names of the explorers who seldom did that for themselves. In this way the Gilbert and Marshall Islands, for example, were named for two officers who sailed that way in 1788 after helping to convoy the first batch of convicts to Australia.

Unfortunately, most of the naval men who made these discoveries, though brave and enterprising in their deeds, were conventional and uninspired in devising names. Samuel Wallis who discovered Tahiti in 1767 showered titles of the royal family and other English notabilities on romantic islands in all directions, but luckily hardly any of them survived; and Captain Philip Carteret, a distinguished gentleman from Jersey (whose ancestor had named New Jersey) had just as little idea of suiting a name to a place. What could be less apposite for a Pacific atoll than 'The Bishop of Osnaburg's Island'? This was taken from the German title of the king's second son who was not yet Duke of York, being only four years old. Naturally it reverted to its own name, Tematengi. Some of Carteret's names that have lasted are New Ireland, New Hanover and Pitcairn. The last is one of his better efforts, being in one word and with a slightly rocky sound. But that was only luck; he named it from the midshipman who sighted it, 'a young gentleman, son to Major Pitcairn of the Marines'. The first white men to inhabit this island were the mutineers from the *Bounty*, whose descendants are there still. Their ship's name remains on the Bounty Islands far to the south which they had passed earlier in their long voyage.

Compared with those of Carteret, Cook's names in the Pacific are on the whole more enlightened. Though he generally gave English names to groups of islands, the Friendly Isles, the Society Isles, the Sandwich Isles and so forth, he was careful to record the native names for individual islands whenever he could learn them, giving new names only to those that were uninhabited, such as Norfolk Island and Christmas Island, which was sighted on Christmas Day, 1770.

Lord Sandwich, First Lord of the Admiralty, in and out of office for over thirty years, had his name planted on many shores and in several oceans. It is no longer used for the Hawaiian group where it certainly was not needed, for the principal island has a name of deep significance for Polynesians (page 262) and in every way fitting for the archipelago that is now an American state. The United States authorities have added a few factual names of their own, such as Pearl Harbor and Midway Island (midway between America and Asia), but they respect the native names and will not attempt to replace them. Nearly all have natural or mythical meanings and musical sounds. Honolulu, for instance, literally 'safe harbour', is full of the sound of lapping water.

Of the Polynesian language that is spoken in many dialects over thousands of miles of ocean some slight impression has been given in Chapter 22 (page 276). On the whole, although Spanish, French, English and American influences have touched them, the vast majority of Pacific islands have kept their own names regardless of ships that came and went, and of missionaries and administrators who often stayed. One curious result of missionary activity may be seen in the form of Pago Pago in Samoa. A century ago the missionaries had a small printing press for issuing a news-sheet; they were somewhat short of type, especially of the letter 'n', and some names had to go without it, including Pango Pango. But the natives and the well-informed still pronounce it in the old way.

There are other islands in other oceans which we must pass quickly. The Falkland Islands in the deep Atlantic, sighted in 1590 by John Davis, were named a generation later by another English seaman in honour of the Earl of Falkland who was then Charles I's chief Minister of State. These have been always British. Islands that have changed hands generally tell the story in their mixed naming. Tristan da Cunha bears the name of a fifteenth-century Portuguese navigator, but its chief and only settlement is Edinburgh. St Helena was also named by the Portuguese, but Jamestown and Longwood proclaim a later allegiance. On the whole the English have seldom changed names inherited from others, when they have been aware of them, but have added thousands of their own.

There is also the Antarctic, where, in the absence of inhabitants, a completely blank page was presented to the explorers of several nations and to the governments to whom they made their reports. The names that have been placed on it are chiefly those of recent royalties, for whom nothing else of sufficient size was left, and of the explorers themselves. Notable among the earliest of these were James Weddell, captain of an English sealing ship who in 1823 sailed further south than any man before him, and James Ross, sent by the Admiralty in 1839 to study polar magnetism, each of whom had his name immortalized in an icy sea. Perhaps the aptest names in Antarctica were given by Captain Ross when he called two active volcanoes after his ships, Erebus and Terror.

A point to admire in Antarctic naming, as far as it goes – for it still lies largely in the future – is the degree of international cooperation that it has shown, the nations concerned having accepted each other's names in a civilized spirit, as they have throughout most of the southern hemisphere. In this respect there was great improvement from the time when the French and English had changed each other's names repeatedly in North America. In the late eighteenth century and early nineteenth, although these two countries were still constantly at war, each respected the other's voyages of exploration and used the other's names in the Pacific, where both sent scientific expeditions, their common heritage of classical learning making such cooperation easy. Polynesia, 'many islands', was invented by the French; Melanesia, 'black islands', for a group with darker skinned inhabitants, coined later on the same pattern by the English.

As for Arctic and Antarctic, they are much older terms used by geographers of ancient times; the former derived from Arcturus, the Great Bear, the latter from its opposite which was discussed hypothetically by scholars long before it was seen by man. Both of these names are mentioned by Chaucer.

In many parts of the world to which Britain has never made any claim there are clusters of English place-names that bear witness to British zeal for exploration. One such unexpected group exists on the southern coast of Chile which stretches with its fringe of islands down to the Horn. These wild and dangerous shores were first charted by a series of naval officers – such as Captain Fitzroy of the *Beagle* – sent out by the Admiralty in the early nineteenth century in search of scientific knowledge. The names they gave remain in use by Chileans, to whom they must have an exotic sound, prefaced now by Spanish words, Seno Deepwater, Seno Langford (*seno* is a cove or inlet), Isla Wellington, Isla Duque de York, Isla Londonderry, and many others.

It was these same naval men who gave the name Drake Passage to the turbulent waters immediately south of the Horn. Drake himself did not use that route, having reached the Pacific on his voyage round the world through Magellan's Straits. However, on emerging from them he was driven south by great gales and saw 'the Atlantick ocean and the South Sea meet in a most large and free scope', being thus the first navigator to discover that this route existed. He named the most southerly land that he saw Elizabeth Island in honour of his queen, but this did not survive and it was left to a Dutch skipper of the next century to give the last cape its permanent name, calling it after his ship, the *Hoorn*, a name that proved more apt than he had realized when later the whole curved shape of the mass of islands was revealed.

As we look at the principal groups of names given all round the world by English speakers we see the differences that give each land its special character but also marked similarities of style. And since in the last two centuries so many places were named from people it might be of interest to consider briefly which individuals have been most honoured in this way.

By far the most named-after person in the world is, as we should expect, Queen Victoria, even though she does not appear in the United States. Apart from cities she has a superb set of natural features, a huge island in the Canadian Arctic, a top-ranking lake and waterfall in Africa, an enormous desert in Australia, and a long river, as well as two states (Queensland as well as Victoria). Her name is to be found in the most exotic places: a mountain in New Guinea, the chief town of the Seychelles, the harbour of Hong Kong, the Antarctic. She names everything except a sea; there have been few of these available since her reign began.

Second is Columbus who piled up a big score in the nineteenth century after having nothing for the best part of three centuries. Even in the States he is just ahead of George Washington, by my reckoning, and British Columbia puts him well in the lead. Or does it? It was named largely from the Columbia River, and that was named from a ship. But the explorer was the inspiration behind them all.

Then comes George Washington, leading a number of American politicians by only a short head, for the habit in the States of repeating any popular name over and over means that any prominent man with a tolerable sounding name who had a town named for him a century or more ago is likely to have at least a dozen more by now.

Every sovereign of England from Elizabeth I to the II is well represented, and nearly all their consorts too, but those of this century are mostly in the Polar regions. The highest score among them, after Victoria, goes probably to George III whose long reign gave him representation in the States, as well as in most of the Commonwealth countries. George IV has his place on American soil too, as Prince of Wales in Alaska where a cape and island were named for him by Captain Cook, and the town of Wales on the cape is known by his title. Looking farther back, both Charleses did well, and also James II whose list starts with New York, State and City, but their adversary, Cromwell, is hardly to be found anywhere.

I believe that every American president has his place on the map down to John F. Kennedy whose name recently displaced

K*

the Spanish Cape Canaveral.* No one would grudge him an honour of this sort, but it is sad that it was at the expense of one of the oldest names in America. The presidential scores are very varied. McKinley has the highest mountain but little else. Monroe, who has the regular quota of about twenty towns, has also a foreign capital, Monrovia in Liberia, which puts him high on the list.

Similarly, there is an almost complete set of English prime ministers dotted round the world, but it falls off in this century, since Commonwealth countries have preferred to use their own names and in England this kind of naming is almost unknown. Again their local honours have varied greatly, depending more on the chances of colonial projects during their terms of office than on their own merit. Those who secured the greatest single prizes were Pitt the Elder (Pittsburgh), the Duke of Wellington, Lord Melbourne and Lord Salisbury, while other famous statesmen such as Peel and Gladstone had only small towns or minor geographical features.† Disraeli had no tributes of this sort until he received the title of Lord Beaconsfield, which was more acceptable than his Jewish name, but even then a small town in Tasmania and another in South Africa made his total.

On the whole the ministers for the colonies have done almost better than their political chiefs, men like Halifax, Sydney, Kimberley, and Bathurst, little remembered now for themselves. Their pleasant sounding titles helped to make their names congenial; the first Lord Halifax, for instance, was by birth George Dunk, and had he been untitled the choice for the town in Nova Scotia might have fallen elsewhere. It must have seemed a regular perquisite of office, a colonial city, but hardly any of the gentlemen in question can have visited their namesakes, nor is it recorded whether they were greatly gratified.

Everyone would agree that if places are to be named from men, then those who first discovered them have the highest claims, and on the whole explorers have been well represented; but again fate has dealt the cards erratically. A lucky one fell

* Out of thirty-seven presidents the only doubt arises in the cases of Andrew Johnson and Benjamin Harrison. There are several American towns named Johnson and Harrison, some called after other men; but it is likely that at least one of each was named in honour of a president.

† The mineral deposits in the neighbourhood of Gladstone (Australia) may yet make it a great city.

to Juan Bermudez who found the island of Bermuda. Nothing whatever is known of him except this one fact. But there his name is forever, while many great explorers of that early period of whom much is known had no commemoration until long after their deaths and sometimes not then. Names chosen long after a man's achievement in places he had never seen – as for instance Raleigh, state capital of North Carolina and the many towns called Columbus – are honest tributes, but they lack the first-hand quality of one like Hudson Bay with its real personal link.

Royalties, politicians, explorers, soldiers and sailors, these are the people whose names have been most often chosen for important places, but for some strange reason neither writers, artists or musicians seem ever to have been thought suitable. Most people would agree that the greatest Englishman of all time is Shakespeare, but in *The Times World Atlas* with about 200,000 entries his name occurs only once – Shakespeare Island in Canada. It has been put forward on several occasions when important names were under discussion, for Canberra for instance, but it was never felt to be right. Nor was it. A city destined for greatness should have a name that will be all its own, one that is not already loaded with significance of another sort. Many colonists have thought of him when they named rivers Avon, or towns Stratford; the creations of his brain, Romeo, Viola, Hamlet, even Othello have named small towns in America, but his own name has been avoided almost everywhere.

Opinions on the merits of place-names will vary with individual tastes, but there are certain standards on which all who give thought to the matter will agree.

As the purpose of naming is to distinguish one place from another, the first essential for any name is to be unique in the region in which it is used, and the more widely it is known the greater its need to be distinctive. If a single word can convey to all the world what place is meant, so much the better, and many great cities have achieved this goal, though the effect can easily be spoilt, as in the case of Quebec, by failure to find a different designation for the surrounding province, so that ambiguity can arise even with a highly distinctive name.

In England the common names that grew in the days when each district was self-sufficient, the Stokes, Hamptons, Westons and so forth, must always be doubled up with something else for the sake of clarity, good names in origin but with this weakness in modern times; but the worst offenders in this class are the popular American town-names that have been repeated in state after state, having been borrowed from England in the first place: fifteen Plymouths, sixteen Dovers, eighteen Oxfords, nineteen Chesters.* Even the most original American creations, such as Minneapolis, Atlanta, Phoenix and Buffalo, have had no immunity from regular reproduction. But such repetition cannot detract from the distinction of the original name in the place where it first began. Dover has still a unique quality to the English; London, standing alone, is still London, England; it is London, Ohio, and London, Ontario, that need qualification. When the name of an obscure village is copied in another land the lack of originality is much less to be deplored, if at all, for the little place is known to comparatively few. Confusion can seldom have arisen between the Irish village of Baltimore and the great American city.

The second most important quality for a place-name is euphony. We cannot expect every name to have a melodious sound, though a great many do and give constant pleasure, but it must not be harsh or awkward to pronounce. Its length too is of great significance. For an important place a single syllable seems inadequate, and two, three or even four are generally liked, but they must flow easily together, the arrangement of stresses being vital. The possible rhythms are very varied, the most widely used for English place-names consisting of three syllables with the stress on the first – Cumberland, Delaware, Salisbury, Kimberley – and these run more smoothly on the tongue than two syllables of equal weight such as Palm Springs or South Bend, while four or five syllables with varied stress – Ontario, Canterbury, California – may seem shorter than the three of New South Wales. Many a well-sounding name has been spoilt by the addition of a second word. Queen Victoria chose Columbia for a Canadian province because she liked its noble sound, but she added British to avoid confusion with Colombia, thereby reducing it in practice to BC.

* In *The Times Atlas of the World*, 1967.

288

The third essential for a name of the highest standard is a link with reality, past or present. Most of the names in the British Isles and a great many that are classed as natural in the younger countries refer directly to physical facts: Little Rock, Detroit, Cape Town, Swan River, Bay of Islands. Many others reflect an historic rather than a geographic truth, telling of human actions or emotions connected directly with those places – Newfoundland, Lake Disappointment (dried up in the Australian desert), Encounter Bay, Blood River, Cape Farewell – or preserving the names of their first discoverers.

But there is another and more abstract truth which is none the less based on reality, on the emotion that inspired the choice. A name like Philadelphia for instance sprang from deep conviction and hope. It may be in fact that there is no more brotherly love in Philadelphia than elsewhere, but Penn intended that there should be. Even a name like Minneapolis, which some might call an incongruous mixture, does truly reflect the tastes and feelings of its inhabitants at that time, which included an enthusiasm for Red Indians as portrayed by Longfellow, and a desire for something poetical with a fine classical sound.

It is easy to dismiss the practice of repeating names from the homeland in remote colonies as nothing more than lack of originality but often it denotes a very real love and loyalty to the native place and tells us where it was. When exiled Highlanders in Ontario or Otago call their new homes by Gaelic names they are expressing an emotional truth. It is interesting to note that the Polynesians who also colonized distant places from which return was difficult were inclined to do exactly the same thing. But all migrating people do not do it; the Anglo-Saxons seem never to have thought of it, which shows that the second great migration of their race in the seventeenth century and onwards was very different in character from the first one rather more than a thousand years earlier.

The very great bulk of royal names also reflects the genuine loyalty that bound the scattered empire together during its chief period of expansion. It is fashionable to decry such sentiments today, and it is true that some of these names were given for mere correctness, but there are far too many of them in every region where men of British descent have settled to be so easily explained away. They too contain a basis of truth.

The names that are least genuine are those given quickly without personal feeling by officials in the course of their duty, and many of the titles of English statesmen and their secretaries scattered round the colonies must be placed in this class. Nevertheless, such names as Sydney and Kimberley atone for this by their other qualities. Even worse as regards any link with reality are those of generals and battles, distant in time and space from the places named. What had Hannibal to do with the Mississippi, or Marlborough and Blenheim with New Zealand? Worse again are some of those given by surveyors who have been left the responsibility of finding names for newly mapped districts and have been known to take them from any list that came to hand or any passing whim. The town of Luther in Ontario was named by a Roman Catholic surveyor who said he gave it that name because 'it was the meanest tract of land' he had yet surveyed; and another in Otago gave the name of Cromwell to a site he had just surveyed 'to annoy some Irishmen' who were camping there and had given trouble.

With the older names it is often impossible to find the origin, but all the evidence suggests that once we are back five hundred years or so all names sprang from something real and mostly of a physical sort. And this brings us to another kind of merit, the attribute of age; for names grow to suit the places they belong to, as associations gather round them. Enough history of its own can enrich the weakest name, and none that has stood honourably for a century or more should be lightly thrown away.

Part Four

OLD AND NEW

Chapter 24

NAMES OF COUNTRIES

The establishing of names for whole countries, whether by slow natural growth or conscious decision, has proved a precarious business. Happy the land that has a name truly related to its history, euphonious and easy in use, unambiguous, and giving offence to none. Some of the English-speaking countries have this amenity to perfection, others have failed in securing it and must make the best of an awkward situation.

Even the name of England, deeply and widely loved as it is, has run into difficulties. The trouble for names of countries is that they are beset by politics, and politics have little to do with the more natural arts. It is a normal speech development for the name of a part to be sometimes used for the whole, at the convenience of the speaker. We say Fleet Street and the whole of London's newspaper world is understood; Grand Bahama is only one of the Bahama Islands; Canada was once the hunting-ground of a single tribe, but because it lay in the very heart of a growing nation it was stretched out to include four million square miles, and it is one of the most successful names. But Scotland and Wales have too much national spirit ever to submit to being included in the word 'England' without an outcry. One sees their point, but it is so natural for people overseas to say England when they mean the whole island that it is impossible to stop them. They do it with no disrespect to Scotland and Wales, but simply because it is easy.

The solution to this problem should lie in the word 'Britain', the correct name of the whole island, but until recently this has been little used except formally. For some hundreds of years after the coming of the Angles and Saxons, it was almost obsolete, except as an historical term used when referring to the period of Roman occupation and before. Geoffrey of Monmouth, compiling his chronicle of semi-mythical kings, called them the Kings of Britain, and Elizabethan writers liked to air the word in a scholarly way. Shakespeare used it in *Lear* and *Cymbeline* and, no doubt, relished its antique quality, but the land as he knew it was always England even when he was thinking of the whole island, 'This precious stone set in a silver sea'. In his lifetime 'Britain' was officially revived by James I, for the union of his two kingdoms. But England remained England; Scotland was still another country; and not many people had occasion to speak of the two in one breath. 'Britain', unused for so long, had an unreal quality that was accentuated by the addition of 'Great'. However, it was not national pride which prompted this addition, but the practical need to avoid confusion with Brittany. Ever since the sixth century when refugee Britons fled there, that corner of France had been known by their name. When the Elizabethans spoke of Britons – as Hackluyt, for instance, does very often – they meant the people we now call Bretons. In France there is still no distinction between the names of their region and our island except James's addition – Bretagne and La Grande Bretagne.

The fact remains that Great Britain has always had a formal, ponderous sound unfitted to ordinary speech, and even Britain alone has been little used colloquially. But now, when people travel so much more than they did and are far more conscious of political susceptibilities, it is at last in the ascendant. Americans and Commonwealth citizens, anxious to be correct, are beginning to speak quite naturally of 'going to Britain'; in fact it is now more fully alive than at any time since the Dark Ages. In contrast, its adjective, British, has had a very different history. From qualifying the island only, it swelled to enormous proportions to include a world-wide Empire and peoples of countless origins. But now that the Commonwealth is tending to break apart, and each member state – except Britain – has its exclusive national adjective, the word 'British' is rapidly shrinking again to apply only to the island where it properly belongs, whose inhabitants, English, Welsh and Scottish, really need it.

Then, because of our entanglement with Northern Ireland, the phrase 'United Kingdom' has been brought into play, for official and diplomatic use. And because nowadays, owing chiefly to television, the whole population is soaked in a flood of official language, hears carefully worded statements, and sees its representatives in sport and other international activities labelled with the letters UK, this ugly abbreviation is spreading insidiously even in common speech. In contrast with the United States, which has no proper name of its own, we have too many and hardly know which to use. But 'the UK' is only a political expedient and as such probably ephemeral; 'Britain' is based on the physical reality of an island, and 'England' has common usage so strongly behind it that surely it cannot be overthrown.

The oldest name recorded for our island is Albion, which was known to Greek sailors in the fourth century BC. It is a name that poets have loved, and because of its likeness to the Latin *albus* it has long been associated with the idea of whiteness, which seems particularly appropriate for an island guarded by white cliffs. However, Professor K. Jackson, now the leading authority on the Celtic language of the pre-Christian era, will not accept this association and prefers a Celtic stem *albio-* which meant simply 'the land'. And the exact meaning is not of great importance, for the antiquity of the name and the thought of Greek sailors speaking it as they sailed to the ends of the earth invest it with as deep a significance as any name can need.

How old this name was when Pytheas heard it, we can never know. When Julius Caesar invaded the island three centuries later, he must have been aware of it, but it may then have seemed old fashioned and out of date. He was more interested in the island's inhabitants, the Brittanni, whom he wished to subjugate; he chose to speak of it by their name as Britannia, and his influence is with us still.

However, 'Albion' was never entirely eclipsed. The Romans never conquered the whole island and in the north where the climate and the terrain aided the Picts in resisting the legions the older name continued in use. In Gaelic and Welsh, Scotland is still Alban, and this name lives on in certain Scottish places, such as Breadalbane (the uplands of Alban) and Drumalbin (Ridge of Alban), the central range of the Highlands. The early Scottish kings used it in their titles, which explains why Albany in later times was the chief royal dukedom of Scotland, and why when James I united the two kingdoms he made his heir the Duke of York and Albany. To English people as well as Scots this name has had a pleasing and noble sound, and has made a popular place-name overseas though few understand clearly to what it refers. *The Times World Atlas* gives seventeen Albanys and twelve Albions in the English-speaking countries, but none in the island that was once known by this name.

Many of the older countries of Europe have names derived from their inhabitants. France is literally 'the Franks', and England, Scotland, Ireland and Wales were all of this same type before the first three received the addition of 'land', rather late in the day. During the restless fifth and sixth centuries, when nations were in a state of flux, it was more practical to use names referring to people rather than their territory since this was so liable to change. Some of the Saxons, for instance, stayed in Saxony, while others brought their name into Sussex, Essex and Wessex. The Angles, according to Bede, left their continental homeland so completely that to his day it remained 'a desert', and now the name of the small district of Angeln in West Germany is the only trace of their past habitation. The Scots of Ireland made only a partial migration but took their name with them; very confusing for their neighbours who were growing more fixed in their habits. As late as the ninth century the word 'Scotland' occurs in the *Anglo-Saxon Chronicle* meaning Ireland. But that usage was a little out of date, for, by that time, most of the Scots were in the north swallowing up Pictland, which lost its place altogether in this game of musical chairs.

Those who try to find the origins of these tribal names must look so far into pre-history that there can be little certainty, but some points are clear. Tribal groups were often known – not by the name they called themselves, but by one given by their neighbours, who viewed them objectively. To this day the French, Italians and English each have their own name for the Germans, all different from what they call themselves. Because relations with others were frequently warlike, some races were known by their weapons: the Franks by their short sword, the *franca*; the Saxons – so it is generally supposed – by their dagger, the *seaxna*. The Scots were first mentioned under that name (as inhabitants of Ireland) by a fourth-century Latin writer. It was a term that other races applied to them for centuries before they took it to themselves, and the chances are that it referred to the throwing of missiles or to some other act of hostility.

Wales is the Old English word *walas*, which meant the enemy, the other people, 'them' rather than 'us' – hard that they should be so called in their own land. As if in answer they spoke of themselves as the *Cymri*, meaning compatriots or brothers, 'us' as against 'them'; and their land, or what they managed to keep of it, was Cymru, as it still is in Welsh. This was rendered in Latin as Cambria, but to the English it was just *Walas*, the Welsh, and this plural form became Wales. They were, of course, also called Britons for some time after the coming of the English, and, logically, the name of Britain or Brittany might more suitably have survived in Wales than across the Channel.

The oldest known racial name still in use in the British Isles is the one that makes the first element of Ireland. Albion and Ierne are the first names mentioned by the ancient Greeks, and, as we have seen, Albion was lost about two thousand years ago and exists now only in modern reproductions. Ierne, sometimes given as Ivernia or Ibernia by classic writers, is very much alive, though further contracted to Ire- or Eire. It had been on record for at least thirteen hundred years before the Vikings added 'land' to it, and in recent times its national leaders have tried to shake off the addition but without success. Their failure to impose Eire on the world is now an acknowledged fact (their cars now bear the registration letters IRL instead of EIR), an example of the impossibility of controlling people's speech habits. Officials of other countries were willing enough to say 'Eire'; it was the millions of Irishmen all round the world who would go on talking of 'Ireland'. As to the meaning of the word, we can only say that it is racial; at the time when others were calling them Scots they spoke of themselves – among several names – as the Erainn. Like Albion the word is too old to be effectively cross-examined.

297

So we come back to the Angles or the English, who are the main pivot of our theme. They were so called because they came from the district known as Angeln, being at the corner or 'angle' where Denmark juts out northward from the main mass of Europe. Surprising, perhaps, that the geometrical angle, the hook that named the art of fishing with a line and the English race and language should all be derived from the same word. It is less strange, really, that being derived from Angle, we spell English with an 'E' and pronounce it Inglish. Language is constantly changing – less so now than formerly – but even the powers of modern education cannot hold it still; and vowels have always been more mutable than consonants. Anyone who doubts the truth of this should think of what has happened to them in Australia.

For a time it must have hung nicely in the balance whether Angles or Saxons would give their name to the new land that they had jointly seized, but by the ninth century the Angles had tipped the scales, and, even in the great kingdom of the West Saxons, men were proudly calling themselves the *Angel cynn* or English nation. The first recorded use of 'England' occurs in the reign of King Alfred about the year 890. Thus, an important conclusion was reached, and not the faintest echo is heard of the sort of troubles we should have today: protest marches by outraged Saxons; violence from small minorities of Jutes; and a final compromise of a United Realm of all three to be known as URSAJ.

The truth must be that the differences between the groups, who at first called themselves Angles or Saxons, were not great. They fused together in making one nation with little trouble over names or language. And it should be noted that their enemies in the British Isles also regarded them as one people, but were more conscious of their sharp daggers than their place of origin. *Sassanach* and *Sassneig* are the Gaelic and Welsh forms of the word 'Saxon' and that is what the Celts still call the English.

By the tenth century England, Scotland, Ireland and Wales were established in name and place. After that there was a long lull before their descendants had any more lands to name.

As soon as the existence of a new world across the western ocean was known in Europe it was at once a subject of eager discussion in royal courts and on the water fronts, and two names came at once into being – with the variations of several languages – West Indies and Newfoundland. These were so widely and vaguely used, before there was any real knowledge of what they referred to, that Sebastian Cabot could write of his father's discovery of 'the West Indies', meaning the Newfoundland region, while the French included all the northern mainland under the term Terre Neuve, which they later restricted to Newfoundland. This sort of confusion is a commonplace in the history of discovery.

West Indies was soon found to be an error but once launched it could not be repressed. Newfoundland (or just the New Land, which is what the other nations call it) was so obvious and general a term that it might have been used just as well for any other part of the two continents or for the whole of them. But the island we know by that name secured it first, and for everywhere else something different had to be found. These two names are more fully treated in Chapter 16.

When one looks at the earliest maps of the new discoveries and sees 'Mondo Novo' (or New World) written across the empty spaces one realizes how easily some name of this sort could have become established for the double continent. But instead of that, an original name was supplied from a most unlikely quarter and accepted by all concerned so easily that it remains one of the oddest freaks of naming on a grand scale. The facts are well known but will bear repetition. In 1501 the Florentine Amerigo Vespucci, employed by the king of Spain, who was growing tired of Columbus, sailed southwards from the West Indies far down a great mainland coast, and on his return published a book about his discoveries entitled *Mundus Novus*. He was only one of many sea-captains who went where Columbus had shown the way and beyond; but he had excellent publicity and made the most of what he had discovered, and perhaps – as some say – made more of it than was justified. In 1506 a German professor in a college in the Vosges, who had been impressed by Vespucci's book, published a Latin work of his own called *Cosmographiae Introductio* in which he threw out the suggestion that since Amerigo – or

Americus as he rendered it in Latin – had 'discovered a fourth part of the world, we may therefore call it Amerige or America'. He can have had little confidence in his own idea for, when he wrote on the subject again, he did not mention it, but reverted to Novus Mundus. But it had fallen among the geographers of Europe, as a spark among the haycocks. Everyone who talked of the new unknown lands that seemed – and were – so enormous wanted a comprehensive name for them, and this would do. No one seems to have considered the merits of the case or given a thought to poor Columbus – who was still alive; no one seems to have said, 'Who is this Martin Waldseemuller? A pedant. A bookman who has never seen the sea. A nobody. By what authority should he give a name of such magnitude?' The name had been tossed to the wind, and was picked up never to drop again.

As a name it is excellent, well sounding and giving a good adjectival form. But – really – two whole continents for one man is out of all reason, and he a man no better than many others, and second in achievement to Columbus who received no such memorial. Posterity has tried to redress the balance by exalting Columbus and turning a cold uninterested eye on Vespucci, and in more recent name-giving the United States has shown its feelings on this subject in no uncertain way (page 200).

That the two great land masses had to share one name was inevitable, for it was long before anyone knew what shape or size they were, how joined or how divided, and the one name qualified by North and South would have been quite satisfactory for both. But an added weight and complication was thrown upon it by the inability of founders of the United States to find another name for their own nation. 'The United States' is a political statement, and not a name. One cannot love it; or put it in a song; or make a human description out of it (United Statians or United Statesman). In general use it is impracticable and, therefore, the world at large and the American people (as I must call them) have been obliged to treat the continental name as if it were their own. Their patriotism is centred on the word America, although they must share it with twenty other separate countries and use something different for formal statements.

This need never have come about if those who drew up the constitution had realized the importance of a name. At that supreme moment of rebirth, a new name would quickly have become a focus of loyalty; but in the general excitement, it seems to have been little thought of by those responsible. Columbia was suggested, and would no doubt have proved popular, but the moment passed. Perhaps too many well-informed men reflected that Columbus had never even seen North America (but neither had Vespucci). But I think the true explanation lies more in the fact that they were already used to being called Americans. The separate colonies had been spoken of as American for a long time, and anything else sounded unreal and fictitious in comparison. Besides, it is always much harder to make a name for oneself than for others. Years later when the American government decided to create a new state in Africa for freed negroes, they called it Liberia, the free land, and had no trouble in agreeing on that. But for themselves, in the critical moment, they failed to take action. Then 'Columbia' was snapped up by others – Colombia in South America and British Columbia over the border – and that possibility was gone for ever. George Stewart who devotes a whole chapter of his *Names on the Land* to this failure calls it 'the worst misfortune in our whole naming history'. It can never be changed now.

In the first rush to seize large portions of the New World the rival nations produced a series of names that were essentially claims to possession: New Spain, New France, New England, New Netherland, and the short-lived New Sweden.

England's first claimant in this field was Francis Drake. In 1597 he reached the Pacific, which only the Spaniards had done before, sailed farther up the coast than they had ever been, and formally took possession of it – no one could say to what extent – in the name of his Queen, proclaiming it New Albion. This was over thirty years before the naming of New England on the more accessible side of America, and it is revealing that a feeling for the romantic past of his country made him choose Albion rather than England. In order to make this name as solid and permanent as possible, he had it engraved on a metal plate and 'sett up on a faire great post', before a crowd of wondering Indians who had gathered on the beach.* Over two hundred years were to pass before another Englishman was to see that coast. All that time Drake's name remained on world maps (at least on those made by the English); and when Captain Cook sailed up that uncharted shore in 1778 to reassert England's claim and make a survey, he consistently wrote of it in his log as New Albion. But, meanwhile, the Spaniards, slowly working their way up that western coast, had naturally ignored Drake's action; and later on, American pioneers further north struggled over the mountains in the determination to occupy the coastal region before the British could make good their claim. So New Albion, always a neglected plant, withered away, replaced by part of California and Oregon.

Of these 'New' lands in America only New England remains alive, and that unofficially. One by one the others were conquered, or otherwise absorbed by the British or their descendants, and their nationalistic names vanished for political reasons. New England, first placed on the map by Captain John Smith in 1614 to describe an indefinite area north of Virginia, has continued in popular use ever since for the six north eastern states, showing how well an informal name can last, if it fulfils a useful purpose. Seven years after its inception, New Scotland (latinized as Nova Scotia) was to join it as a northern neighbour.

Although few of these early 'national' names were to attain permanence, they set a fashion for navigators when discovering coasts and islands, about which they often knew no more than could be seen from a ship's deck. And so it is that among the islands of the western Pacific we find such names as New Britain, New Ireland, New Caledonia and New Hebrides. They are not appropriate by any standard. In a region where natural grace abounds, they are stiff and formal, and totally unrelated to the islanders to whom they are applied. In North America, where the first names of this sort were given, they had much more significance, for, besides being possessive, they expressed

---

* In 1937 a bronze plate bearing Drake's inscription was dug up in a bay just north of San Francisco. Doubts cast on its authenticity have been dispelled by recent scientific tests; it has been accepted as the original, and the place is now called Drake's Bay.

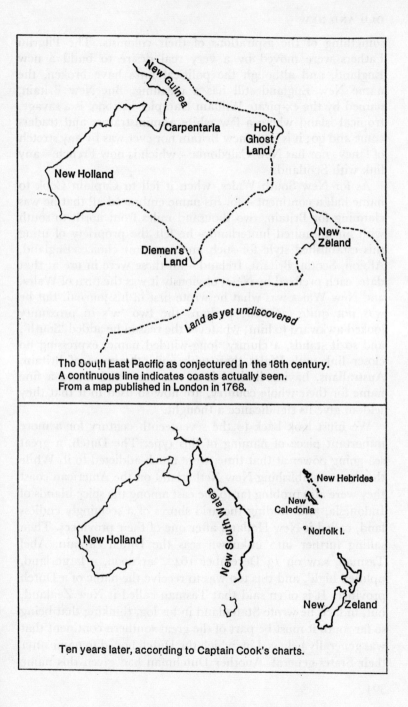

The South East Pacific as conjectured in the 18th century.
A continuous line indicates coasts actually seen.
From a map published in London in 1768.

Ten years later, according to Captain Cook's charts.

something of the aspirations of their colonists. The Pilgrim Fathers were moved by a very real desire to build a new England, and although the political links have broken, the name New England still has a meaning. But New Britain, named by the ex-pirate William Dampier in 1699, is a savage, tropical island where a few white administrators and traders come and go; it is not a new Britain nor ever was by any stretch of fancy; nor has New Caledonia – which is now French – any link with Scotland.

As for New South Wales, when it fell to Captain Cook to name half a continent – for his name embraced all that he was claiming for Britain, two thousand miles from north to south with an unlimited hinterland – he felt the propriety of using this established style for such an important choice. England, Albion, Scotia, Britain, Ireland – all these were in use at that date, each prefixed by New; obviously it was the turn of Wales, and New Wales was what he wrote first in his journal. But he was not quite satisfied; perhaps the two 'w's in proximity looked awkward to him; whatever the reason he added 'South', and so it stands, a clumsy, long-winded name, expressing no closer link with Wales than with any other part of Britain. Australians, having limited it to one state and found a fine name for their whole country, are now so used to it that they seldom give its significance a thought.

We must look back to the seventeenth century for a more important piece of naming of this type. The Dutch, a great sea-going power at that time, were much addicted to it. While they were establishing New Netherland on the American coast they were also probing far to the east among the spice islands of Indonesia, and, finding the arid shores of a seemingly endless land, called it New Holland after one of their provinces. Then sailing further into unknown seas the Dutch captain, Abel Tasman, saw on 13 December 1642, 'at noon, a large land, uplifted high', and this too was to receive the name of a Dutch province. It is often said that Tasman called it New Zealand, but, in fact, he wrote Statenland in his log, thinking that being so far south it must be part of the great southern continent that was generally believed in, which the Dutch hoped to name after their States-general. Another Dutchman had given this name to the island at the tip of Cape Horn* in the same mistaken belief and Tasman thought it might all be joined together, but after his return to Holland, officials there preferred *Nieuw Zeeland*.

Thus a temperate land, bigger than Britain, and the young British nation that has grown up in it were named in Holland by men who had never been near it. In Australia the British colonists rejected New Holland, shaking it off as completely as New Netherland had been discarded in America; but New Zealand remains as an inappropriate left-over from a race who cared nothing for it. The link with Holland is minimal – non-existent one might say – except for the name. Neither Tasman nor any of his crew set foot ashore, and the Dutch authorities, who named it on his return, did not know whether they were naming a continent or a group of islands, and never sent another ship to find out.

For the next hundred and twenty-seven years New Zealand was nothing but a name on world charts. The next Europeans to see it were Cook and his ship's company in 1769. He spent many months in making a complete survey, formally annexing the islands for Britain, and it would have been quite within his powers to have given a new name of a more British or local character. But he, who gave many names himself, had respect for those given by others, and he let the Dutch one remain with no further change than a slight modification of spelling, writing it variably as 'Newzeland' or 'New Zeeland'. However, another seventy years were to pass before the British government confirmed his annexation.

During that interlude the Dutch name became established by use among the adventurous seamen who visited this dangerous no-man's-land, while in Britain it became a romantic synonym for the remotest ends of the earth. When at last the unwilling government did take responsibility, the only uncertainty about the name was how to spell it. Apparently 'Zee' looked too Dutch for a British possession, and a half-hearted compromise turned it into 'Zea'. The alteration of just one more letter (with only a slight change of sound) would have effected a complete translation into English as 'Sea-land'. This would have been truly appropriate, and in breaking the link with the Dutch province

* Now Staten Island.

305

it could have shed the unwanted 'New' and stood as an original name in its own right. But nobody seems to have given it a thought.

If anyone had wanted a more individual name for the new colony, one that really belonged to it, it was there ready to hand. The Maoris had their own name for their country, one of honoured antiquity (see page 278); but, again, no one seems to have questioned that the land could be anything but New Zealand, and its colonists accepted the double-barrelled hybrid and even grew to love it, as people will love what is their own, however ill-favoured it may be.

Compared with New Zealand, Australia is fortunate in its name – or so one might say – a single word, of sufficiently apt meaning, easy to say and providing a good adjective. But it was not luck, rather the good judgement of an able man, Captain Matthew Flinders, that produced it in this form when it was needed.

Terra Australis, 'land of the south', had been in the general geographical vocabulary for centuries before any actual locality could be found for it. The ancient Greek philosophers, who believed that the world was a sphere, had deduced that a large southern continent must exist to balance the land mass of the north. At the Renaissance these ideas were revived, and the cartographers of Europe, using Latin as their international language, often wrote across the bottoms of their world maps 'Terra Australis Incognita'. When Magellan discovered his route to the Pacific in 1519 it was widely agreed that the land to the south of his straits must be part of this polar continent, but in 1579 Drake dispelled this assumption when he was blown past the land's extremity and saw the oceans meet beyond it. On the chart made on the *Golden Hind* the region south of the straits is shown as an island group, with the words written ironically across it, 'terra Australis bene cognita'.

By the end of the century the Dutch were sending ships to the East Indies, and in 1597 Cornelius Wytfliet published a map showing a vast Terra Australis stretching from around the Pole almost to Java and New Guinea. This could have been based on some actual sighting of the northern coast of the land that would become Australia, but when a few years later the

Dutch began to make landings on it they called it possessively New Holland.

In 1606 a Spaniard named De Quiros, a mystic and a dreamer like Columbus, discovered land in the Pacific which he called Australia del Espiritu Santo, the Southland of the Holy Ghost, but Cook later identified this with the group of islands that he named New Hebrides. No one sought more diligently for the elusive polar continent than Cook himself, but his hazardous voyage into the Antarctic proved only that if it existed at all it was much smaller than had been imagined. Being no classical scholar himself, he wrote of it generally as 'the South land', but was familiar with the Latin form. He would not have given either name to land that did not extend into polar regions.

So at the start of the nineteenth century 'Terra Australis' was still unplaced, and when young Matthew Flinders proved by his voyage of 1801–2 that New South Wales and New Holland were one land, he used this old name for it in the official account of his discoveries, and suggested the shorter form, Australia. The Admiralty who were sponsoring his book rejected this, and, worn out by hardships, he barely lived to see his book in print. But his suggestion was taken up by those who had a right to judge of it, the colonists themselves, and within a few years of his death it had come into general use, his last gift to a land he had served unstintingly.

Another country that is entirely happy in its name is Canada. In Chapter 18 it was told how the Breton Jacques Cartier first heard the name in 1535. He obviously felt that it was the most important of the three Indian kingdoms of which his guides told him, because in the map made in France soon after his return it is written in much larger letters than the others. From that time it was used for the region on both sides of the St Lawrence, of which Quebec became the chief city. This was at first a French colony, a part only of New France, but when it was conquered by the British and, not long after, there came thousands of English refugees from the American Colonies to settle further up the river, the name was stretched westwards making Upper and Lower Canada, later known as the provinces of Ontario and Quebec. For a time Canada was only one of several loyal colonies in North America, and not till 1866 was the name adopted for the Federation of most of them, the others joining in soon after.

This was an excellent arrangement, far better than having yet another great country called a Union of this or that. There are far too many of them. The virtue of the name Canada was that it was a native word to begin with, and had been used for both French and English settlements from their foundation. Therefore, it was acceptable to all.

As to its meaning, many theories have been advanced. Much the most likely is that it comes from the Algonquian *kanata* which means 'huts'. If this is so, the original sense must have been extended from a small village to the whole tribal territory before Cartier heard it, for he consistently speaks of it as a *royaume*. It has been extended far further since. With an old name of an indigenous sort, the actual meaning is of secondary importance to the historical associations that have gathered round it. Canada truly belongs to the country that it names, and has grown in meaning as it has swelled in size. Indeed there is a positive advantage in obscurity of meaning for a national name, for then there is nothing to make it inappropriate to any part of the country.

Another geographical term that has grown from small to great is Africa. The name is first recorded by the Latin writer Ennius in the third century BC, when it referred only to the central strip of the southern Mediterranean coast, including the city of Carthage. Its origin is unknown. The whole great continent, which it now names, was then known as Libya; however, after many centuries the relation between these two ancient names has been reversed.

It was the Portuguese who carried the word 'Africa' southwards. They knew it first in the Mediterranean, and, as they explored farther and farther round the great Atlantic bulge, in their speech they took 'Africa' with them, until at last they rounded its southern extremity, and still they thought of that interminable coast as Africa all the way.

The Dutch who followed the Portuguese to the Indies were the first to make a permanent settlement on the great southern promontory, whose physical presence so dominated the route to the east that the single word 'Cape' – which is practically the same in all the relevant languages – was sufficient to name the colony there; indeed, so strongly were the expressions 'Cape Colony' or just 'the Cape' established in the nineteenth century, that the whole British dominion might have developed as Capeland. But the situation was too complicated for such a simple solution. As the Cape grew predominantly English, the Dutch founded other provinces, and preferring to identify themselves more closely with Africa than with Holland were proud to call themselves Africans, in their own word Afrikaners. With so many races and different loyalties to be satisfied, it was not possible that the name of any one province would be acceptable for all, as had happened in Canada, and when the time came for a comprehensive name, the only solution was the factual, but unoriginal, South Africa.

The use of the continental name invites comparison with America, but the qualification 'South' does limit the meaning to the part intended, avoiding America's ambiguity. And though it is a great advantage for a national name to consist of one word only, it must be admitted that South Africa runs easily on the tongue while South African is hardly longer in sound than American. It was probably the best choice in the circumstances, but it would have surprised the Romans who thought Africa was in the Mediterranean.

Only one African country – at the time of writing – retains an English name, Rhodesia, so called in 1895 after its famous founder, Cecil Rhodes, the son of an English clergyman, who by his own ability and enterprise exerted a remarkable influence on this continent. The surname Rhodes has a slightly foreign look due to its spelling, but this is misleading. It is derived from the Old English *rod* ('a clearing', page 56) and belongs to the same regular type as Hills and Brooks. The 'h' is a relic of the Saxon tendency to aspirate an initial 'r', and its preservation in this case is probably due only to the chance resemblance to a famous Greek island with which it has no connection. Apart from the Latin ending, Rhodesia is a purely English word. Will it survive? Probably, because, anomalous though it is, the Rhodesians have broken the political link with England in order to preserve the English tradition that they value, and, in standing alone, their loyalties are more concentrated on their own name than before.

L

In writing of the names of 'countries', I have made no attempt to define the word precisely. My main purpose in this chapter has been to inquire how the English-speaking peoples have acquired names for the principal territories that they now inhabit, and in following this theme, and noting the different styles of naming used at different periods, I have lingered here and there over names of lands that are not now sovereign states, since some of these 'might-have-beens' are significant parts of the story.

As for the many other countries that have grown to statehood in Africa in recent years, they are hardly within the scope of my subject. Many of them have native names derived from natural features, great rivers or mountains – Kenya, simply means 'the mountain' in Swahili. Other districts were named in English traditional style from their principal inhabitants with the addition of 'land', Nyasaland, Basutoland, Bechuanaland, and so forth, exactly as England, Scotland and Ireland were named, but in every case when such 'lands' reached independence, they cast off this nominal debt to the English language and found themselves African names.

There are other countries in the world where the British have had enormous influence in general, but almost none on names. We think at once of India whose name, derived from its great river the Indus, is given by Herodotus in the fifth century BC. In contrast, its neighbour Pakistan has an ultra-modern name, made up in 1933 out of the names of its provinces, *P*unjab, *A*fghan, *K*ashmir and Baluchi*stan*. This was the choice of its own people, and has already won their loyalty.

Returning to the names of the principal countries for which English-speaking people are fully responsible, we see that they are enormously varied, as a result of the somewhat haphazard and easy-going approach to names that has characterized the British and their descendants. They have always shown great readiness to use native materials and names given by others, and, failing that, have simply stated the facts, with results that range from excellent to poor.

They are a polyglot collection. The United States is an English phrase but hardly a name; America is an Italian name given a Latin form by a German; Canada is North American Indian; Australia Latin; New Zealand Dutch, only half anglicized; the principal part of South Africa Phoenician, while Rhodesia is nearly English but has a Latin tag. But all these names were adopted or confirmed by English-speaking assemblies and made part of the English language.

Chapter 25

THE NEW VOCABULARY

The basic ingredients of all original place-names are the common nouns and adjectives of natural speech. But where do they all come from, and why do some disappear while others rise to take their places? Having looked at the way in which the British and their descendants have been combining words to name places during the last two thousand years, let us pause to consider these questions in a general way, and particularly to look at some of the changes in the topographical vocabulary of the younger countries for they can help to throw light on similar changes in England.

When a race moves into new physical surroundings its old vocabulary is stretched to meet new needs, and in some respects must prove inadequate. New conditions cry out for new words to describe them, and human beings, wonderfully inventive in this respect, seem always able to supply them. One method is to use an old word in a new sense, so new that it seems like a different word. Another is to take words from another language, not necessarily using them in their correct foreign sense but making them do just what is wanted. Yet another is to create an onomatopoeic sound, but this is rare compared with the other two ways.

In Anglo-Saxon England old Germanic words often acquired new meanings, as the English settled down and shaped the land to their desires. We have seen earlier that *wald* which meant 'wood' on the Continent changed (as 'wold') to bare upland, and *lēah* which had been part of a wood became (as 'lea') open grass-land. In the younger countries the same sort of thing often happened. Take 'creek', for example. In England it means an inlet of the sea, more enclosed than a bay, a tidal back-water. It is not English in origin, but was picked up on the coasts of Europe during the Middle Ages by seafaring men such as Chaucer's Shipman who knew 'every cryke in Britayne and in Spayne'. (Britayne at this time meant Brittany.) It was never much used in England and is not found in English place-names, but being essentially a seaman's word was carried by English sailors to America and used by them on that unknown coast as they nosed their way among rocks and sandbanks, seeking safe anchorage. At first they used it as they would at home for some sheltered arm of the sea, not knowing if it was purely tidal or fed by a river. Later on, when they explored 'up the creek' and found the water narrowing and flowing more strongly they still used the same word, and when those who came after penetrated further inland it went with them all the way. Look at it now. To the whole of North America and the British countries of the southern hemisphere a creek is a small river, even hundreds of miles from the sea. Its water is always fresh and no American or Australian would use this word for a salt-water inlet.

The fact of the word's being carried gradually inland from the coast is only part of the explanation of this change of meaning. The magnitude of the physical features of America created a need for more words to cope with the range of size. If 'river' was reserved for the biggest waterways, those of the next size were still too big to be called by any of the English words for little streams – or so the first settlers seem to have felt. The word 'stream' which was not very common in England before the sixteenth century was used to some extent, but as they pressed westwards and the land seemed less and less like England even this word was abandoned and almost anything that flowed – barring the great rivers – became a creek.

They found other words for flowing water too; a small stream in the south is often a 'run' (which in Australia means sheep-grazing land), and throughout the country a tributary stream may be a 'branch', a simple metaphor whose meaning seems obvious to Americans, although to others it may not be instantly apparent that a town called Roaring Branch stands by a noisy river.

The making of metaphors is as old as speech itself, and the

readiest source for topographical metaphors has always been the human body. The head has been used in every language: *pen*, *cap*, *kop*, and so on; but the Northmen saw promontories more as noses, hence the many 'nesses' round our coasts. We speak of the breast of a hill, an arm of the sea or a neck of land, and such expressions have helped to make names everywhere. The Teton Mountains of Wyoming (named by the French) and the Paps of Jura in the Western Isles have the same significance, while Joe Batt's Arm and Herring Neck are typical Newfoundland names.

One metaphor that has been used in many forms and many countries is that of a deep cleft down which water runs being likened to a throat. We know this best in England as 'gorge', a late borrowing from French in this sense, used in only a few places. An earlier word, perhaps also from French, but possibly from a cognate Germanic source, was *goule*, the ancestor of the modern 'gullet'. This was the origin of Goole, a Yorkshire town on the banks of a deep-cut stream. From 'gullet' sprang the more colloquial 'gulley' which spread rapidly in America, with its even more slangy variant 'gulch'. This last is a most expressive word with its gulping, swallowing sound, suggestive of the roughest kind of manners and of country. It has remained exclusively American, but 'gully' like 'creek' was carried to Australia and New Zealand in their several gold-rushes, and there too every small valley is now a gully, just as every stream is a creek.

The Spaniards had much the same idea when they used the word *cañon* for the enormous fissures that they found in the American South West. Literally it meant a pipe – much the same thought as a gullet – and as the early explorers peered down into the depths of the greatest one, they found no words to describe it but *grande cañon*, or great pipe.* English-speaking Americans have been content with these words, slightly anglicized as Grand Canyon, for one of their greatest natural wonders; and, fortunately, no one has insisted on naming it after Washington or Columbus.

'Canyon' is a case of borrowing, 'gully' of making a new word from an old one, 'gulch', a bit of onomatopoeic creation starting from the same base. Other words seem to have sprung

* The word 'cannon' is derived from the same source.

from nowhere when required, and this generally means that they began as slang and worked upwards. One that has just the right sound for its purpose is 'swamp' which appears first in the writings of Captain John Smith in 1624. It seems that neither the English 'marsh' nor the Irish 'bog' was adequate for some of the conditions in Virginia.

Another useful word of unknown origin is 'bluff'. Like 'creek', it was a seaman's word, and is first found in a nautical manual of 1627, meaning 'broad-fronted' as applied to cliffs. In the next century we find it in America as a noun, signifying a blunt, rugged headland, whether inland or jutting into the sea. The meaning is clearly connected with that of the adjective and the verb, all expressing the idea of a bold front; expressing it well, too, sounding as it does like a cross between 'blunt' and 'rough' with just a touch of 'bluster'. In America it has helped to name many towns, such as Pine Bluff, Bluff City and several Blufftons, while American whalers ranging over distant seas carried it far afield, even to the southernmost headland and harbour of New Zealand.

The English have always been greedy for words and take them from all their neighbours, constantly building up their un-rivalled vocabulary. In the early period of settlement in North America, their many contacts with their principal rivals, the French, provided a rich source of word material. For instance, the rivers dashed down so violently from the mountains that more ways were needed of describing their behaviour, and the English 'falls' – still much used – was reinforced by 'rapids' and 'cascades', while a dry water-course became a 'coulee'. With such words, it was natural to take over the French *grand*, which soon became interchangeable with 'great' and 'big'; and so there were many ways of saying the same thing – always an asset for place-names – and there are towns called Big Falls, Great Falls, Grand Falls, Big Rapids, Grand Rapids, and so on, all good names and all dating back to the days when exploration was largely by river, and falls created an enforced stopping-place, where a camp was made and later a town grew.

Then the mountains and rocks reared up in such strange shapes that they too demanded new words. 'Hill' was still serviceable for the milder features, and 'peak' for the pointed ones, while the French *mont* brought into England by the Normans, but not very much used there, has gone round the world as 'mount', making titles for the greatest heights. But there was no word in English for the sudden steep eminence with a flat top, and for this the French *butte*, literally a stump, came into use. In the south the Spanish *mesa* served the same purpose, seeming much more romantic than the equivalent English 'table', though this too holds an honourable place in world geography, especially as Table Mountain in South Africa.

But perhaps the most useful local word that we have taken from the French in America is 'prairie', which is identical in meaning with our gentle 'meadow-land'. In the first stages of colonization the English and French each used their own words for the grass-lands that they found, which were not extensive among the forests and mountains of the east. But when they reached further westwards and saw the limitless plains where the herds of bison grazed, the English pioneers, groping for some way of expressing this enormous phenomenon, seized upon the Frenchman's 'prairie'. In its own language it must serve the double purpose of moderate sized meadows at home and something much larger and wilder abroad, but in English it was a new word for a new thing, and one to which it is beautifully suited with its long drawn-out vowels that give a feeling of space.

In South Africa, English settlers, wanting new words for landscape features that were strange to them, found those of the Cape Dutch readily available, and so to them the rough, open country that seemed to stretch forever in the clear, bright air became 'veldt'. This word is first cousin to the English 'field', springing from the same Germanic origin, and to the Anglo-Saxons it had the same meaning of open land (as opposed to woods) that it retains in Africaans. But in England, as time passed and waste-lands were brought under cultivation, it had changed its nature with the land until 'fields' came to signify that patchwork of ploughland and pasture, hedged about in neat enclosures, that is so typical of the countryside. This would not do at all for untamed virgin lands, but 'prairie' and 'veldt' filled the gap.

Other borrowings at the Cape include 'kop' or 'kopjie' for

a rocky outcrop, and 'kraal' for a native village. The latter, which had earlier been borrowed by the Dutch from the Portuguese, is nearly related to the Spanish 'corral', well known as an enclosure for horses in the American west. Its basic idea of protection given by an encircling fence lies at the root of many common place-name elements, the French 'court', the Norse 'garth', the Welsh 'llan' and our own 'town', to name but a few that each began as an enclosure.

Most of the Cape Dutch words used by the English have remained exclusively in South Africa, but *bosch*, meaning originally a wood and anglicized as 'bush', has spread enormously throughout the southern hemisphere. We will return to it presently.

In Australia there was no second European language to supply new words, and English settlers in another unfamiliar landscape had to find them as best they could. When first they crossed the Blue Mountains that had penned them in near the coast, and saw mile upon mile of gently undulating country, sparsely dotted with trees but open to the sun, the rise and fall of the land made them think of the chalk downs of southern England. So in this hot, dry land, so unlike England in general, this word that is almost archaic in its homeland, except in special localities, has taken on a new life. Most people know of the Darling Downs, because the surname of Governor Darling helps to make a pleasant alliteration that sticks in the mind, but there are many more Downs in Australia, all of them rolling sheep country.

But something more was needed for the vast spaces and white Australians found it in the unlikely word 'bush'. This has been much misunderstood in the northern hemisphere, owing to confusion with the English 'bush', a word of Norse origin whose meaning implies a single growth of very limited size. Australian 'bush', Dutch in origin, with its basic sense of woodland greatly extended, stretches as widely as the prairies and includes trees of magnificent height. As in South Africa it is used primarily for virgin forest, but also very vaguely for wild, undeveloped land and this second usage has almost outrun the first. But the Australians had it from the Dutch before the establishment of an English colony at the Cape. On the long

L*

voyage out, all the early fleets of convict ships called there for water and other supplies, and in these brief contacts with Dutch settlers the word must have been heard. At their journey's end the first Australians saw a land whose vegetation was more reminiscent of the Cape than of England; someone among them must have said the word 'bush', and others taken it up. This is not clearly recorded (one would not expect it) but can hardly have happened otherwise.

A new word can spread very quickly in a small community and certainly did so in this case. By the turn of the century it was in general use, and in 1806 appears officially in the first reports of trouble with 'bush-rangers'. Since then it has been the universal word for rough country all across the continent, excepting absolute desert, and particularly for the areas where most trees grow, but its use is very elastic and a dozen tall, gaunt, blue-gums lifting their mottled trunks and silvery drooping leaves in a wide landscape are enough to classify it all as bush. It is universal to a fault.

The same word was carried on to New Zealand by missionaries, escaped convicts and others, and because the physical conditions are so different from those of Australia its meaning there is different again. Bush in New Zealand is the dense, virgin forest in which some of the tallest trees in the world grow, and grow so closely that the light can barely filter through. There is nothing vague about the use of the word. One moment you are outside the bush on the bright, bare hillside, and when you step into it you enter another world, cool, dark, damp, and tangled with foliage. 'Forest' would be more appropriate, and this is used in a limited way, but the colloquial term is 'bush', and New Zealanders like Australians are only too easily content with a small vocabulary worked hard. So the false impression continues to be given to the rest of the world. 'We camped in the bush', one says, relating an adventure, and then one is aware of English listeners picturing only bushes no higher than oneself, thinking in fact of 'scrub' which is quite another thing. Words can only be judged by their power to convey impressions, and by this standard 'bush' as used by Australians can be misleading, and by New Zealanders a total failure.

These two young peoples of British stock have been even more inclined to break away from traditional English words than the Americans. Of course the variety of speech habits in the States is enormous, but in many areas Americans still talk of woods, fields and villages while Australians and New Zealanders can hardly bring themselves to use these words. The fields 'down under' are all paddocks. Why? A paddock in England is a very small enclosure for keeping a horse conveniently close to the house. In Australia it may serve any agricultural use and stretch to the horizon. Was it irony perhaps, or just a chronic tendency to understatement?

As to 'village', it is thought of as a picturesque word, belonging like 'woods' and 'fields' to England, something one reads of in books and hopes to see one day on a trip 'home'. But the group of bungalows beside the road, with one or two stores, a hotel, a wooden church and busy garage – these do not constitute a village, but a 'township', the southern diminutive of 'town'. But 'town' itself, having reached its maturity in England, has spread unchanged around the world.

A big farm in either of these southern lands is a 'station', a stiff sounding word for a family home perhaps, but not more so than the 'plantation' of the American south which has long been accepted as both homelike and romantic. The Australian station comes from the time when land for settlement was being apportioned in lots, and a man's station was at first only an area on the map. One would not call it a farm when there was nothing there; it was only a place, and this word too is much used in the same sense, 'My place' being a very common way of saying 'My home'. There were stations in Australia before there were railways in England, and the modern English usage has tended to make the southern one seem odder, but cannot change it. If an Australian wants a train he goes to the 'railway station'.

The local vocabulary of these two countries is very similar, the only variations being those dictated by geography. Australians have the more expressive phrases for great space: the 'outback', the 'never-never' and so on. New Zealanders use more words for mountain features. 'Gorge' is very common for precipitous valleys that would be 'canyons' in America, and where these open into the sea the Norwegian 'fiord' had to be imported for nothing in English was sufficiently dramatic; and so a whole district has become Fiordland. Because Australia is mainly low-lying any eminence is made much of, and the title Mount has been given freely. Mount Lofty, near Adelaide, named by Flinders after following hundreds of miles of low coastline, is little over a thousand feet, and many other mounts are much lower. In New Zealand anything under about four thousand feet is likely to be called a hill, and the 'high country' lies between peaks of eight to twelve thousand. It follows that because the land is so mountainous a piece of level ground is generally worth mentioning as a 'flat', and many townships such as Hawea Flat include this in their name.

The English language in its homeland, even though it has lost the use of many old words, has still a richer vocabulary for describing the natural scene – with its wood and forest, thicket, copse and spinney, heath and moorland and so forth – than the speech of these two young nations. Even today in Britain there is still much regional variation. In the South the brook flows down the valley, or the coomb; in the North the beck runs down the dale, while over the border it is the burn in the glen. But right across Australia, and New Zealand too, the creek flows down the gully and across the paddocks, and to speak of it otherwise would mark one as a stranger.

But although these southerners are chary of using old English words, even such regular ones as wood and field, their inhibitions can disappear when it comes to finding a name for a place. Then they can show a preference for traditional terms, coining names like Woodbourne, Glenbrook and Meadowbank out of materials they would never use in speech. And though this type of name, which is found all round the English-speaking world, is somewhat artificial, somewhat reminiscent of the Romantic Revival which is over now, yet there is merit in keeping old words in use. Natural naming, to be effective, must spring from a rich vocabulary, and since these southern British have borrowed few words from other languages, they would be well advised to retain a wide selection from their own.

Chapter 26

RETURN TO BRITAIN

In the first part of this book we followed in outline the naming of England to the Tudor period, and the rest of the story must be told briefly.

During the seventeenth and eighteenth centuries, when agriculture flourished exceedingly, the chief events that gave rise to more naming were the enclosing of more farmland from woods and wastes, and the building of more farm-houses. Many of our field- and farm-names date from that period, small country houses often preserving the names of Jacobean yeomen, while field names echo the sardonic humour of farmers who liked to disparage their land with such expressions as Pinchgut Close, Starveacres, Cold Comfort, Cold Christmas, or – where the mud was deep – Pease Pottage or Pudding Lane. Some of these have graduated to village status in later times.

The gentry building new country houses in the prosperous eighteenth century were more inclined, if a new name was wanted, to choose something gracious like Mount Pleasant or Fairfield, and these names have been more acceptable for modern housing estates, but far more often they used a name that was already on the land, that of an earlier farm or natural feature. All the great old houses held in highest honour have names that are Anglo-Saxon if not earlier – Chatsworth, Knole, Longleat,* and so forth – and it was slightly *parvenu* to invent a new one.

If we had space to deal, even generally, with minor names of fields and farms, there would be much to report from the eighteenth and nineteenth centuries, but the large scope of this

---

* 'Ceatt's farm', the 'knoll' or hillock, and a 'long stretch of water'.

book must have its limits. However, it should be borne in mind that this richness of detailed naming over all the land has meant that not a field, or piece of waste land, not a farm or clump of trees exists that cannot be spoken of by an individual name. So whenever a new project is started on the land a name is there ready for it.

The English are more conservative about their place-names than almost any other nation; and this may be demonstrated in the street-names of our cities. In other European capitals the principal streets and spaces commemorate national leaders or political or military triumphs, and are liable to change with new events. The Place de l'Etoile becomes Place Charles de Gaulle overnight. In London we are content to go on with the Haymarket and the Strand for ever, and if we do name a newly laid-out feature from a public event – Trafalgar Square for instance – once there it is immutable.

This conservatism arises partly from a genuine fondness for old familiar things, but also and very largely from an absent-minded approach to the matter. Although we have created so many successful names and exported them in hundreds to distant lands, we have done so with the minimum of conscious thought. We are in fact, as nations go, not very name-conscious. Our tradition has always been the same in regard to places, to call them what they are and leave it at that. It was a hay-market; that was the truth once, and we prefer it to any substitute.

Since the English habit is to retain old names however much the places may change, and since by the Middle Ages every acre of land and every work of man in the land had a name, it follows that few have been needed in later times, even for the enormous growth of towns, cities and other developments in the last two centuries. The great industrial cities of the north all grew from villages or market towns and their names grew with them. Leeds has a pre-English tribal name; Preston was the priests' farm; Halifax a field of rough grass (OE *feax*) which was perhaps spoken of as holy, but the nature of the first element is unsure. There are as yet no modern names among our cities.

Occasionally some completely new enterprise in a hitherto unoccupied spot produced a new coinage in the old factual style, as at Ironbridge in Shropshire where the first bridge in the world to be made of iron was begun in 1777, and the village that grew by it was known in this way. Rather more deliberately the inhabitants of Plymouth Dock, when it was enlarged in the early nineteenth century with a residential area added in the current regency style, decided to call it Devonport. This was such an unusual event, the choice of a new name, that they put up a column to mark the occasion; but it was only stating a truth.

The late eighteenth and early nineteenth centuries saw an enormous growth in the built up area of London. Squares and streets, systematically laid out, were named largely after the aristocratic landowners whose property was thus developed, but the newly built suburbs retained in almost every case the ancient names of the villages and hamlets that were thus swallowed up. Paddington, Kensington, and Islington, are of the early English settlement type; Chelsea was a 'chalk hythe' (*Cealc hyth*) as early as 785, though why they were loading or unloading chalk is not known; Finsbury and Bloomsbury are not recorded until the thirteenth century when they must have been fortified manors, their first elements giving names of early owners, Finn (probably a Dane) and a Norman whose surname was de Blemont. Hammersmith was 'the hammerer's smithy' in 1312. One of the very few new developments where the whole district took the name of its landowner is Camden Town, laid out on the property of the Earl of Camden, then Lord Chancellor, in 1791. (This title has recently been raised to borough status.) But the neighbouring Kentish Town is on record as *Kentisston* in 1207.

A recent rearrangement of parliamentary boroughs has brought some unfamiliar names to prominence in London, but few of them are really new. Nearly all are former borough names, although their boundaries have been rearranged. The cases where a complete change of name has taken place have resulted from respect for local loyalties and the difficulty of preferring one name before another. Thus the boroughs of Wembley and Willesden have been united as Brent, taking the name of the river that runs through both of them, and, far from being a new name, Brent has existed here in unbroken continuity from prehistoric times (page 16). For a similar amalgamation between Wanstead and Ilford the name of Redbridge was chosen, which might be classed as new since it was formerly written in two words. But the bridge has been there, linking the two districts, and so called, for several centuries, though a youngster compared with Brent.

The joining of East Ham and West Ham produced Newham, a new name here, but formed so naturally and traditionally that it hardly seems so. In this case the basic word is not a 'home', but a 'meadow' (page 43). Although it is such a simple concept it is not of common occurrence in this form, because in Anglo-Saxon England, when meadows were often newly cleared for use, they were spoken of with grammatical inflections that produced different results. The dative form '*æt niwan hamme*' produced Newnham, the more usual form to have survived.

The phrase Tower Hamlets which embraces the old boroughs of Stepney, Poplar, and Bethnal Green is a revival of words used by local officials in the eighteenth century (and probably before) to describe these three outlying parishes which had, since Norman times, belonged to the feudal estate of the Tower of London. The word 'hamlets', revived here after an interval, strikes a slightly unnatural note, but it is used only in an administrative context, and will not prevent the inhabitants of the three parishes from using their old names. Stepney was Stibba's landing-place (*Stibbanhythe*) before the Tower was built.

The fashion for seaside pleasures that began in the late Georgian period encouraged the growth of new resorts on the coast, but even where there was no previous habitation there was always a name. Bournemouth, for instance, has no history before 1811 when a local gentleman built a cottage there for his delicate wife who had been recommended sea air. The stream that ran down the break in the cliffs was known simply as the Bourne, and the point where it entered the sea was naturally its mouth. Just across the Solent the fashionable yachting resort of Cowes grew up with the name of two sand banks at the river mouth, which had long been called 'the Cows' by local fishermen, though exactly why would be hard to say. Both these names were recorded for these localities in the fifteenth century. Older seaside towns might receive additions to their names in traditional style as their importance grew; Lyme (a Celtic river-name) became Lyme Regis when visited by George III; Bognor assumed its 'Regis' after the convalescence there of George V.

With the great increase of travel in the eighteenth century a few new village names arose, originating from busy coaching inns and the hamlets that grew up around them. Indian Queens and London Apprentice, both crossroad hamlets in Cornwall, owe their odd names to picturesque signs; there are several Waterloos scattered about the country; while Nelson in Lancashire, now a large town, began as the Lord Nelson Inn.

One might expect a greater influx of new names from more modern methods of communication, but although the railways created busy junctions in places that had previously little or no distinction, there was always a name there if little else, and these now took on a new character. Swindon was the 'swine hill'; Crewe, a Celtic word, left there by the Britons, meant the 'stepping stones'. So also with airports, modern in everything except their names. In other countries they are frequently called after prominent men but in Britain they only tell what they once were: Gatwick, the 'goat farm'; Prestwick, the priests' farm; and if one is built at Foulness it will probably still be the 'birds' cape'.

Since the Second World War a new phenomenon in Britain is the deliberate creation by official policy of 'New Towns'. Here, if anywhere, one might expect new names, but of the twenty-seven listed by the Ministry of Housing up to 1972, only two have names that did not exist on the sites before; of these more presently. In every other case the new development has continued the name of an earlier town, village or hamlet, even when eclipsing it completely.

Ever since the Angles and Saxons landed in Britain in the fifth century they have been calling their latest settlements 'new towns', in just those words and are doing it still in the same spirit. No wonder this is the commonest English place-name. The *AA Book of the Road* for the British Isles gives over sixty unqualified Newtons and Newtowns, without counting any of the far more numerous examples that are combined with other names. Newtown is of course the later of the two forms and is found chiefly in Scotland, Ireland, and Wales where settlements were founded under English influence in the Middle

325

Ages and even later. The Newtons are mostly in England and pre-Conquest. Their profusion does not deter us from using the same words again whenever they seem applicable; but in most cases the use is only temporary, and the matter adjusts itself automatically in a few years. At first, the people of Harlow, for instance, talk of their 'New Town' as a matter of course, while those at a distance say 'Harlow New Town'. But as soon as the new centre with its better amenities becomes more important than the old it takes over the unqualified 'Harlow', while the original village on its outskirts becomes 'Old Harlow'. So the adjustment is complete and another double name added to the land, without the need of any decision being taken.

In the Celtic countries with their much sparser population new towns were occasionally planted and named deliberately by those in authority even before the present century, and a larger number of modern names can be found in these lands than in England, but even so they are a tiny sprinkling among those of ancient origin. Campbelltown in Scotland was founded in 1667 by the Duke of Argyll, Portmadoc in Wales by the wealthy William Maddocks in 1800; both took their founder's surnames which superseded old natural names. This is unusual anywhere in the British Isles and practically unknown in England, where old names may receive additions and subtractions but go on and on.

The habit of adding to old names to fit them to new circumstances is second nature to us. We subdivide them by the additions of East and West, Upper and Lower and so on, and have our methods too for extending their range as required. In some districts where the spread of population has made a need to speak of larger units than single towns or cities, the official authorities call them 'conurbations', but the simple, old-fashioned 'side', as used with pleasant vagueness in 'countryside', has combined happily with old river-names to meet the case with such useful expressions as Tyneside, Clydeside and Merseyside. These districts are now becoming separate counties and their names are ready for them as a natural growth.

In the centuries since they were coined, many English place-names have had something more added to them than words and syllables, something of historic significance that has totally changed their character. The name of Oxford means many things to many people but does one in a million think of it as a convenient cattle-crossing, obvious though the etymology is? This matter of association has affected most of our old city names, especially those that became titles of royalty and the nobility, to whom genuine feelings of honour and respect have been accorded for centuries. As far as the world at large goes this secondary meaning far outweighs the first which was often humble and has generally been forgotten. The true origin of Windsor may be a gadget for drawing boats up a river-bank, but that was not what caused it to be reproduced in seven countries overseas and several times in each.

In the same way the names of ordinary farms could rise in dignity with their owners if the latter grew rich and distinguished and rebuilt them as stately mansions. Clarendon means the 'clover-covered hill' but its connotation in the world is purely aristocratic; Melbourne in Derbyshire meant the 'mill-stream' but when its squire became Prime Minister it seemed a noble name.

No English place-name has changed more in significance than Sandwich. Its origin could not be simpler, 'village in the sand', but during the Middle Ages it was an important port – before the sea receded from it – and later came to be the title of an earldom. It was the dissipated fourth earl whose life had most effect on it. As First Lord of the Admiralty he was held in respect by naval captains, among them Captain Cook, who in the course of his voyages placed the title on distant islands, thinking in that way to give it lasting honour. Meanwhile the Earl's passion for gambling was so strong that being unable to tear himself away from the tables ever to eat he would call for 'a slice of beef between two slices of bread', thereby giving his title a very different immortality from anything that he or Captain Cook had intended. It is no exaggeration to say that this English place-name must be spoken millions of times every day all round the world, perhaps in every hour. The thing has gone so far that visitors to the charming little town of Sandwich often think it has a funny name.

This is a freakish development, but it illustrates the sort of thing that can happen. Sandwich in England means what it says; Sandwich in Massachusetts is called after the English town; Sandwich Bay in Labrador and a Cape in Queensland are called after the earl; nowhere that I know of is yet called after the edible snack, but there may be such a place; if not there surely will. There is already a town in America called Hot Coffee, and Sandwich Bar would be just as reasonable.

So many British place-names have been carried overseas that we may well ask if there has been any return of the same commodity, but so far it is minimal. There is, for example, a hamlet in Gloucestershire, hardly more than a single farm, named Pennsylvania by an American colonist who returned to his native land, and two or three, equally small, named Bunker's Hill. No doubt a diligent search up and down the country would produce more in this class, but very few, and those that might be thought American are generally older than they seem. Strata Florida in Wales, for instance, is the Latin version of the Welsh Ystrad Fflur, 'flowery valley'. It was so called in the twelfth century by monks who built a monastery there.

The return has been more one of vocabulary than of actual names. The use of 'ville' as a town-name ending had such an enormous vogue in America that it was bound to appear occasionally in England under that influence, but it has never been much liked here because it seems pretentious. This does not apply in America where it has been used wholeheartedly without inhibitions. In England 'ville' seems quite natural as a surname ending because that was how it came into the country with the Normans; nobody, however socialistic, objects to a family being called Melville or Sommerville, such names being genuine survivals from the past; but to tag the suffix onto a place-name where it does not belong seems like snobbery. When Margate spread along the cliffs in the nineteenth century and the new growth could not be content with Clifton, but must add 'ville', the choice was censured, and justly, by the discerning. Coalville in Leicestershire is better in having no redundancy, and perhaps the neighbourhood of a colliery gave its inhabitants a just cause to want something that sounded elegant. But 'ville' has never taken root (except of course in the Channel Islands which as part of the old Duchy of Normandy are its natural habitat).

Another American usage out of place in England is that of 'City' in Welwyn Garden City. In America this word is used very freely, but in England it has the exact meaning of a cathedral town (the seat of a bishop) or one to which the title has been given by royal grant. There are forty-three cities in England and Welwyn is not one of them, nor has it any of the qualifications. This again was pretentious naming, and will not last. Already the place is spoken of simply as Welwyn, and its little parent town as Old Welwyn.

A much more serviceable word that has lately come from America and is being widely used is 'centre'. We already talk naturally of the 'civic centre' and the 'shopping centre' and so forth, and as it expresses an idea in a clear and practical way it has probably come to stay, and to make a useful ingredient for future naming. But American influence on our local vocabulary has, so far, been slight.

However, a new trend in name-giving has appeared recently in England in the choice of two entirely original names for new towns. This has come about not from any lack of old names on their sites, but because in each case the new development was planned to absorb two or more villages of equal standing and – as with some amalgamations of London boroughs – local rivalry enforced a search for a 'neutral' name. In Shropshire the surname of the famous engineer, Thomas Telford, was chosen, he having been at one time official surveyor for the county; in Durham, where the new town occupies a former mining district, the name of Peterlee had been put together to honour one of the miners' leaders in times of past distress, Peter Lee. These two men, both of humble origin, have attained a distinction rare in this country.

Incidentally it may be noticed that the two personal names that have been accorded this modern prominence as place-names are both acceptable as such to the English ear because they end with regular place-name elements, 'lee' being identical in origin and similar in sound to the common ending -ley. However it so happens that the last syllable of Telford is not what it appears. The surname is a variant form of Telfer, the final 'd' being excrescent, and is well recorded as a descendant of the Norman *Taille-fer*, literally 'cut-iron', a nickname for a strong fighter. The first man killed at Hastings was William's

329

warlike minstrel, Taillefer. This is by-the-way and does not affect the appropriate sound of Telford as a local name, but it explains why it does not exist locally except in this new town.

This style of commemorating individuals in place-names, long a commonplace in the younger countries, shows a complete departure from English tradition. But its appearance is, I believe, not so much attributable to overseas influence, as to the changed conditions of modern England, in which large towns are deliberately planned, and decisions on their names required, in a way that is new to us. There is no longer time, as there used to be, to wait for a name to grow. But although we undoubtedly see the beginning of a new movement, it can hardly move very far or fast, because the profusion of old names is so great in every district, and our preference for them so strong. It is only as a last resort in cases of special difficulty that the planners are forced to devise something original, and then it is always done with the greatest respect to geographic or historic suitability.

Whatever happens to Britain, short of total obliteration, the mass of ancient place-names will remain. Towns will be rebuilt, old landmarks destroyed, landscapes remodelled, but most of the names will survive it all, as they have in past upheavals. In almost every town, however rich in ancient monuments, the name is the oldest of them all. There may be ruins of a Norman Castle and Saxon foundations to the church, but the name is almost certain to antedate them; and even if there are Roman remains, it may be older still. In a world where so much changes, place-names are among the most enduring things.

APPENDICES

Appendix I

A CHRONOLOGICAL TABLE OF EVENTS THAT HAVE INFLUENCED PLACE-NAMES

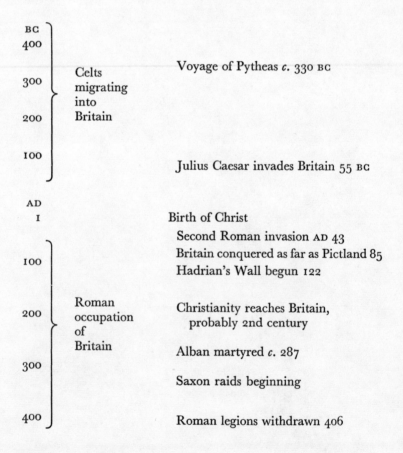

BC		
400		
300	Celts migrating into Britain	Voyage of Pytheas *c.* 330 BC
200		
100		Julius Caesar invades Britain 55 BC

AD		
I		Birth of Christ
		Second Roman invasion AD 43
100		Britain conquered as far as Pictland 85
		Hadrian's Wall begun 122
200	Roman occupation of Britain	Christianity reaches Britain, probably 2nd century
		Alban martyred *c.* 287
300		Saxon raids beginning
400		Roman legions withdrawn 406

		Patrick preaching in Ireland *c.* 432
		Landing of Saxons in Kent 449
500	Angles and Saxons invading	Britons victorious at Badon *c.* 500
	Britain. Scots invading Pictland	Columba in Iona 563
		Saxons reach Severn estuary 577
		Augustine lands in Kent 597
600		
		Angles defeat Britons at Chester 605
		All England Christian, on death of Penda 655
		Scots win control of Lowlands from Northumbria 685
700		Bede's history finished 731
		Offa's Dyke built *c.* 785
		First Danish raid on England 793
800		
		Vikings capture Dublin 841
		Scotland united under Kenneth I 848
		Alfred defeats Danes, establishes Danelaw 878
900	Viking raids round British Isles	
		Viking settlement in Normandy 911
		Danelaw reconquered, England united 937
1000		Vikings reach North America *c.* 1000
		Battle of Hastings 1066
		Domesday Book compiled 1086
1100	Norman rule in England	
		Anglo-Norman conquest of Ireland 1171
1200		French possessions lost 1204
		English conquest of Wales 1283

1300

1400

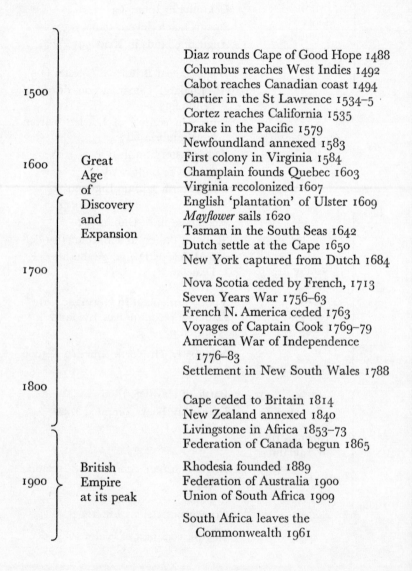

1500

Diaz rounds Cape of Good Hope 1488
Columbus reaches West Indies 1492
Cabot reaches Canadian coast 1494
Cartier in the St Lawrence 1534–5
Cortez reaches California 1535
Drake in the Pacific 1579
Newfoundland annexed 1583

1600

Great
Age
of
Discovery
and
Expansion

First colony in Virginia 1584
Champlain founds Quebec 1603
Virginia recolonized 1607
English 'plantation' of Ulster 1609
Mayflower sails 1620
Tasman in the South Seas 1642
Dutch settle at the Cape 1650
New York captured from Dutch 1684

1700

Nova Scotia ceded by French, 1713
Seven Years War 1756–63
French N. America ceded 1763
Voyages of Captain Cook 1769–79
American War of Independence
        1776–83
Settlement in New South Wales 1788

1800

Cape ceded to Britain 1814
New Zealand annexed 1840
Livingstone in Africa 1853–73
Federation of Canada begun 1865

British
Empire
at its peak

1900

Rhodesia founded 1889
Federation of Australia 1900
Union of South Africa 1909

South Africa leaves the
    Commonwealth 1961

Appendix 2

COMMON PLACE-NAME ELEMENTS IN THE BRITISH ISLES

These selections are listed by languages rather than regions. (L) indicates a word borrowed from Latin during or after the Roman occupation. The original words are given on the left; the right-hand columns show how they most commonly appear in modern place-names, but more variations exist than can be shown here. They overlap, and are easily confused. For each separate place-name only a study of the early evidence can give a certain etymology.

(A) OF OLD ENGLISH ORIGIN
(i.e. English as spoken before about 1100)
The words listed are obsolete, archaic, or changed in form. Other common elements that are more easily recognizable, such as 'ford' or 'hill', have not been included. þ is the OE symbol for 'th'.

āc	oak	Ac-, Aik-, Oak-, Oke-, -ock
bearu	grove	Barrow, -bere, -beare
beorg	hill, burial mound	-berrow, -borough, -bury
bere	barley	Ber-, Bar-
bold, boþl }	a building	Bolt-, -bold, -bottle, Bootle
burh	a fortified place	Bur-, -borough, -burgh, -bury
burna	a stream	Bourne, Burn-, -burn, -borne
cēap	trade, market	Chip-, Chep-
ceaster (L)	Roman town or fort	Chester-, -caster, -cester

ceorl	churl or free man	Charl-, Carl-, Chorl-
cot	hut or cottage	Coat(e), -cot, -cote
denn	swine pasture in woods	-den (chiefly Kent & Sussex)
denu	dene or valley	Dean(e), Den-, -den
draeg	drag or slipway	Dray-
dūn	a hill	Dun-, Down-, -down, -don
ēa	water, river	Ea-, -ey, Ya-
ēg	island	Ea-, Ey-, -ey, -y
grāf,	grove, small wood	Graf-, -grave, -greave, -grove
haga	hedge, enclosure	Haw-, Hag-, Haigh-, -haw, -haugh
halh	nook, corner	Hal-, Hale, Haugh-, -hall, -all
hall	hall, large building	-hall (not as common as above)
hām	a homestead	Ham-, -ham
hamm,	a watermeadow	Ham, -ham
hlāw	mound, hill	-low, -law
hōh	spur of high land	Hough, How(e), Hoo, Hu-, -ow, -oe
holt	thicket	Holt, -holt
hop	a small enclosure	Hop-, Hope, -hope, -op
hyrst	small wooded hill	Hurst-, -hurst
hȳþ	landing-place	Hythe, -hithe, -ith, -eth, -ey
lēah	glade or clearing	Leigh, Lee, -leigh, -ley
mere	lake	Mer-, Mar-, -mer, -mere
ōra	bank, edge	Oare, Or-, -or(e)
sceaga	a small wood	Shaw, Shaugh, -shaw
scīr	bright	Shir-, Sher-
sealh	sallow (kind of willow)	Sel-, Sil-, Zeal (Devon)
stān	stone	Stan-, Stain-, -stone, -ston
stede	place, site	-sted, -stead
stoc	meeting place, holy place	Stoke, -stoke, -stock
stocc	tree trunk	Stock, -stock (not so common as above)
stōw	(same as *stoc*)	Stow(e), -stow(e)

strǣt (L)	Roman road	Strat-, Stret-, Streat-, Street
tūn	enclosure, farm, village	-ton, -town
walh	foreigner, a Briton	Wal-
wīc	a dwelling, a farm	Wick, Wyke, -wick, -wich, -ick, -ich
worþ, worþig	enclosure, farm	Worth, -worth, -worthy

Pronunciation of Old English

a as in German mann		ā as in father		
æ ,, ,, at		ǣ ,, ,, fare		
e ,, ,, set		ē ,, ,, German see		
i ,, ,, it		ī ,, ,, English see		
o ,, ,, hot		ō ,, ,, French beau		
u ,, ,, put		ū ,, ,, rude		
y ,, ,, French tu		ȳ ,, ,, French pur		

In diphthongs both vowels were sounded with the stress on the first. The consonants were largely as in modern English, the chief differences being:

c before e or i was like ch, as in child, otherwise like k.
g before e or i was like y, as in yet, otherwise as in go.
h was initially as in hat, but otherwise like ch in loch.
sc was like sh in shall, with a few exceptions.
þ represented th.
All consonants were sounded, hl being very similar to Welsh ll.

(B) OF SCANDINAVIAN ORIGIN

Only the most distinctive of these are given. Many others merged with cognate English words, from which they can hardly be distinguished. This is true of some of those listed, but in these cases their frequent occurrence in Britain is due principally to the Northmen.

bekkr	a stream	-beck
by	farm, village	-by
dalr	dale, valley	Dal-, -dale
ey	island	-ey, -ay
fjall	fell, hill	-fell

fjorth	fiord, inlet	Firth (Scot.), -ford (Ir.)
garþr	enclosure	Garth-, -garth, -guard, Gart-(Sc.)
gil	narrow ravine	-gill
haugr	mound, hill	How(e), -how
holmr	small flat-topped island	Holme, -holme
melr	sand-bank	-mel
nes	nose or cape	-ness
saetr	a hill pasture	-set, -side
scãli	a temporary hut	Scale(s), Scole, -scale, -skill
sker	a rock or reef	Skerry, -scar, Sgeir (Sc.)
staþr	a place or site	-ster (Sc. and Ir.)
þorp	farm, village	Thorp(e), -thorpe
þveit	glade or clearing	Thwaite, -thwaite
vik	an inlet of the sea	Wick, -wick (chiefly Sc. & Ir.)

In the writing of Old Norse j represented the sound of y, as in yet, and v that of English w. Otherwise its pronunciation is presumed to have been similar to that of Old English.

(C) OF WELSH OR BRITTONIC ORIGIN

The left-hand column gives Welsh words common in place-names. In Wales they are generally unchanged from their originals, except for the usual mutations. The column on the right shows the same elements in the forms in which they are found in other parts of Britain, and in English versions of Welsh names. Cornish words are very close to their Welsh equivalents, but have been more subject to English spelling. In other parts of England the same elements are descended from the older form of Welsh, known as British or Brittonic, and a few of these postulated root-words are indicated (B).

aber	river mouth	Aber-
afon (B. abona)	river	Avon
ar	near	
bach, bechan fach, fechan	little	-fechan, vean
bre, fre (B. briga)	hill	Bre-
bryn, fryn	hill	Bryn, -vern
blaen	end or head	Blan-
caer, gaer	fortified place	Car-
cam (B. cambo)	crooked	Cam-
celli, gelli	a wood	-gethly, -gelly

coed, goed (B. ceto)	a wood	Chat-, -chett
craig, graig	a rock	Creake, Creigh-
crug, grug	small hill, mound	Crick-, Creech, Crewk-
cwm (B. cumbo)	deep valley	Co(o)mb(e), Comp-, -combe
derw, pl. derwen	oak tree	Derwent, Darwen, Dart
din, dinas (B.dunon)	fortress, town	Din-, Den-, Tin-
du, ddu (B. dubo-)	black	Dove, Dou-, -dew
dwfr (B. dubro-)	water	Dover, Dour, -dovery
eglwys (L)	church	Eccles, Eglo-
glan	bank, shore	-lan
glas	greeny blue	Glas-, -glas
glais	a small stream	Glais-, Glas-, -glas
glyn	a narrow valley	Glen-
gwyn, wyn	white	Win-, Wen-
heli	salt water	Hayle, Hel-
llan	enclosure, church	Lan-
llech	a flat stone	
llyn (B. lindon)	a lake or pool	Lin-, Lynn, Lyn-, -lin
llys	a court or hall	Lis-
maen, faen	a stone	-maine
mawr, fawr	great	-vor
moel, foel	bald or bare hill	Mal-, Mel-
mor	the sea	Mor-
mynydd	mountain	Mine-, Mynd
nant	brook or valley	
pen	head or end	Pen-
pont, bont (L)	bridge	
porth, borth (L)	harbour	Port-, -port
pwll	pool, anchorage	Pol-, -pool
rhiw	slope or hillside	Ru-, -rew
rhos	moorland	Ros-, Ross, -rose
rhyd	a ford	-rith
rhyn	a cape	-ryn
tir	the land	-tire
traeth, draeth	sands	
tre(f), dre	a farm or village	Tre-
ty, dy	a house	
y, yr	the, of the	
ynys	island	
ystrad	a wide valley	

Pronunciation of Welsh

c is always hard	ll has no English equivalent; the nearest is thl
ch as in loch	
dd as th in then	th as in thin
f as English v	w is a vowel, oo as in wood
ff as English f	u has no English equivalent; the nearest is a short i as in did
g always hard	
	y has two sounds, either like u in run, or i in did

All letters are sounded.

Mutation. In certain circumstances some consonants make regular changes. Some are shown in this list. The most common mutations are b to f, c to g, d to dd, f to dd, m to f, p to b, and t to d.

(D) OF GAELIC ORIGIN

Irish and Scottish Gaelic are so similar that one list can suffice for the principal local elements of both. The right-hand column shows the forms in which they generally occur in English versions of Gaelic names.

abhain	water, river	Avon
achadh	field	Ach-, Auch-, Auchin-
an	of the	
-an	diminutive suffix	
al, ail	a rock	All-, Ail-
ard	high or height	Ard-, Aird-
baile	farm or village	Bally-, Balla-, Bal-
barr	summit	-bar
beag	little	-beg
bealach	crossing-place	Bel-, Bal-, Balloch
beinn	peak, mountain	Ben, Ban-
bri, braigh	upper slopes	Brae-, Bray, Bre-
cam	crooked	Cam-
caol	strait	Kyle
carn	heap of stones	Carn-, Cairn-
carraig	a rock	Carreg, Carrick
caseal (L)	fort	Cashel
cill (L)	monastic cell, church	Kil-
clach	a stone	Clack-
cluain	meadow among woods	Clon-, Cloon-
cnoc	a small hill	Knock-
coille	wood	Killi-

dal	meadow by a stream	Dal-
daire, doire	oak-wood	Derry, -dare
droichead	bridge	Drogh-, drochit
druim	ridge	Drum-
dubh, dhu	black,	Dub-, Dou-
dún	a fortified place	Dun-, Down(e), Doun(e)
gaill,	a stranger	Gal-, -gal
glais	a stream	Glass-, -glas
glas	green or blue	Glas-, -glas
gleann	a narrow valley	Glen
imbhir	river mouth or junction	Inver-
innis	an island	Innis, Inch
lough, loch	lake or sea inlet	Loch
magh, machair	a plain by the sea	Magher-, -magh, Moy-
meal, maol	bald or bare hill	Mel-
monadh	mountain	Mon-
mór	great	-more
rath	a small fort or court	Rath-,
ros	moorland	Ros-, -rose
sleibh	range of hills	Slieve
srath	a wide valley	Strath-
tobar	a well	Tipper-, Tober-
tigh	a house	Ty-,
tir	land	Tyr-, -tire
tom	a round hill	Tom-
traigh	shore, sands	-trae, -try
uiscge	water	Usk, Esk

Pronunciation of Gaelic

It is not possible to give simple rules for the pronunciation of Gaelic, but the most helpful thing to understand is aspiration, which is indicated by an h following a consonant. This either changes or nullifies it, as follows:

bh and mh are pronounced as v
dh, fh and gh are silent or sounded as h only
ch as in loch or in German nacht
ph as f, and th as in thin or often silent.
c and g are always hard.

Note on the Welsh and Gaelic lists

A comparison of these two short selections shows many similarities and many more could be given. It is also of interest to notice that both have a closer relationship with Latin (quite apart from the loan words borrowed in historic times) than with the Germanic languages. This is apparent in a comparison of some of the most essential words for natural features:

LATIN	WELSH	GAELIC	
terra	tir	tir	(land)
mare	mor	muir	(sea)
mons	mynydd	monadh	(hill)
insula	ynys	innis	(island)

These Celtic words are not descended from Latin, but from a common linguistic ancestor.

A SELECT BIBLIOGRAPHY

I. THE OLD WORLD

The Anglo-Saxon Chronicle, Everyman revised edition, London, 1954

D.Attwater, *The Penguin Dictionary of Saints*, London, 1965

S.Baring-Gould and A.Fisher, *The Lives of the British Saints*, 4 vols., 1907–13

The Venerable Bede, *The Ecclesiastical History of the English Nation*, Everyman edition, London, 1930

E.G.Bowen, *The Settlements of the Celtic Saints in Wales*, Cardiff, 1954

K.Cameron, *English Place-Names*, London, 1961

N.K.Chadwick (ed.), *Studies in Early British History*, Cambridge, 1954

— *Celt and Saxon*, Cambridge, 1962

— *The Celts*, London, 1970

R.G.Collingwood and J.L.N.Myres, *Roman Britain and the English Settlements*, Oxford, 1936

H.C.Darby (ed.), *Historical Geography of England*, Cambridge, 1951

B.Dickins, 'English Names and Old English Heathenism', in *Essays and Studies*, English Assoc. XIX, Oxford, 1934

W.Croft Dickinson, *Scotland from the Earliest Times to 1603*, London, 1963

M.Dillon and N.K.Chadwick, *The Celtic Realms*, London, 1967

E.Ekwall, *English River-Names*, Oxford, 1928

— *The Concise Oxford Dictionary of English Place-Names*, 4th edn, Oxford, 1960

— 'The Scandinavian Settlement', in *Historical Geography of England*, see H.C.Darby

The English Place-Name Society Publications, Cambridge, 1923 – 45 volumes (up to 1970) dealing with 22 counties

J.E.B.Gover, 'Cornish Place-Names', in *Antiquity* II, 1928

C.A.Gresham, 'The Book of Aneirin', in *Antiquity* XVI, 1942

K.Jackson, 'On Some Romano-British Place-Names', in *The Journal of Roman Studies*, vol. 38, 1948

— *Language and History in Early Britain*, Edinburgh, 1953

— 'The Arthur of History', in *Arthurian Literature of the Middle Ages*, ed. R.S.Loomis, Oxford, 1959

J.B.Johnson, *Place-Names of Scotland*, London, 1934

SELECT BIBLIOGRAPHY

P.W.Joyce, *Irish Names of Places*, Dublin, 1883
J.E.Lloyd, *History of Wales*, vol. 1, London, 1954
W.F.H.Nicolaisen, M.Gelling and Melville Richards, *The Names of Towns and Cities in Britain*, London, 1970
M. and L. de Paor, *Early Christian Ireland*, London, 1958
Liam Price, *The Place-Names of County Wicklow*, Dublin, 1945
P.H.Reaney, *The Origin of English Place-Names*, London, 1960
A.H.Smith, *English Place-Name Elements*, EPNS publications, vols. xxv, xxvi.
F.M.Stenton, *Anglo-Saxon England*, Oxford, 1947
W.J.Watson, *History of the Celtic Place-Names of Scotland*, Edinburgh, 1926
The Ordnance Survey *Map of Roman Britain*, 3rd edn, 1956, gives a list of all known Roman names and sites, and other useful information
The Irish Encyclopedia, Dublin 1968, has articles on Irish place-names and the Gaelic language
The *Blue Guides* to Ireland and Wales (latest editions) and the *Shell Guides* (Ireland 1962 and Wales 1969) also have useful articles on these subjects, with word lists

2. THE NEW WORLD

G.H.Armstrong, *The Origin and Meaning of Place-Names in Canada*, Toronto, 1930
Graham Botha, 'Place-Names in the Cape District', in the *Collected Works of Graham Botha*, vol. 2, Cape Town, 1962
J.B.Brebner, *Explorers of North America* (1492–1806), New York, 1933
Sir Peter Buck, *Vikings of the Pacific*, London and Chicago, 1959
Sir Alan Burns, *History of the British West Indies*, London, 1954
C.E.Carrington, *The British Overseas*, Cambridge, 1950
Hugh Carrington, *The Life of Captain Cook*, London, 1939
Le Voiage de Jacques Cartier, Relation Originale, ed. J.C.Pouliot, Quebec, 1934
The Voyages of Christopher Columbus, consisting of his journals and letters, trans. and ed. Cecil Jane, London, 1930
The Journals of Captain James Cook on his voyages of Discovery, ed. J.C.Beaglehole, 3 vols., London, 1955–67
S.E.Dawson, *The St Lawrence Basin* (with reproductions of early maps), London, 1905
A.P.Elkin, *The Australian Aborigines*, London, 1938
Richard Hakluyt, *Principal Navigations, Voyages, and Discoveries of the English Nation* (first published 1589), London, 1903

344

Sir H.Johnson, *The Colonisation of Africa*, Cambridge, 1930

A.E.Martin, *Romance in Nomenclature*, Sydney, 1945

A.P.Newton, *The Great Age of Discovery*, London, 1932

F.Parkman, *The Discovery of the Great West*, London, 1962

Charles Pettman, *South African Place-Names*, in the *Report of the South African Association*, Cape Town, 1914

D.W.Prowse, *A History of Newfoundland, from the English, Colonial and Foreign Records*, London, 1895

A.W.Reed, *The Story of New Zealand Place-Names*, Wellington, 1952

— *A Dictionary of Maori Place-Names*, Wellington, 1961

Sir Ernest Scott, *Life of Matthew Flinders*, London, 1914

Andrew Sharp, *The Discovery of the Pacific Islands*, Oxford, 1960

— *The Discovery of Australia*, Oxford, 1963

Keith Sinclair, *History of New Zealand*, revised edn, London, 1969

R.A.Skelton, *Explorers' Maps*, London, 1958

P.R.Stephenson, *History and Description of Sydney Harbour*, London, 1967

The Works of Captain John Smith (1608–1631), ed. E.Arbor, London, 1884

G.R.Stewart, *Names on the Land*, An Historical Account of Place-Naming in the United States, New York, 1945

— *American Place-Names*, A Concise and Selective Dictionary for the Continental USA, New York, 1970

Alan Villiers, *The Western Ocean*, London, 1957

The following all give valuable information on place-names:

The Australian Encyclopedia, ed. A.H.Chisolm, 10 vols., (especially vol. 7), Sydney, 1965

Encyclopedia Canadiana, vols., Ottawa, 1956

An Encyclopedia of New Zealand, 3 vols., ed. A. H. McLintock, Wellington, 1966

The Encyclopedia of Southern Africa, ed. Eric Rosenthal, London, 1961

Subject Index

In order to avoid repetition the names of persons who are mentioned only on the same pages as places named recognisably after them are not included here but may be found in the Place-Name Index.

Cook, Captain James, 178, 226, 246–51, 260, 263–6, 276, 282, 285, 327
Cornwall, 7, 73, 125, 131–4, 151–2
Cortez, Ferdinando, 175

Dampier, William, 246, 256, 304
Danes, invasion of England, 76–7, 82, 92–4; language 77–80, 337–8; personal names, 80–2; *see also* Vikings
David, St, 125, 150, 154
Diaz, Bartholomew, 233
Domesday Book, 34, 53, 98
Drake, Sir Francis, 175, 211, 284, 301–2, 307

Edwin, of Northumbria, 135, 138
Elizabeth I, 175, 180, 285
Elizabeth II, 285
England, place-names in, 4–118, 321–30
   the commonest, 44; contractions, 50, 109–11; spelling, 105; redundancies, 20, 199, 104; folk-etymology, 110–11; back-formation, 111–12; compound names, 78, 80, 102–5, 112–17; new towns, 325–6, 329–30; new county names, 97, 326; *see also* Anglo-Saxons and Old English

Flinders, Captain Matthew, 251–2, 307
Frontenac, Comte de, 229

Gaelic language, 9, 122–30, 144–9, 340–2
Gama, Vasco da, 233
Geoffrey of Monmouth, 17, 294
George II, 183
George III, 223, 240, 285
Gilbert, Sir Humphrey, 173
Gildas, 131–3
Gododdin, 146
Gold rushes, 237, 258, 275
Gosnold, Captain B., 180
Grant, Captain James, 251

Grenville, Sir Richard, 178–9
Greeks, the ancient, 3, 6, 8, 164, 295, 306
Guinea, 232

'Heptarchy', 89
Hackluyt, Richard, 171, 294
Hobson, Captain William, 268–9
Hudson Bay Company, 222, 229

India, 28, 243, 280
Ireland, 297; early history, 141–3, 145–8; Viking raids, 83–8; language, *see* Gaelic

James I, 180, 220
James II, 182, 222, 285
Jefferson, President, 199, 204, 211–2
Jolliet, Louis, 194
Julius Caesar, 7, 8, 14, 295

Kenya, 242–3

La Salle, Sieur de, 192–3
Lewis and Clarke expedition, 211–2
London boroughs, 323–4

Man, Isle of, 84, 87, 125, 135
Marquette, Pere, 194
Mason, Captain John, 186

Nennius, 11
Newfoundland, 165, 171–4, 219–20
New Zealand, early history and naming, 245, 247, 249, 262–79, 304–6; local words, 318–20; Maori names, 262–3, 276–9
Nicholls, Colonel R., 182
Normans, their origin, 83, 98; influence in England, 93–4, 98–105; in Wales, Scotland and Ireland, 106

Offa, King, 46, 52
Old English, inflexions: 42, genitive, 37, 48; masculine and feminine, 47; vocabulary: *-ing*, *-ington* etc,

M*

Place-Names Index

Llanfair, Wal, 155
Llanfairfechan, Wal, 155
Llanfair p.g., Wal, 155
Llanfihangel, Wal, 155
Llangattock, Wal, 156
Llangollen, Wal, 156
Llanpumpsant, Wal, 156
Llantrisant, Wal, 156
Llantwit, Wal, 155
Loch Ness, Sc, 145
Londesborough, Eng (Yorks.), 81
London, Eng, 6, 29
  Can, 226
  US (Ohio), 288
London Apprentice, Eng (Corn.),
  325
Londonderry, Ir, 129
Looe, Eng (Corn.), 133
Long I., US (N.Y.), 190
Long I., WI, 168
Longleat, Eng (Wilts.), 321
Long Mynd, Eng (Salop.), 20
Los Angeles, US (Cal.), 210
Louisburg, Can, 171
Louise, L., Can, 224
Louisiana, US, 193
Louis Trichart, SAf, 237
Louisville, US (Ky.), 202
Ludwell, Eng (Wilts.), 60
Lulworth, Eng (Dorset), 47
Lundy I., Eng, 86
Luther, Can, 290
Luton, Eng (Beds.), 16
Llyallpur, Pakistan, 280
Lybster, Sc, 87
Lyme Regis, Eng (Dorset), 324-5
Lyndhurst, Eng (Hants.), 64
Lyttelton, NZ, 271

Mackenzie R., Can, 225
McKinley, Mt., US, 286
Macquarie R., Aus, 255
Madison, US, *f*, 199
Maiden Bradley, Eng (Wilts.) 114
Maiden Castle, Eng (Dorset), 23
Maidenhead, Eng (Berks.), 111
Maiden Newton, Eng (Dorset), 114
Maids Moreton, Eng (Bucks.), 113

Maidstone, Eng (Kent), 113
Maine, US, 186
Main Topsail, Nfd, 173
Malmesbury, Eng (Wilts.),
  SAf, 239
Malte Brun, Mt., NZ, 274
Malvern, Eng (Worcs.), 20
Man, I. of, 135
Manapouri, L., NZ, 279
Manchester, Eng (Lancs.), 23
Manhattan, US (N.Y.), 179
Manly, Aus, 249
Manitoba, Can, 218
Maple Creek, Can, 228
Mapledurham, Eng (Oxon.), 65
Marathon, Can, 227
Marble Bar, Aus, 258
Margate, Eng (Kent), 63
Maria's I., Aus, 245
Marie Galante, WI, 169
Marlborough, NZ, 273, 290
Marshall Is., Pacific O., 281
Martha's Vinyard, US (Mass.), 180
Mary R., Aus, 255
Maryborough, Aus, 255
Maryland, US, 181
Marylebone, Eng (Lond.), 111
Massachusetts, US, 178
Matlock, Eng (Derbs.), 64
Maui I., Hawaiian Is., 263
Mawgan, Eng (Corn.), 151
Mayo, Ir, 142, 158
Mayor I., NZ, 265
Meadowbank, Aus, 320
Meath, Ir, 142
Medicine Hat, Can, 228
Medway, R., Eng (Kent), 15
Melanesia, Pacific O., 283
Melbourne, Eng (Derbs.), 327
  Aus, 254, 257
Melbury Bubb, Eng (Dorset), 117
Melrose, Sc, 128
Melton Mowbray, Eng (Leics.), 103
Memory Cove, Aus, 252
Memphis, US (Tenn.), 197
Mendips, The, Eng (Som.), 20
Mercia, Eng, 96
Mercury Bay, NZ, 265

367

Wednesbury, Eng (Staffs.), 67–8
Wednesfield, Eng (Staffs.), 68
Weedon, Eng (Nthants., Bucks.), 69
Weeley, Eng (Essex), 69
Weenen, SAf, 235
Wellington (Herefs., Salop, Som), 69–70
  NZ, 269
Wells, Eng (Som.), 76
Welwyn, Eng (Herts.), 64, 329
Wendover, Eng (Bucks.), 15
Weoley, Eng (Worcs.), 69
Wensum R., Eng (Norf.), 61
Wessex, Eng, 90, 96, 296
West Bromwich, Eng (Staff.), 65
West Camel, Eng (Som.), 11
Western Australia, 260
West Indies, 166, 299
Westminster, Eng (Lond.), 71–2
Westmorland, Eng, 88, 93, 97
Weston, Eng, *f*, 39
Westray, Orkneys, 87
Wexford, Ir, 147
Wey Rs., Eng (Sy., Dorset), 15
Weymouth, Eng (Dorset), 15
Whangaroa, NZ, 277
Whitchurch, Eng, *f*, 72
Whitchurch Canonicorum (Dorset), 114
White Horse, Can, 228
Whittingham, Eng (Lancs., Nthumb.), 36
Whittington, Eng, *f*, 36
Whitwell, Eng, *f*, 60
Wick, Sc, 85, 208
Wicklow, Ir, 85, 147
Widdicombe, Eng (Devon), 59, 64
Wight, Isle of, Eng, 18–19
Wildboarclough, Eng (Ches.), 63
Willey, Eng (Salop.), 69
Williamsburg, US (Va.), 183
Willoughby, Eng (Notts., Warks.), 64
Willoughby-on-the-Wolds (Notts.), 117
Willoughby Waterless (Leics.), 117
Willowmore, SAf, 236
Wilton, Eng (Wilts.), 18

Wiltshire, Eng, 18, 91
Wimbledon, Eng (Sy.), 50
Winchester, Eng (Hants.), 24
Windermere, Eng (Westm.), 63, 110
Windrush R., Eng, 110
Windsor, Eng (Berks.), 53, 102, 327
Winnipeg, Can, 229–30
Winterbourne Gunner (Dorset), 116
Winterbourne Steepleton (Dorset), 116
Wisconsin, US, 194
Witcombe, Eng (Glos.), 64
Withycombe, Eng (Som.), 64
Witless Bay, Nfd., 173
Woburn, Eng (Beds.), 60
Wolfe, Can, 225
Wolferton, Eng (Norf.), 49
Wolfe's Cove, Can, 225
Wolfeville, Can, 230
Wolstanton, Eng (Staffs.), 49
Wolverhampton, Eng (Staffs.), 50, 53
Wolverton, Eng (Worcs.), 49
Woodbourne, NZ, 320
Woodbridge, Eng (Suff.), 34
Woodnesborough, Eng (Kent), 67
Woolfardisworthy (Devon), 50
Woodstock, Eng (Oxon.), 204
Woolley (Berks., Hunts., Yorks.), 56
Wooloomooloo, Aus, 259
Woolwich, Eng (Kent), 40
Wootton, Eng, *f*, 103
Wootton Bassett, Eng (Wilts.), 103, 113
Woomera, Aus, 260
Worcester, Eng, 23
  SAf, 239
Wormley, Eng (Herts.), 56
Worth, Eng (Kent, Sx.), 337
Worthing, Eng (Sx.), 36
Wrekin, The, Eng (Salop.), 19
Wroxeter, Eng (Salop.), 19, 32
Wye R., Wal/Eng, 15
Wylye R., Eng (Wilts.), 18, 91
Wynot, US (Neb.), 212
Wyoming, US, 205–6

Yarmouth, Eng (Norf.), 18